"O SISTERS AIN'T YOU HAPPY?"

Women and Gender in North American Religions
Amanda Porterfield *and* Mary Farrell Bednarowski, *Series Editors*

Shaker sisters on a visit to Fruitlands Farmhouse in 1914.
Courtesy of the Fruitlands Museums, Harvard, Massachusetts.

"O Sisters Ain't You Happy?"

Gender, Family, and Community among the
Harvard and Shirley Shakers, 1781–1918

Suzanne R. Thurman

Syracuse University Press

First Edition 2002
02 03 04 05 06 07   6 5 4 3 2 1

The paper used in this publication meets the minimum requirements of
American National Standard for Information Sciences—Permanence
of Paper for Printed Library Materials, ANSI Z39.48–1984.∞™

Library of Congress Cataloging-in-Publication Data
Thurman, Suzanne Ruth.
    "O sisters ain't you happy?" : gender, family, and community among the Harvard and
Shirley Shakers / Suzanne R. Thurman.—1st ed.
        p. cm.—(Women and gender in North American religions)
    Includes bibliographical references and index.
    ISBN 0-8156-2906-0 (alk. paper)—ISBN 0-8156-2934-6 (pbk. : alk. paper)
    1. Shaker women—Massachusetts—Shaker Village—History. 2.
Shakers—Massachusetts—Shaker Village—History. 3. Shaker Village (Mass.)—Church history.
    4. Shaker women—Massachusetts—Shirley (Town)—History. 5. Shakers—Massachusetts—
Shirley (Town)—History 6. Shirley (Mass. : Town)—Church history. 7. Family—Religious
aspects—Shakers—History of doctrines. I. Title. II. Series
BX9768.H3 T48 2001
289'.8'097443—dc21   2001032833

Manufactured in the United States of America

In loving memory of my grandparents,
Beulah Brunson Zimmerman,
Elnora Loomis Thurman,
and
Charlie Thurman,
*who taught by example
the value of faith, hard work, and integrity*

Suzanne R. Thurman teaches history at the University of Alabama—Huntsville. Her publications include articles on the Shakers in *Journal of Women's History, Church History, Communal Societies,* and *Nineteenth Century Studies.*

Contents

Acknowledgments

WRITING IS A SOLITARY ACT, but turning out a completed manuscript requires many hands. Having discovered the truth of this statement more times than I can count, I would like to thank a number of individuals and institutions that contributed to the formation of this book.

Above all I must acknowledge my debt to Stephen J. Stein, originally my dissertation adviser, now a valued colleague. More than ten years ago he introduced me to the Shakers in his graduate class on American religious history. He oversaw my master's thesis on the Shakers, directed my doctoral dissertation on the same, and has been a source of calm support in the long process of turning that dissertation into a book. More than anyone else, he taught me what it means to be a writer. His exacting standard of scholarship, reflected in his own work, is, I hope, apparent in mine as well.

Many others also made valuable contributions to this book. The probing questions that Bernard Sheehan, Muriel Nazzari, and J. Samuel Preus asked during my dissertation defense helped me create the framework of the book that I eventually wrote. Etta Madden's friendship and mutual interest in the Shakers made an enormous difference in the early and middle stages of this project. I am particularly grateful to Etta and her husband, Neil Guion, for taking me in while I was conducting research in New Hampshire. Their graciousness in the midst of their own hectic schedules was greatly appreciated.

I am also indebted to my dear friends Erika and Paul Marer, whose home has been my temporary abode on many occasions. Their interest in my project and their frequent words of encouragement have been a source of strength on some rather dark days. Thanks, too, to the students in my women's history classes at Mesa State College and the University of Alabama–Huntsville for their spirited discussions and moral support.

I have been very fortunate in the financial assistance that I received for this project. Grants and fellowships from the History Department, the Graduate School, and the Women's Studies Program at Indiana University enabled me to conduct research throughout New England and New York and to finish my research at IU. A fellowship from the Henry Francis du Pont Winterthur Museum, Winterthur, Delaware, allowed me to use the Andrews Shaker Collection housed there.

Many librarians, archivists, and staff people helped me locate sources and made my task of writing an easier one. I would like to thank the following in particular: Diana Hanson, Marty Sorury, and the Reference and Interlibrary Loan staff at Indiana University; Jane Heitman at Mesa State College, the most efficient interlibrary loan coordinator I've ever met; Jerry Grant of Emma B. King Library, Shaker Museum and Library, Old Chatham, New York; the late Robert F. W. Meader and Magda Gabor-Hotchkiss, formerly of Hancock Shaker Village, Inc., Hancock, Massachusetts; Stephen Paterwic, who graciously allowed me to use his census material on the Harvard and Shirley Shakers housed in the library at Hancock Shaker Village; Sylvia B. Kennick and Lynne Fonteneau-McCann of Williams College Library, Williamstown, Massachusetts; Maggie Stier, formerly of Fruitlands Museums, Harvard, Massachusetts; Mary Fuhrer, formerly of Fruitlands Museums; Robert Farwell, director of Fruitlands Museums; the staff of the American Antiquarian Society, Worcester, Massachusetts; Renee Fox of Shaker Library, Canterbury Shaker Village, Canterbury, New Hampshire; Anne Gilbert, formerly of the Shaker Library, the United Society of Shakers, Sabbathday Lake, Maine; and the staffs of the Case Western Reserve Historical Society, Cleveland, Ohio, and the Manuscripts and Special Collections, New York State Library.

The following people made my stay at the Henry Francis du Pont Winterthur Museum both productive and enjoyable: E. Richard McKinstry, Mary-Elise Haug, Iris Snyder, Pat Elliott, John Krill, and Bert Denker. The time I spent there will remain a highlight of writing this book.

The final stages of this project were facilitated by the hard work of many people at Syracuse University Press. Thanks are due especially to Amanda Porterfield and Mary Bednarowski for their enthusiastic support of the manuscript from day one and to Mary Selden Evans for seeing the project through the initial hurdles.

In closing, I want to recognize those who enrich my life beyond words. Gender equality begins at home, and I thank my parents, Eldon and Carole Thurman, for never hesitating to support their only daughter in her intellectual pursuits. My mother, in particular, deserves special notice. Twice she accompanied me on research trips for this book, navigating us through the countryside of New England (including those pesky rotaries) and restoring my sanity after long days in dusty archives. Her help was invaluable. I thank my stepdaughters, Anna and Kristina Makowski, for sharing many hours of their summer visits with my manuscript. Finally, words cannot express my love and appreciation for my husband, George Makowski, who gave me the space to think and write and loved me in spite of it all.

"O SISTERS AIN'T YOU HAPPY?"

Introduction

The opportunity to criticize American family life destructively has been given to many men, but the true test of criticism comes with the opportunity to present one's concept of the ideal family.
—Alma J. Payne,
"The Family in the Utopia of William Dean Howells"

IN 1774 ANN LEE, a visionary from Manchester, England, landed in New York City with a handful of followers. For the first several years they worked at odd jobs, remaining an inconspicuous part of the New York landscape. By 1779 they had acquired land in Niskeyuna, New York, northwest of Albany, and it was here in 1780 that Ann Lee "opened the gospel" in America. Capitalizing on the upheaval caused by a recent religious revival, Lee told the world what she claimed God had revealed to her: sexual intercourse led to Adam and Eve's fall from grace in the Garden of Eden. Thus, humanity could achieve salvation only by casting off the desires of the flesh and living a celibate life. Around this core belief Ann Lee built a religious system that emphasized each person's ability to experience a direct and immediate relationship with God, expressed through ecstatic behavior such as dancing and speaking in tongues.[1]

Ann Lee's "gospel" message resulted in the formation of a new religious sect—the United Society of Believers in Christ's Second Appearing— whose adherents were commonly known as Shakers or Believers. Central to her plan was a radical restructuring of society based on a reorganization of the family. In other words, Lee visualized the "ideal family," and she seized upon the chaos immediately following the American Revolution to pro-

1

mote her vision. Her message was well received by some, and at her death she left behind clusters of Believers who would soon gather into structured and well-planned villages.

Oddly enough, for all the importance that life in community had for the Shakers, there are few in-depth examinations of these villages available to scholars today. Edward Deming Andrews's *The People Called Shakers* ranks as the classic history of the movement, and Stephen J. Stein's recent book *The Shaker Experience in America* will remain the definitive history of Shakerism for years to come, but there are almost no analytical local histories.[2] John Wolford's dissertation on South Union, Kentucky, is one of the few community studies to use a scholarly paradigm (in his case, folklore) as a larger context for understanding the Believers; Julia Neal's book on the same village, *By Their Fruits*, is an older, somewhat romanticized, history. Deborah Burns's book *Shaker Cities of Peace, Love, and Union*, on the Hancock bishopric, and Edward Horgan's *The Shaker Holy Land*, on Harvard, Massachusetts, although informative, are written for a popular audience and provide little analysis of Shaker behavior.[3]

To fill this gap in the literature, I decided to write a comprehensive account of the founding, "golden years," and eventual demise of Harvard and Shirley, Massachusetts. The result, however, is more than a narrative history. Within the framework of a community study I discuss how gender, family, and community functioned in those two villages. I focus on these three themes because they get at the core of the movement. They highlight key ideas of Shakerism and help explain what made the Believers similar to their neighbors as well as what set them apart from the rest of the world.

My decision to write about Harvard and Shirley was not random. There are both administrative and historical reasons for choosing these particular sites as the focus of my study. First, because the two villages were only seven miles apart, they made up a bishopric and shared the same top leadership. Thus, issues and events that affected one community almost always affected the other.

Second, Harvard and Shirley constituted the historical center of Shakerism. Though Niskeyuna was the first place where Shakers gathered under Ann Lee, Harvard and Shirley served as her "headquarters" during her New England missionary tour from 1781 to 1783 and were the source of some of her earliest converts in "the east." The persecution of Believers at Harvard and Shirley, more virulent than that experienced in other places and recorded for posterity in oral histories such as the 1816 *Testimonies,* further enshrined those communities in Shaker memory. As late as the 1920s, Josephine Jilson remembered the Square House, Ann Lee's residence at Harvard, as a special place where spirits congregated.[4]

Third, Harvard and Shirley were geographically close to Boston, one of the most important cities in early America. Locating Shaker villages close to established towns or cities was a guiding principle in the formative years of Shakerism. Villages were generally situated within a twenty- to forty-mile radius of a larger town that served as a hub for the Shaker market in that area. These towns, varying in size and character from one bishopric to another, affected the economic development of the Shaker village. The religious and cultural milieu of the surrounding area also influenced the Believers. Thus, one would expect that Harvard and Shirley, thirty-odd miles west of Boston, would be shaped by their proximity to one of the four major commercial and cultural centers of nineteenth-century America.[5] Closer than any other Shakers to an influential urban center (an advantage that was lessened with the advent of the railroad), the Believers of Harvard and Shirley entered easily into the economic, intellectual, and social life of America. Given the frequent visiting done between these Shakers and people from Boston or its environs, a phenomenon documented in this book, it is no surprise to find that the Harvard and Shirley Shakers were often liberal in their opinions and progressive in their outlook.

The flip side of the Believers' frequent contact with the world was the exposure it gave to Shaker ideas and social organization. Of particular interest to nineteenth-century reformers was the Shaker family and its social ramifications for women. Indeed, the family, both biological and spiritual, was central to the Shaker enterprise.[6] Initially the Shaker family served a largely protective function by shielding the Believers from physical attack and economic adversity and by providing the emotional support necessary to live a celibate life in a society that considered it abnormal. The Shaker family also served an emancipatory function, restructuring work and childcare duties to achieve a more equitable distribution of labor and time between men and women.[7] Over the years, the Shaker family expanded its roles. It provided shelter to abused wives and desperate widows and took in orphans and children of indigent parents, all the while challenging the "traditional" and patriarchal American family. What makes the Shaker endeavor so important is that nineteenth-century critics of the patriarchal family were voicing their concerns after the Shakers had already tackled a problem that, Carl Degler argues, has plagued the American family "for at least two centuries"—reconciling women's growing sense of autonomy with the role of "family guardian" that society continued to assign them.[8] As I will show, the Shakers offered an outlet for the tensions created when women's personal expectations outpaced the family structure of middle-class America.

Degler's analysis of the family is based on a notion of domesticity that developed over the course of the late eighteenth and nineteenth centuries, a view shared by many historians of the American family.[9] The general outline of the story documents the privatization of the family and the bifurcation of men and women into separate spheres. These changes began in the postrevolutionary world where men worked outside the home and managed the new republic, while women anchored the family, and by extension the country, through their roles as mothers and moral guardians. To oversee this newly emerging family structure, legal theorists constructed a body of legislation aimed at protecting the republican family.[10] Less patriarchal than the colonial family but still controlled by men, the ideal family that evolved by the middle of the nineteenth century was rooted in what historians have labeled the Cult of Domesticity or the Cult of True Womanhood.[11] This domestic ideology was not uniformly implemented in America's various cultural regions, nor was it a possibility open to all races and classes, but for most middle-class Americans the notion of separate spheres took on biological and theological sanctions and became the prevailing family model.[12]

Recently, however, scholars have begun to question the explanatory function of the Cult of Domesticity, positing that this notion has outlived its usefulness, clouded the complexity of male and female relations in American history, and overshadowed the continued economic role that families played at a time when they were supposedly divorced from that function.[13] Indeed, some would argue that it is time to replace the "interpretive fiction" of domesticity with a paradigm that takes into account the idea that "manhood and womanhood are not metaphorical polar opposites."[14] The social construction of gender is a complex process and cannot always be reduced to the model of public versus private or home versus work. Gender relations are, like life itself, often unclear and full of ambiguity.

This was an idea that I believe the Shakers at Harvard and Shirley understood fully. In restructuring the family, these Shakers were forced to confront notions of gender as well. Just how were men and women to act in spiritual families, stripped of their biological roles as mothers and fathers, in communities where the dual notions of public/private and home/work did not exist as they did in the world at large? The very basis of the Shaker concepts of family and community rested on an intricate interweaving of notions about gender. Celibacy, combined with what I have identified among the Shakers of Harvard and Shirley as the "androgynous ideal"—the belief that a whole person has both male and female characteristics—allowed women and men to move beyond expected roles and empowered them to develop other sides of their personality. In the spiritual sphere, the Harvard and Shirley Shakers' use of a "gendered spirituality" encouraged both brothers and sisters to emulate the notion of "spiritual motherhood" modeled on socially constructed female traits.[15] In the temporal world, the Shaker construction of community collapsed the whole notion of public and private spheres, forcing women's work and actions into the public realm on a par with male activity.[16]

The Shaker notion of community required that both women and men act androgynously, an idea that was liberating for both sexes, but particularly for women. According to Donald Yacovone, antebellum American society accepted a notion of "romantic manhood" that sanctioned close male friendships and encouraged expressions of female sentimentality by men.[17] But women were rarely if ever encouraged to "act like men." By positing an androgynous ideal that emphasized boundary crossing by both women and men, the Shakers at Harvard and Shirley opened the way for a greater expression of personhood for everyone.

If gender equality was the keystone of Shaker society, then why do I emphasize women throughout this book? The answer is simple: because the Shakers did. The Believers recognized the importance of their system for the sisters. They touted their communities as havens of peace for abused wives, and argued that their ideas empowered women. Conscious of their position as elevators of female status, the Shakers were years ahead of most of their contemporaries. Thus, when possible, I illuminate the particular influence of Shakerism on women, while always keeping the larger, inclusive notion of gender in the background.

The Shakers' attempts to alleviate gender inequalities by redefining the family did not go unnoticed by some intellectuals and reformers who

tween Shakers and their nonbelieving relatives continued on a regular basis. Journals reveal a constant flow of visiting in and out of Harvard and Shirley.

The strength of the biological family in these two villages sheds new light on the Shaker venture itself. Americans castigated the Shakers for destroying the fabric of society; a mob claimed to have beaten Abijah Worster of Harvard for "breaking up churches and families." Yet the Shakers were not like the religious "enthusiasts" described by Richard Lovejoy, the Quakers and New Lights who left their homes and families to work as individuals in God's service.[27] Although the Believers advocated renouncing ties with biological families, they never intended that Believers live in isolation from each other. They merely replaced one type of family with another. As far as the Believers were concerned, they were not destroying the family; they were only improving it.

The continued importance of the biological family in Shaker life, moreover, highlights the ever-present conflict between the Believers' separation from the world and their ties—biological, cultural, religious, ideological, social, and economic—to that same world. The Shakers fostered the belief that they were different from other people, physically separating themselves from the outside, wearing distinctive clothing, and adopting special speech patterns. The Believers, in essence, developed a "rhetoric of separatism" in which they characterized themselves as possessors of the "truth" who could not be sullied by contact with the sinful world.

Yet from the very beginning, the Shakers adhered to an ideological system shared by most Americans, a mix of republicanism, market capitalism, and a deep faith in the perfectibility of humankind.[28] Aware that their distinctiveness was not as clear-cut as they would have others believe, the Shakers struggled with the biblical injunction to be in the world but not of it. Yet by the middle of the nineteenth century they had strengthened their intellectual, cultural, and financial ties to the outside. It is out of these sometimes conflicted interactions that the Shakers constructed their notions of community. Building on the Shaker family and Shaker gender roles, the Believers sought to create a larger communal ethos, a sense of community that promoted their radical mission yet protected them from the "slings and arrows" of the world.

I emphasize the ambiguous nature of the Believers' relations with the outside because scholars too often portray the Believers as marginalized

Americans and overlook the many similarities between the Shakers and their worldly counterparts. Indeed, as R. Laurence Moore argues, religious "outsiders" are at the heart of American religious life. Their very "otherness" causes mainline groups to react to them and rethink their own positions. Yet these same outsider groups also vie for legitimacy on the constantly shifting spectrum of American religious life.[29] The Shakers fit this pattern well. Provoking Americans to reconsider traditional Christian beliefs and values and claiming a place for themselves in Christian and American history, the Shakers tied themselves to the intellectual, social, and religious concerns of nineteenth-century America.

In the following chapters I discuss and analyze the similarities, as well as the differences, between the Harvard and Shirley Shakers and other Americans. My aim is neither to claim full mainstream status for these Shakers nor to argue that their lifestyle was ever popular or considered "normal" by most Americans but to highlight the complexity of the Shaker identity, an identity not merely conceived in isolation *from* the world, but developed in reaction *to* and in interaction *with* the world. By focusing on three areas of particular concern to the Believers at Harvard and Shirley I will show how Shaker concepts of family and community helped reconceptualize ideas of gender and how their ideas about gender helped reconceptualize Shaker notions of family and community. Given the increasing attention paid by scholars generally to issues of gender and family, it is important to look closely at how the Shakers at Harvard and Shirley dealt with these ideas. Their stories can add much to the increasingly complex picture of gender that emerges from our study of the past.

Chapters 1, 2, and 3 examine the foundations and early history of Harvard and Shirley, from Ann Lee's missionary tour of New England (1781–1783) to the establishment and gathering of the two villages. Central to these chapters is the issue of community formation, how the Shakers decided to establish themselves as a group separate from the world. Chapters 4 and 5 look at the ways in which the theoretical underpinnings of Shaker community helped the Believers reformulate notions of gender and how those ideas created an environment that fostered the empowerment of women.

Chapter 6 tracks the next step of community development, the creation of an identity, and chapter 7 evaluates the internal testing of that identity as Shaker villages everywhere experienced an intense period of revivalism known as Mother Ann's Work. This chapter also looks at how the era of spiritualism reflected Shaker values and how it enhanced the position of Shaker women. Chapter 8 examines the legacy of female empowerment after the revival ended.

Chapters 9 and 10 illuminate the ways in which Harvard and Shirley tested the bonds of community through their increasing accommodation to the world and explore the cost of that accommodation for both villages. Shirley suffered a severe economic setback, while Harvard experienced a devastating schism that involved prominently placed sisters. Finally, chapter 11 looks at the last years of the two villages as declining membership undermined the Believers' sense of community and forced the remaining Shakers to sell their property and move elsewhere.

Ultimately, my goal is to uncover the deeper meaning of Shakerism for the lives of the Believers at Harvard and Shirley. The title of this book comes from the lively Shaker hymn "Followers of the Lamb." After the first verse inquires "O brethren ain't you happy?" the second asks the same of the sisters.[30] The question is provocative. Were the Shakers happy? Had we only account books and statistics this would be difficult to answer, for it is impossible to quantify happiness. But the Shakers at Harvard and Shirley addressed this question in many different ways in their own writings. Despite the problems these Believers faced, despite the disgruntled apostates who left, the majority of Shakers at Harvard and Shirley were content with their life choice. This was especially true for women, who found opportunities at Harvard and Shirley that they did not have in the outside world. As I will show in this book, the sisters knew they were fortunate. At the end of her long and fruitful life as a Harvard Shaker, Eunice Bathrick wrote, "I love the pure gospel as taught by Jesus, and Mother Ann, because it has yielded me all the true comfort and solid happiness I ever enjoyed."[31] To uncover and examine this "solid happiness" is the task to which we now turn.

A Note about *sic*

Because most of the primary material in this book dates from the late eighteenth and nineteenth centuries, many of the quotes that appear in this text contain the vagaries of spelling and punctuation that were common to those periods. To preserve the integrity of the original documents, I have omitted the use of *sic* except in isolated cases.

1

Planting the "Gospel"

ON A SPRING DAY IN 1781, Ann Lee, her natural brother William Lee,
and one of her English followers, James Whittaker (the latter two known as
"the Elders"), set off for New England, "a journey [which] had been upon
[Ann Lee's] mind for some time."[1] Though portrayed as a response to God's
call to spread the gospel, Ann Lee's decision to travel through New England
was a well-calculated plan based on her knowledge that a network of followers already existed there through the efforts of a zealous convert, a former follower of Shadrach Ireland, who had taken Lee's message home to
Massachusetts. Indeed, Ann Lee's early success in Massachusetts was due
largely to her assimilation of former Irelandites into her movement and her
ability to capitalize on existing religious tensions in New England. Many of
Lee's converts already had experience with living in sectarian groups,
preparing them well for life as Shakers and contributing to the phenomenon of "clustering," a process that provided the Believers with a solid familial base on which to build after Ann Lee returned to Niskeyuna, New York,
in 1783. The movement also encouraged the participation of both men and
women, setting the stage for later communal development.

Daniel Wood of Upton, Massachusetts, was the first to spread the message of Shakerism in that state. During the winter of 1780–1781, spurred
by reports of religious stirrings among a group of "Shaking Quakers" gathered at Niskeyuna, Wood journeyed there to see for himself the woman
called "the Elect Lady." He was impressed by Ann Lee, became a Believer,
and returned to Massachusetts at her behest to spread her message of salvation and pave the way for her forthcoming missionary effort. Wood was the
first Shaker many people in Massachusetts had met. Apparently he pos-

sessed a charismatic personality himself—his voice was likened to the sound of a trumpet—and he converted many of his friends, family, and neighbors to Shakerism before they ever saw Ann Lee in a process that Stephen Marini identifies as "residential evangelism." Wood's link to these converts was strong; many of them, including Wood, had been followers of Shadrach Ireland, a New Light preacher from Charlestown, Massachusetts.[2] Patterns of working and worshiping together, then, were already in place when Lee arrived. To her was left the task of consolidating her new followers and establishing her authority over them.

In the middle of June 1781 Ann Lee arrived at the home of Isaac Willard of Shirley, Massachusetts, a former Irelandite. From his house Lee could see a building known as the Square House, located on the outskirts of the town of Harvard, where the remaining followers of Shadrach Ireland lived. Ann Lee chose to make this house her headquarters while she remained in New England, and it is likely that Daniel Wood's and Isaac Willard's connections with the Irelandites helped her achieve her goal.[3]

Ireland's followers built the house as a hiding place for their notorious leader in 1769. Ireland began his checkered career in Charlestown as a New Light minister, but the town expelled him in 1753 when he claimed immortality and sought to create his own church. Abandoning his wife and children, he moved to Harvard to pastor the small flock of separatists there. Already suspect in the eyes of the locals, he enraged them even further by living with a "spiritual companion," Abigail Logee (the natural grandmother of Eleazer Rand, the male founder of the Harvard-Shirley bishopric). Fearing retribution for his scandalous behavior, Ireland's followers hid him in their homes while they built him his own house, complete with a lookout and a secret hiding place. Several future Shakers contributed to the building of the Square House, as it came to be known, including Isaac and Hannah Willard, Zaccheus Stevens, Abel Jewett, Samuel and Abigail Cooper, Jonathan Cooper, and Ethan Phillips. Hannah Willard's contributions were especially important. As the daughter of a wealthy landowner, she had inherited a large amount of land, some of which she donated as the site for the Square House. When the house was finished, Ireland and Logee, as well as Samuel and Abigail Cooper and their two daughters, Beulah and Deliverance, moved in.[4]

Accounts of Ireland appeared frequently in the mid- to late eighteenth century. His followers were located throughout Massachusetts and seem to have been concentrated in the very places where Ann Lee became popular. Isaac Backus, in his *History of New England,* noted that in 1749 about twenty followers of Ireland in Easton and Norton, Massachusetts, baptized each other, traded spouses, and bore "bastard" children. Abijah Marvin, in his town history of Lancaster, Massachusetts, recorded the presence of Irelandites who tried to raise people from the dead.[5]

Ireland's exploits were well known in Harvard, so it is no surprise that his followers built the Square House in the isolated northeast corner of the township, minimizing his risk of attack from irate citizens. Despite his extreme religious views, however, by 1777 Ireland had achieved a measure of tolerance in the community, signaled by Harvard town's exemption of three of his followers—Isaac Willard, Zaccheus Stevens, and Abijah Worster—from payment of their minister's rates.[6]

Ireland and his followers lived quietly in the Square House until, his claims of immortality notwithstanding, he died in 1780. His followers temporarily buried him in the basement wall of the house, anticipating his imminent resurrection, but the stench eventually forced them to move his body to a cornfield. Left without a leader, shocked and confused by Ireland's unfulfilled prophecies, his followers remained at the Square House, unsure of their next step.[7]

Certainly aware of the turn of events at the Square House, information easily gotten from Isaac Willard or Daniel Wood, Ann Lee and the Elders lost no time in establishing their authority with the remaining Irelandites. The story of their first visit to the Square House in 1781, resulting in the conversion of Abigail Cooper, may be apocryphal, but it illustrates the determination of Ann Lee and the Elders to claim the Square House and its inhabitants as their own. When they knocked on the Square House door, as the story goes, Abigail Cooper answered but refused to let them in because they were English. Undaunted, the three pushed their way in and began to question Cooper about her religious beliefs and to tell her about theirs. Cooper, disillusioned by her experience with Ireland and his "false religion," informed the Shakers that she was not interested in what they had to say. At this pivotal point in the story, Ann Lee legitimated her presence in the Square House through prophetic revelation. She looked at Cooper and said, "I have seen you before," and then remarked that she had seen this entire scene in a vision while she was still in England. Cooper remained unconvinced, and the Shakers left, but not before asking Cooper if she loved them. She replied that she did not. William Lee said that they would make her love them and gave her an apple. She put the apple on the fireplace mantel, she later testified, and picked it up whenever she walked by it. Soon, she confessed, she felt a deep love for the Shakers and hoped that they would visit again. When Ann Lee and the Elders did return, Cooper became a Shaker.[8]

The other inhabitants of the Square House converted soon after and invited Ann Lee to move in with them. Though this arrangement contained potential problems—it was not clear who owned the property since Ireland had died intestate—it worked well until David Hoar, whose bid for the leadership of the group had been unsuccessful, informed Ireland's heirs of the situation. They demanded their share of their deceased father's estate, and the house and property were deeded to them for £78.10.0 on February 7, 1782. They sold it back to the Believers in April for £500 ($1,666.86). One Shaker document indicates that the Believers raised £161.0.4 ($568.48) toward the purchase of the Square House, but it does not mention where the remaining money came from. Because Ann Lee was credited with providing the largest individual sum—£43.5.0 ($144.17)—the Square House was traditionally known as Mother's House.[9]

With legal possession of the house, Ann Lee established a physical center for her operations in New England; through revelation and prophecy, Lee created a sacred center for her ministry. She revealed the "sacred origins" of the Square House to Abigail Cooper and told Jonathan Slosson that she had had visions of Harvard before leaving England and recognized the spot as soon as she saw it in America.[10] Lee also used her prophetic powers to establish herself as the God-appointed successor to Ireland. Soon after she came to Harvard, Ann Lee told the people: "God has a people in this place; he has heard their cries; they have had great light. Their Leader [Ireland] got overcome; God has taken him away and sent me here. The wicked seek my life; as they did in England, so do they here; but heed it not; for God will establish his work here, and the wicked cannot overthrow it."[11] She also claimed to have talked with Ireland's spirit, which was in hell because he had refused to believe in her. His punishment was awful, she observed, "and the souls in hell were frightened at him, because his torment was so much greater than theirs. But he will never come out until some of his people find their redemption."[12]

It is not surprising that Ann Lee exploited both her supernatural rela-

tions with Ireland's spirit and her earthly friendships with his former followers to facilitate her journey into New England. Common sense dictated
making use of existing networks. As news of Lee's teachings spread among
families and friends, the number of possible converts increased, until the
Believers began making inroads among other denominations. In 1783 the
Baptist church at Harvard lamented that "for twelve months we had but two
persons added, and several left us, and joined the Shakers."[13]

Ann Lee's success probably surprised many people. What could an illiterate woman possibly have to say about religion that had not already been
said? Indeed, her message was not, in itself, new. She taught celibacy, pacifism, compassion for others, frugality, and moderation, all of which were
part of a much older Christian tradition. Yet these teachings, when combined with ecstatic worship and the novelty of a woman "preacher,"
touched a nerve among residents of the New England countryside, and
people flocked to hear Ann Lee speak.[14] Although detractors challenged
her gender, she was always able, according to Shaker lore, to confound her
accusers and prove the validity of her message.

The Believers' success did not endear them to the local populace, and
virulent opposition to and persecution of the Shakers soon developed. The
anger that Baptists felt as the Believers enticed away their members was
only one of the factors contributing to an increasingly hostile view of the
early Shakers. Their doctrine of "implicit obedience" worried others. In
1782 Amos Taylor, himself a former Shaker whose brother lived at Harvard
for several years, viewed them as a threat to the newly independent United
States. In his opinion, a group of people who relinquished their freedom
and willingly placed themselves under the authority of a handful of En-
glishmen and women were "deluded" and dangerous examples to the American public. He particularly detested Shaker dancing and singing, seeing
them not as modes of worship but as examples of mass hysteria. Such behavior, warned Taylor, was dangerous. When a person lost control of himself or herself, when the Shakers infringed upon an unwary individual's
most basic and "natural" right of self-possession, then, Taylor believed,
America's independence was most at risk.[15]

Amos Taylor was only one of many outside observers who commented
on the extremes of Shaker behavior, extremes that often led to violent persecution. One of the earliest accounts of the Harvard Shakers—written by
William Plumer, a future governor, chief justice, and United States senator

from New Hampshire who visited Harvard in June 1782—highlights their odd conduct. He noted their practice of kneeling in silent prayer and commented upon the dancing, whirling, and "unintelligible jargon" of ecstatic speech that he witnessed at a worship meeting. He was not, however, especially critical of what he observed. He did find that "their love and tenderness for each other degenerate[d] into fondness and ridiculous weakness," yet he also noted their knowledge of scripture. Overall, Plumer viewed the Shakers as sincere, if silly, and, while noting their oddities, he refrained from maligning them.[16]

Other contemporaries of the Shakers were not so circumspect. Many stories about the Shakers' bizarre behavior passed from town to town, including the oft-repeated accusation that the Shakers danced in the nude. Another story that made its rounds involved a Shaker ship. Isaac Backus, an unsympathetic Baptist and contemporary of the Shakers, recounted that in 1782 residents of Norton and Rehoboth, Massachusetts, sold their homes and property and used the proceeds to help the Shakers build a ship. In return for this financial help, the Shakers promised to take the people to "New Jerusalem." When the ship was finished, however, the Believers left their backers behind and sailed to the West Indies, where they loaded up with a variety of trade goods. They then allegedly sold the ship and cargo and kept the money, bilking the trusting people of Norton and Rehoboth.[17] Similar stories appear in *An Account of the People Called Shakers,* by Thomas Brown, who had once lived with Shakers—generally considered a reliable source—and in George Faber Clark's town history of Norton, Massachusetts.[18]

Such stories, whether true or not, riled non-Shakers, especially when added to the growing store of information about the Believers' ecstatic dancing and speaking in tongues. Because of their strange behavior, many people associated the Shakers with witchcraft. When Jemima Blanchard's sister was gathering firewood one morning, she dropped her end of a large stick when James Whittaker picked up the other end; she was afraid that he would "bewitch" her. On another occasion, a young man confided to Believer Amos Buttrick that the first time he visited Ann Lee he placed a silver coin in his mouth to protect him from her powers.[19]

Observing the Shakers or listening to them describe their experiences may have lent credence to the suppositions of witchcraft. When Sarah Whittemore, the young daughter of Harvard Shaker Samuel Whittemore, died in 1786, her father reacted quite strangely. According to a town history of New Ipswich, New Hampshire, Whittemore believed that Sarah was so "possessed of supernatural powers, exerted upon his cattle and other subjects, that when she died she was placed in a box of rough boards, and denied the common rites of burial." Jemima Blanchard, herself a Believer, claimed that she had flown through the air "supported by the power."[20]

Unfortunately for the Believers, they suffered more than witchcraft accusations. Nonbelievers were frightened by the Shakers' uncontrolled dancing, angered by their inroads into other denominations, threatened by the Believers' adherence to celibacy, and suspicious of the Shakers' pacifism and their English origins. Out of fear and apprehension, the world's people attacked the Shakers verbally and physically. The resulting violence influenced the Believers' early living patterns. Because conversion was based on personal contacts in the form of family and religious ties, Shakers clustered together in towns and neighborhoods. These clusters served a protective function, providing physical and economic security against hostile nonbelievers, and isolated Believers felt the absence of such a support network. The 1816 *Testimonies* recounts the trials of Peter and Abigail Bishop, the only Shakers in the town of Montague, Massachusetts. This couple, who earned their living by weaving, dying, and pressing cloth, took seriously their non-Shaker neighbors' threatened boycott of their business. Separated from other Believers, the Bishops had no one to whom they could turn for emergency financial support.[21]

Living near each other also provided Shakers with some protection against physical violence, though large numbers of Believers did not always deter the mobs from their intended course of action. The Shakers' experiences in Harvard are a case in point. After several "warnings out" and unsuccessful attempts to drive the Shakers from Harvard in 1781 and 1782, violence finally erupted in August 1782 when a large group of Believers gathered at the Square House to worship and visit with Ann Lee. Taking matters into their own hands, an angry mob converged upon the house and drove all nonresident Shakers out of Harvard. Enraged townsmen whipped and beat many of the Believers, including Jonathan Bridges and the elderly Jonathan Clark. They broke Eleazer Rand's arm and whipped Abijah Worster for "breaking up churches and families."[22]

Such persecution, rather than stopping the Shakers, actually encouraged their efforts by convincing them that they were beaten for speaking the truth. They continued to gather at Harvard, prompting another "warning out" in January 1783. Ann Lee left but returned in May. On June 1 another mob gathered, this time outside Elijah Wilds's home in Shirley, and remained in position all night. The following day William Lee and James Whittaker accompanied the crowd back to Harvard at the request of the mob leaders. When they neared the house of Believer Jeremiah Willard, the mob tied Whittaker to a tree limb and whipped him "till his back was all in a gore of blood, and the flesh bruised to a jelly." Whittaker survived, but Shaker tradition maintains that the tree limb withered and died soon after. The mob next went for William Lee, who knelt for his lashing. In the course of Lee's beating, Whittaker jumped on Lee's back, Bethiah Willard, who had been watching from the sidelines, jumped on Whittaker's back, and other Believers piled on top of Willard. The mob whipped them "inhumanly . . . without mercy." Willard's beating, which left her with a black eye, was so severe that she bore its scars for the rest of her life.[23]

Mob violence occurred in other towns that Ann Lee visited, but no attacks were as brutal or involved as many Believers as those at Harvard and Shirley. There are several explanations for this. Thomas Hammond, a mid-nineteenth-century Harvard Shaker, attributed the attacks to displaced hostility against Shadrach Ireland. He thought that the townspeople of Harvard associated Ann Lee with Ireland and felt justified in persecuting her, being "one generation older in bitterness" than people in other places where the Shakers had proselytized. Henry Nourse, a nonbeliever who wrote a nineteenth-century history of the town of Harvard, attributed the violence to the recent military experience of many of the mob members. Because flogging with cat-o'-nine-tails was still a common form of punishment in the military, Nourse thought it no surprise that angry men would resort to this same type of "brutality." Stephen J. Stein suggests that the townspeople were merely following standard practice in "warning out" poor nonresidents to prevent them from becoming a financial drain on the taxpayers. In fact, a combination of all three factors best explains the severe attacks at Harvard and Shirley.[24]

The physical violence of these early years took its toll on the Believers, especially Ann Lee and the Elders. After two and a half years of grueling evangelism, Ann Lee, William Lee, and James Whittaker returned to Niskeyuna in September 1783, physically and emotionally exhausted. William Lee died the following July, followed by Ann Lee in September.

Fortunately, her death, however trying it was for the Believers, did not seriously threaten her work in New England. When she returned to Niskeyuna, hundreds of Believers remained behind, clustered together in various towns and already developing mechanisms for living in community.

These clusters became important as a main source of members when it came time to organize the villages of Harvard and Shirley. Many Shakers, of course, were natives or residents of Harvard and Shirley. Many others came from nearby towns and villages, including Rowley, Lancaster, Petersham, Littleton, Westford, and Chelmsford. Another group of converts came from the towns of Rindge, Mason, and New Ipswich, New Hampshire, close to the New Hampshire-Massachusetts border. More isolated were Believers from the towns of Belchertown, located further west and a little south, and Grafton and Sutton, south of Worcester. Yet another cluster of Believers centered on Cambridge and nearby towns such as Woburn, Medford, and Lexington. Other Believers came from the area of Bridgewater, Taunton, and Norton, southeast of Harvard and Shirley. All of these localities were close to the original route traveled by Ann Lee on her missionary journey through New England.[25]

Shakers not only clustered in particular towns but also within certain parts of a town. Many people converted to Shakerism in Lancaster, Massachusetts, when Ann Lee visited in 1781; most of them resided in the north part of town. By 1783 Shaker converts in this area included the families of Aaron Cook, John Clark, Aaron Johnson, Samuel Barrett, Moses Hayward, Thomas Beckwith, John Melvin, and Samuel Whitney; the Whittemore sisters; Mr. Worcester; and Mrs. Manasseh Knight. Other converts soon followed. Most of these people were landowners, and the homes of some of them—Elijah Wilds, Aaron Lyon, and the Phillips family—became places of worship for the Shakers. A majority of these converts remained with the Shakers after the gathering.[26]

Several residents of New Ipswich, New Hampshire, including John Melvin, David Melvin, Jonathan Kinney, Amos Whittemore, and Nathaniel Williams, became Believers in 1784. Most of them lived in the southern part of New Ipswich. Again, many, if not all, were property owners and opened their homes to the Shakers. As many as forty or fifty Believers sometimes gathered to worship in the home of Amos Whittemore, "the leading man among them." The Shakers also held meetings at Samuel Whittemore's house.[27]

As Amos Whittemore's position suggests, Shakers organized clusters and appointed leaders over the various groupings of towns even before they gathered into communities. Aaron Williams of Lexington is another example of this pattern. He was head of the Cambridge cluster until, for an unspecified breach of conduct, he was removed from his position. (He later took his family to gather with Believers at Harvard.)[28] It is not clear if Ann Lee instituted this early system of leadership during her New England journey or if it was an ad hoc response to the needs of the group after she returned to Niskeyuna. It is also not clear if the power for appointing leaders lay with the local cluster or with the leaders at Niskeyuna.

Despite the ambiguity surrounding the origins of "clustering," it is clear that during their time in New England Ann Lee and the Elders taught the idea of communal responsibility for Believers. While they were at Harvard, Lee and the Elders reprimanded several Harvard Believers for caring more about the financial security of their married, nonbelieving children than of their children who had become Shakers. Jemima Blanchard recalled that when the missionaries were preparing to return to Niskeyuna in 1783, James Whittaker encouraged those with "considerable" property, such as Zaccheus Stevens and Jeremiah Willard, to share the burden of caring for others. He held up Aaron Jewett, who lived at the Square House, as an example of appropriate behavior: "This is a dry barren land, and hard to get a living on; and there is Brother Aaron Jewett, he takes in all the needy, and how charitable he is to them; and you must be kind to him and help him."[29]

Feeding the Believers was, in itself, a monumental task. Jemima Blanchard recalled that many times Ann Lee insisted on providing meals for the hundreds of people who would gather for worship. Unprepared for such crowds, Shaker women served food in shifts, without washing the plates or utensils between sittings. Finding enough food was another problem. According to the *Testimonies*, the Harvard Shakers were poor and providing a daily meal for the steady stream of visitors was a major undertaking. They could procure cheese and flour from fellow Believers in Hancock, Massachusetts, and the New York communities, but the bulk of their supplies had to come from Shakers in the area.[30] It was important, therefore, to share temporal responsibilities; a few people could not afford to care for the needs of the entire Shaker community.

Sharing temporal responsibilities also meant sharing individual resources, and evidence indicates that Believers pooled their property and received property as a community as early as 1786. In that year Timothy Phelps deeded seventy-three acres to Daniel and Oliver Burt. The Burts were specifically listed as Shakers in the transaction, indicating that they received the property for the Shaker community and not as private individuals.[31]

In that same year, James Whittaker wrote to Elijah Wilds at Shirley, advising him on how to deal with a group of rebellious Shakers. Whittaker wrote Wilds that he (Wilds) could release the "pr[i]est and his People[,] the Teacher & his Publicken[,] Provided they a gree to Relese you according to this Rule[,] that they make no more Demand upon us to Support Their Worship or any thing that appertains there unto for the futer." After the seceders had time to calm down, Wilds was to make an equitable settlement with them, insuring that both sides were happy with the exchange. "[T]hey can do you Justice according as it is written to Do Justice."[32]

An account of the Shirley Shakers, written by an outsider, also provides evidence about the early living patterns of the Believers. When William Bentley visited the Shirley Believers in their "infancy" (probably during the 1780s), he noted that "as soon as they had made converts sufficient for little societies, they became fond of settling together. These settlements did not appear to be a part of any original plan, but a dictate of fanaticism, & directed by numerous conveniences which they proposed."[33]

Thus, it becomes apparent that the Shakers under Joseph Meacham were experimenting with communal living arrangements in the earliest years of the movement. The Shaker community at Harvard was officially gathered in 1791 and at Shirley in 1793. Yet consolidation had been taking place among these Believers long before the orders from New Lebanon instructed them to do so. From the beginning of the movement, single Believers in particular had lived with Shaker families. Some were probably employed as servants or had been shepherded out by their parents to family or friends. Upon his conversion in October 1784, Amos Buttrick moved in with Elijah Wilds's family; he was twenty-seven. Betty Druse was residing at the John Maynard home in Grafton, Massachusetts, perhaps as a servant, when she became a Believer. At one point she moved to Believer David Dwinnel's house in Sutton, Massachusetts, before finally uniting with the South family of Shirley Shakers.[34]

The extent to which Believers were living together before the gathering of the Church is clear from the first United States census, taken in 1790, which reveals the large size of several households headed by Shakers.

Aaron Jewett's household contained five males sixteen or older, four males younger than sixteen, and fourteen women. Jeremiah Willard's home held nine men sixteen or older, two boys younger than sixteen, and fifteen women. Ethan Phillips of Lancaster had two men older than sixteen and eleven women living at his place. Nathan Willard housed three men older than sixteen, two boys younger than sixteen, and nine women. Finally, Elijah Wilds of Shirley, the "father" of the Shirley Shakers, housed ten men sixteen or older, four boys younger than sixteen, and twenty-two women.[35] A total of one hundred and twelve people were living among five Shaker households by 1790.

Some of the residents of these combined households were probably Shakers who had originally lived outside of Harvard and Shirley and who sold their land to move closer to Believers. There was a general "clearing out," for example, of the Believers in Lancaster, who sold their property to several families from Reading in 1796. Another option for Shakers who left their hometowns was to buy property near Harvard and Shirley and set up private residences. Joseph Wyeth bought twelve acres of land from fellow Believer Solomon Cooper for $168 in 1785 and moved his wife Eunice and their family to this property from Cambridge. Eunice's father and mother, John and Mary Bathrick, moved with the Wyeths to be near the Shakers but eventually discontinued their affiliation with the Believers.[36]

With an increasing concentration of Believers near Harvard and Shirley, the Shakers had accomplished much by the last decade of the eighteenth century. Beginning with clusters of Believers who could support each other emotionally, spiritually, and financially, the Shakers moved to the next phase of establishing community—a loosely organized polity of shared residences. With the Square House as the physical and religious center of this newly burgeoning community, the gradual accumulation of Shakers living in proximity to Harvard and Shirley on their own farms, the pooling of property, and the integration of households created a sense of order among the Believers. Their actions also seemed to impress their neighbors. By creating village-like settings and ordering their lives around a central place of worship, the Shakers must have appeared less threatening, for in 1787 Harvard town allowed the Believers to "draw their Money which they pay for Schooling and appropriate it to that use as they shall think proper." The goodwill of the townspeople was not always consistent—having once made this concession to the Shakers, the town did not renew the privilege most years—nor did it mean that all tensions between the Shakers and the "World" had disappeared, but it does suggest a certain degree of acceptance of the Shakers only a few short years after violent mobs had risen against them.[37] Thus from the very beginning, "families," whether united by blood, common cause, or persecution, played a pivotal role in the Shaker movement. How these families, and the men and women in them, dealt with the specifics of community formation is the subject of the next chapter.

2

Gathering the Believers

THE OFFICIAL GATHERING OF BELIEVERS began in 1787 at New Lebanon and Watervliet, New York, under the guidance of Joseph Meacham and Lucy Wright, the leaders of the Central Ministry of the United Society.[1] Meacham was the architect of Shaker village organization, and he devised a scheme for dividing villages into three orders or families, each family representing an increasing level of commitment to the society. The highest order was the Church family, a select group of members who were to give all their money and property to the society and renounce all ties to the world; because of the seriousness of this decision, minors could not join the Church.[2]

With this village "blueprint" in mind, Meacham and Wright selected pairs of leaders, known as "parents," to found Shaker communities throughout New England and New York. In 1791 they sent "Father" Eleazer Rand and "Mother" Hannah Kendall to gather the village of Harvard, followed in 1793 by Shirley. Both leaders were chosen because of their devotion to Ann Lee and the early Shaker movement, but in temperament and background they represented opposite ends of the wide range of people who were attracted to Shakerism.

Eleazer Rand was born in Charlestown, Massachusetts, on September 18, 1763, into a modest but "respectable" family. He never knew his father, a seaman who died before Rand's birth. Rand lived with his mother and siblings until he was eight, at which time he took a job as a servant in a Boston boarding house. He was still working in Boston four years later when the American Revolution broke out. Even as a twelve-year-old he was deeply concerned about the wounded soldiers and donated money toward their care. He lived in Boston two more years, but the war upset his delicate emotional balance, compelling him to leave his job. He ended up in the town of Harvard, working for Zaccheus Stevens, a wealthy farmer.[3]

In 1781 the Stevens family, including eighteen-year-old Rand, converted to Shakerism. Rand was appointed the "principal singer" at worship meetings and soon became one of Ann Lee's trusted traveling ministers. Committed to Lee's gospel, he suffered severely in one of the mob attacks at Harvard. Not only did members of the mob whip him, punch him, and throw him against a wall, but they also beat him so fiercely that they broke his arm. He survived the attack and in 1784 moved with the Stevens family to Niskeyuna to live with Ann Lee. He moved to New Lebanon in 1787, and from there he was sent to Harvard in February 1791.[4]

Hannah Kendall's childhood and youth were very different. Born on December 30, 1760, into a wealthy family in Woburn, Massachusetts, she grew up surrounded by finery and the latest fashions. In 1781 or 1782 she, her parents, and six siblings became Believers. In accordance with Shaker principles, the Kendall family disposed of its luxuries; Hannah "began to strip herself of her fine cloths and to put on a garment of humiliation suitable for a handmaid of Christ and Mother Ann."[5]

Kendall, who became a favorite of Ann Lee's and traveled with her extensively in New England, was known as "friend Hannah" who was "valient for the truth by standing boldly in its defence." Many of the stories recorded about Kendall's early years as a Shaker depict her as a clever and playful young woman, strong in her convictions and unafraid of the mobs. When Lee died, Kendall moved back to Woburn to live with her family until they sold their property and moved to the New Lebanon Shaker village. It was from here that Kendall, too, was sent to Harvard in April 1791.[6]

As soon as Rand and Kendall began to translate Meacham's idealized plans into a workable reality, they encountered difficulties. Despite Meacham's penchant for uniformity, it became clear quite early that Harvard and Shirley would evolve at their own rate and not always in accordance with his neat divisions. In 1791, for example, the Harvard Shakers formed only one group, "the Family." Not until October 1793 did they divide themselves between the Family (which became the Church family) and the South House, carefully returning to those who would be living at the latter the land, cattle, and other property they had given to the Church when they entered. The registers of the Harvard and Shirley Church families, furthermore, indicate that children were members of both families, despite Meacham's prohibition.[7] Years later a New Lebanon Believer who was visiting Harvard noted this trend in his journal. Unused to the practice, the author surmised, "This is something quite new—it may be profitable."[8]

Despite such deviations, Harvard and Shirley developed along the general lines set forth by Meacham. Committed to communal living, they relied heavily on their own resources and talents to meet the needs of the new villages. Early records indicate that many Believers contributed to the Shaker enterprise according to their means. The "Manifest Journal," the earliest financial record of Harvard covering the years 1791 to 1806, lists donations of money, food, and other articles made by individual Believers, as well as the settlements the Shakers made with those who left, and it provides a detailed inventory of the Harvard community in the first year of its existence. By listing each gift by name, the journal also allows us to assess the contributions made by men and women, providing a window onto the early importance of women to the Shaker endeavor.

The significant role that the sisters played is borne out when one looks at the cash that Believers gave to Harvard over the course of the first year. In the form of dollars, pounds, and promissory notes, Harvard Shakers donated approximately £370 ($1,233). A major portion of that money came from one person, the widow Deborah Prentice, who gave more than £160 to the Church, the single largest amount given by an individual and most likely her inheritance from her husband. But other women, too, gave generously, and the total amount of cash and promissory notes donated by the sisters was £245, or 66 percent of the total amount of money taken in by the Harvard society in 1791.[9]

Other donations recorded in the journal represent typical food items and articles found in rural New England households at that time. Approximately 95 bushels of rye and 24 bushels of Indian corn, staple ingredients in the bread common to rural households; more than 255 pounds of cheese; approximately 1,100 pounds of beef, veal, and pork; and nearly 27 barrels of cider made up some of the food donations of the year. Of this amount the sisters gave 6 bushels of rye and 46 pounds of cheese. Women also provided butter, chocolate, and tea to the Shaker larder. Household items given to the Shakers included three beds and assorted furniture, teaspoons, an iron skillet, and a variety of dishes. Many of these items came from Elijah Wilds, a wealthy farmer from Shirley, but entries

that list Mercy Clark's gift of two pewter plates or Elizabeth Crouch's dona-
tion of one "large earthen plate" leave the reader wondering if such gifts
could be analogous to the story of the widow's mite found in the New
Testament.[10]

Matching the fervor of the Believers' financial donations was an initially
quick growth spurt in both villages, attested to by detailed membership
rosters, found in appendix A, that I have compiled from archival registers,
journals, and town histories. Between January 1791 and January 1793 the
Harvard community took in 185 people: 130 adults, 44 children, and 11
whose ages are unknown. The gender balance was almost even, 96 females
and 89 males. Most of the converts, 140 or 75.7 percent, had at least one
other family member who was a Shaker, most likely living at either Harvard
or Shirley but sometimes living at one of the other Shaker communities.
Shirley's gathering population (1792–1793) was somewhat smaller at 124
people—90 adults, 28 children, and 6 whose ages are unknown. The gender ratio was much less balanced than Harvard's with 76 females and 48
males. Even more than Harvard, however, most residents, 108 or 87.1 percent, had family members among the Believers.

Further examination of these rosters reveals important information
about the nature of the early communities, showing who stayed, who left,
and who moved to other Shaker villages; at what age the individuals came
into the Shaker communities; and whether or not the individuals came with
their families. Based on these figures, which may be found in tabular form in
appendix B, it is possible to determine how gender, age, and family connections affected retention at Harvard and Shirley.

One of the most surprising pieces of information revealed by these figures is the relative fluidity of the villages. From the beginning both Harvard
and Shirley experienced a steady stream of incoming and outgoing residents, and overall retention was low. In the years under consideration for
Harvard the retention rate (assuming that those people whose names simply disappear from the records ultimately left the Shakers) was 51.9 percent, whereas Shirley's retention rate was slightly better at 62.9 percent. An
additional 6.5 percent of the residents at each village moved to another
Shaker village.

Breaking down the numbers of those who left Harvard and Shirley by
age and gender reveals that both factors had a significant impact on retention rates. Of those who entered as adults, 66.9 percent from Harvard and

77.8 percent from Shirley remained in those villages for life, whereas of those who entered as children under the age of eighteen, only 20.5 percent from Harvard and 28.6 percent from Shirley stayed in those communities for life.[11] Moreover, women were much more likely than men to spend their lives with the Shakers. Retention rates of males at Harvard and Shirley were 36 percent and 46 percent respectively. But 67 percent of the women at Harvard and 74 percent of the women at Shirley remained in those villages until their deaths.[12]

Contrary to my expectations, however, family relationships did not seem to have a dramatic effect on retention. Despite the large numbers of family conversions, family connections did not guarantee that members would stay with the Shakers. In fact, the number of adults with family who left and the number of adults without family who left were very similar, 28.3 percent and 22.6 percent respectively at Harvard, and 15.2 percent and 18.2 percent respectively at Shirley. A similar situation occurred with children. Of the children who came with families to Harvard, 75.7 percent left, whereas of the children who came alone, 71.4 percent left. At Shirley, 65.4 percent of the children who came with families left, compared to 50 percent who came without families. In each case, the difference between the percentage of those who came with family and left and those who came alone and left was statistically insignificant.[13]

The obvious conclusions to be drawn from these statistics are that adults who came to live with the Believers were much more likely to stay than those who came as children, and that women were more likely to stay than men. Both of these observations reinforce the conventional wisdom that adult women are more pious or religious than adult men and thus more likely to be attracted to a religious community. The imbalanced sex ratios noted by later commentators such as Charles Nordhoff, who found that most Shaker villages in the 1870s had one-third men and two-thirds women, seems to have been an ongoing problem at Harvard and Shirley. This by no means implies that men did not play an important role in those two villages or that they did not make good Shakers. On the contrary, men contributed equally with women to the creation and maintenance of Harvard and Shirley. Yet on the whole, more women than men of the founding generation committed themselves to Shakerism.[14]

Clearly, the problems with retention of children and adult males that would eventually jeopardize the Shakers' communal endeavor began in the earliest years of the movement. Although later Shaker records treat the inability of the Believers to keep children in their communities as a new phenomenon, explained by the fact that the children had never known Ann Lee and lacked the zeal of the early Believers, the Shakers at Harvard and Shirley had never been particularly successful at keeping the younger generation interested in communal life.[15] Many of the youth who were brought to these villages during the gathering period could have conceivably met Ann Lee before she died, yet this did not stop the exodus of young adults from the villages. When given a choice, those who came to the Shakers involuntarily more often than not chose to leave. As Rosabeth Moss Kanter explains, "As committed as [the second generation] may be to the community, their commitment stems from different life experiences from that of their parents." Thus, "children often rebelled against the commitment made for them by their parents."[16]

Certainly the persecution suffered by the first adult converts was a strong bond that tied adults to the villages. Many men and women who gathered at Harvard and Shirley, including Eleazer Rand, Hannah Kendall, Mary Hammond, Bethiah Willard, Abijah Worster, Jonathan Clark, and Jonathan Bridges, had suffered verbal assaults and physical abuse at the hands of angry mobs. Others left unnamed could be added to the list. Many of the testimonies of the early Believers verify that the physical and verbal persecution convinced them that the Shakers were the people of God: if the Believers did not speak the truth, then people would not feel the need to silence them. The argument was circular—the Shakers were persecuted for their beliefs because their beliefs were true, and their beliefs were true because the Shakers were persecuted—but to the Believers this logic made perfect sense and strengthened their commitment to Shakerism. Indeed, as Kanter has also noted, persecution binds a group together by clarifying the boundary between "us" and "them" and acts as a "social vaccine," prompting the group to work together as it fortifies itself against future threats.[17]

A third conclusion one can draw from these statistics is that the conversion of biological families did not guarantee an individual member's retention. Indeed, many factors other than biological relationships can help explain why people chose to stay with the Shakers. Women, especially, who defied their family and social convention by leaving their spouse and children to make a life with the Shakers invested much in their decision and were unlikely to leave the community. Others who came alone, such as widows or orphans, may have felt compelled to stay, having nowhere else to go.

Nevertheless, to say that family relationships were not statistically significant in the retention of Believers is not to say that families did not play an important role in the early stability of Harvard and Shirley. Many families, such as the Babbitt, Bridges, Crouch, and Jewett families at Harvard and the Warner and Willard families at Shirley, brought in large numbers of converts, mainly adults, who remained faithful Shakers. Many of these family members became the backbone of Shaker society and took on positions of responsibility. They also provided a numerical buffer against those who would leave in the future.

Because these first adult converts, whether they came with their families or not, were responsible for organizing and administering the villages, their social and economic backgrounds are very important for understanding early Shakerism. Although their lives changed dramatically in many ways after conversion, the Believers still carried with them deeply ingrained preconversion beliefs and attitudes. These beliefs were shared by their non-Shaker neighbors, for the religious and cultural background of Shaker converts was similar, if not identical, to other New Englanders. The religious upheaval of the Great Awakening, the rise of "Radical Evangelicalism," and the social, political, and economic dislocation of the American Revolution provided a common backdrop to individual lives. Some found comfort in joining one of the new sectarian groups, such as the Shakers, that emerged from the "turbulent paroxysm of religious, political, social, and economic unrest" of late eighteenth-century America.[18] Yet despite the Believers' break with their past, their past continued to shape their understanding of basic Shaker precepts.

Most Shaker converts had some sort of religious background. Those at Harvard and Shirley came mainly from three religious groups—Irelandites, Baptists, and Congregationalists. The Irelandite converts represented those whose spiritual quest had already led them far from Congregationalism, and so they seemed the most likely to follow Ann Lee with her emphasis on celibacy and the spiritual family. Isaac and Hannah Willard separated from the Congregational Church in 1751 before becoming followers of Ireland and then converting to Shakerism. Abijah Worster made a similar spiritual trek. He first joined the Congregational Church, then worshiped with the Baptists, next became an Irelandite, and finally decided that Ann Lee possessed the true gospel. Other former Irelandites among the Harvard and Shirley Believers were Beulah Burt, Jonathan and Sarah Cooper, Samuel and Abigail Cooper and their two daughters Beulah and Deliverance, Abel and Mary Jewett, Sarah Jewett, Ethan Phillips, and Deborah Williams.[19]

Other Believers first sought spiritual enlightenment among the Baptists. Jemima Blanchard was one of the original members of the Baptist society formed in Harvard in 1776. Eunice Wyeth, Oliver and Rachel Adams, Sarah Burt, and Elizabeth Woodward also joined or worshiped with the Baptist churches in their communities. Nathan Willard and John Robinson were raised as Baptists from infancy.[20] Still other Shaker converts, like the Crouch and Warner families, seem to have remained in the Congregational Church until they became Believers, though one of the Crouch sons attended the Baptist Church for two years after a revival broke out there.[21]

It is no surprise that Irelandites, Baptists, and even Congregationalists were attracted to Ann Lee's radical alternative to the prewar social order following the dislocation and confusion engendered by the Great Awakening and the American Revolution. Her appeal was strengthened, moreover, by the familiarity many aspects of Shakerism would have had for her followers, given their shared religious milieu. The emotional religious services of the Believers were similar to the volatile revivals of the Great Awakening. And Lee's emphasis on industry, frugality, prudence, and moderation—the cornerstones of her conception of social order—were traits already practiced by many New Englanders, legacies of their Puritan ancestors.

Even those teachings that seemed most Shaker contained elements of familiarity. The use of oral confession of sins as a precondition for admission into the Shaker community was similar to both the Congregational Church's confession of faith and the Baptists' emphasis on personal testimony as mechanisms for monitoring group membership.[22] Even renunciation of the flesh was not an entirely new idea to New England Calvinists. Although Stephen Marini argues that "the local sects [including the Shakers] unmistakably modified the Calvinist theological tradition,"[23] Ann Lee's doctrine of celibacy was largely an extension, rather than a modification, of Calvinist ideas. Lee's renunciation of sexual intercourse and castigation of the flesh took the doctrine of physical and human depravity, a central tenet of Calvinism, to its logical extreme. On the intellectual plane, then, moving from a previous religious affiliation to Shakerism was not necessarily a large step. Those who joined the Shakers, whatever their religious background, did not have to reject entirely their religious belief system. Rather, caught up in the millennial expectations so much a part of the religious landscape at that time, those who became Believers could seek the fulfillment of their religious hopes, not their negation, by choosing to follow Ann Lee.

If it is true that the Shakers were a haven for religious dissenters, it is not true that they were a congregation of indigents. The Believers at Harvard and Shirley were frequently characterized as poor or lower-class, both by the Shakers and by outside observers.[24] In the early days, when hundreds of people gathered at the Square House from miles around, such a characterization may have been accurate, because Lee's message and personal magnetism appealed to all classes. But biographical information about the early converts who gathered at Harvard and Shirley indicates that most of them were, in fact, typical "middling class" rural New Englanders—business-minded, subsistence-level-plus, yeoman farmers—who were "virtually indistinguishable [economically] from the rest of the community"[25] and whose background influenced the early organization of the Shaker communities.

In the late eighteenth century, Harvard and Shirley were typical small New England towns. Most male residents were yeoman farmers who owned a fair amount of property, real and personal. In Worcester County, where Harvard is located, four-fifths of the men owned at least £100 worth of property. Seventy percent of the population occupied "a great middle class of small property owners. . . . [N]early two-thirds of the estates belonged to farmers." In 1771 the average farm in Concord, still a sleepy rural town near Harvard, consisted of 57 acres, with 20.2 percent of the land under tillage. The typical farmer owned approximately one horse, three oxen, four cows, two pigs, and six sheep.[26]

It was out of this environment that the first Shakers came. At least twenty-one individuals or families at Harvard were known property owners, and at least twenty Shirley individuals or families owned property or came from propertied families. Often the exact amount of land is not specified in the records, but in several cases it is clear that Shakers were substantial property owners. Seth Babbitt, who owned at least 120 acres; Jonathan Bridges, who owned at least 116 acres; and the Jewett and Willard families were some of the largest landholders to gather at Harvard.[27] Reuben Barrett, a husbandman who owned at least 80 acres; Nathan Willard, a prosperous bachelor with a "competent" share of property; and brothers Elijah and Ivory Wilds were substantial property owners at Shirley.[28]

Representing the middling class of average landholders in rural Massachusetts were men like David Dwinnel and Samuel Cooper of Harvard, who owned about 64 acres and 75 acres respectively. Samuel Kilbourn, who owned more than 43 acres, and Ethan Phillips, who owned at least 31 acres, were among the average landholders at Shirley. Some of the younger Believers also came from propertied families, including Asa Brocklebank, whose father sold a 70-acre farm to the Harvard Shakers; Sheffield and Lavina Haywood; and Lydia Longley, whose father was a landowner and miller.[29]

In 1810 a general accounting took place at Shirley, and members certified what they had donated to the Society in 1792 and 1793. In 1792, even before the community was officially gathered, Daniel Clark and David Melvin each donated property valued at $333, and Abel Beckwith consecrated $800 worth of property. Jonathan and Susanna Kenny gave the community property worth $500. Other real-estate donations include those made by Ruth Robbins, Dorothy Merrell, Ruth and Susanna Whittemore, Mercy Buttrick, and the six Warner sisters, who each gave their 9-acre share in the farm that they had inherited. Hannah Knight gave thirteen sheep, four beds, and other furniture.[30]

The items that people donated to the Shaker communities in 1791— typical products of New England farms—also suggest that many of the Believers owned land. Tenant farming was uncommon in rural New England, and the quantity of items donated indicates that people were relying largely on their land and not on the Shakers for food. Given that the total average yearly meat allowance in the widow's portion of Middlesex County wills from 1781 to 1799 was between 178 and 195.9 pounds and the average quantity of grains was 10.9 bushels of Indian corn and 6.3 bushels of rye, the Harvard community would have been destitute if all the members were dependent on the society for their meat and grain.[31] The 1,100-odd pounds of meat donated to the Church would not go far among 185 members, nor would the 96 bushels of rye or the 24 bushels of Indian corn. Some Believers were probably dependent on the Shakers for all their needs, but many families, like Joseph Wyeth's, Oliver Adams's, and David Dwinnel's, remained on their own property. They contributed to the society, but they certainly relied on their own farms for most of their food and other necessities.

Other Believers, such as Abijah Worster, came from less prosperous backgrounds. Worster was born in Harvard in 1745. His father died when he was nine, he later recounted, so he "was put out to strangers" and "suffered many hardships and by unkind dealings . . . lost [his] health." To escape this life, Worster entered the military, helping garrison Crown Point and Halifax after the French and Indian War. He also served as a fifer in the early days of the American Revolution but deserted on August 25, 1775. He joined the Shakers when Ann Lee came to Harvard and moved to Niskeyuna, where he lived until the Shakers gathered at Harvard, at which time he moved there. He did not bring property or much money to the community, but he did bring a fervent zeal for Shakerism and became one of Harvard's most beloved members.[32]

Considered together, this information provides a useful key to understanding the early Shaker movement. One characteristic of these early Believers stands out in particular—many were from Yankee farm families, sharing a common background and common values with their non-Shaker neighbors. Like all New England farmers, they lived in a surplus export economy, raising enough crops to support themselves, trading or selling what was left over, and priding themselves on their independence from others. This concept of independence, however, did not imply total self-sufficiency, a situation that was impossible for the average farmer. Realizing that they could not survive alone, argues Christopher Clark, New England farmers understood independence as the act of maintaining "control [over] the means both to make a living and to pass the resources for independence onto their offspring." They also understood that this control had to be conducted within a system of "interdependence" where neighbors and family members exchanged goods and labor. These reciprocal exchanges were facilitated by the use of account books in which farmers kept track of the various relationships among themselves. If a man needed help, his neighbors were expected to come to his aid, but the work was recorded, and he was expected to repay his debt when he was able. Repayment was almost always in goods or services; cash payments implied finality and a break in the web of interdependence.[33]

The Shakers were an integral part of this rural network. They had been yeoman farmers long before they became Believers, and they continued to work within this web of rural life with their non-Shaker neighbors after their conversion. Thus, it is not surprising to find that their ideas of communal living were influenced by their previous experience as independent farmers. Nowhere is this observation more clearly illustrated than in the

Shakers' implementation of communal ownership of real and personal property. Shaker villages were organized on the principle of "community of interest" or "joint interest" developed by Joseph Meacham. Probably a part of the oral covenant to which Believers assented when they first gathered in 1788, the principle was codified in the 1795 written covenant. Each Believer was guaranteed "an Equal right and privilege, according to their Calling and needs, in things both Spiritual and temporal." Those who joined the Church family agreed to turn over all their property, real and personal. Joint interest was, according to Stephen J. Stein, "not merely a right, but a duty, given that they [the Believers] had 'received the grace of God in Christ by the Gospel, and were Called to follow him in the Regeneration.' "34

But the implementation of a joint interest at Harvard and Shirley was not an easy task. The earlier informal communal arrangements probably worked better for Believers, since compliance was voluntary and could be modified to fit the needs of the particular community. Once the Central Ministry made communal living a requirement, the local Ministries were faced with recalcitrant members who refused to comply. Indeed, a close look at the real-estate transactions at Harvard and Shirley shows that not all Believers gave of their land or goods freely. Many Shakers did make sizable land donations to Believers, but the Shakers also spent a significant amount of money on land. In the 1840s the Harvard Shakers began to keep a list of land transactions dating back to the Believers' purchase of the Square House farm in 1782, and they continued this list into the 1850s. Although the list does not always indicate if a person acted as a private individual or as an agent for the Shakers and missing information leaves some transactions unclear, the records do provide a sense of the real estate passing through the hands of the Harvard Shakers and illustrate the ambiguity that existed from the beginning in Shaker economic arrangements.

One of the first problems the Harvard Shakers faced was consolidating ownership of the Square House farm. The Shakers were not a legally constituted body at the time of the purchase, and apparently the property was bought in shares by individual Believers. One of the original owners was Aaron Jewett. Sometime before 1799, Aaron Jewett deeded sixty-four acres of the Square House farm and some other property to his eldest son, Abel. In 1799 Abel Jewett then deeded all of this property to Aaron Jewett and Seth Babbitt as representatives of the Church for $100. Solomon Cooper must also have been an original owner of the Square House farm, because in

April 1784 he deeded to Aaron Jewett, for $53.33, eight acres included in the original deed of the Square House farm as well as some other property.[35]

These transactions reveal two characteristics of early Shaker communal life. On the one hand, it appears that the earliest Believers were committed to the idea of communal property and trusted certain individuals to purchase land for the group even though they were not acting as official agents. Apparently, it was understood that at the proper time these men would transfer the property to the community. On the other hand, the Square House transactions also point out the ambiguity of Shaker notions of communal property. In both cases, money changed hands between the Shaker community and the owners of the Square House property. It is true that the money paid by the Shakers often seems well below market value for the amount of acreage concerned. Unfortunately, the lack of records from this early period makes it impossible to determine why the Believers made these payments. One surmise is that the payments had something to do with the internal mechanism of land transactions in Massachusetts and indicate that the Shakers understood and worked within the land-tenure system that was developing at the end of the colonial period.

The ambiguity of the Shakers' concept of property is heightened if one takes into account further real-estate transactions in which Shakers sold, rather than donated, their property to the communities. Joseph Wyeth, who was admitted into the Church in 1824, sold his estate of twenty acres and an additional fourteen acres of woodland to the Church family trustees in 1829 for $200. Mary Hammond, Nathan Kendall, and Benjamin Winchester also sold land to the Believers. In 1801 even Isaac Willard, a patriarch of the Shirley Shakers, and his son Jeremiah, who left the Shakers in 1796, sold the Believers a piece of property adjacent to one of the Shaker residences for $500.[36]

Even more surprising were the times when private ownership of property seemed to be sanctioned by the Church. In 1804 the Shirley Church deacons sold Ivory Wilds, a prominent Shaker whose property had become the site of the North family, a piece of swamp land for a dollar. Wilds had previously deeded the land to the Church. The year before, the Church had agreed to return a plot of land in northern Lancaster to Ivory's brother, Elijah, who was also a prominent Shaker and whose property had become the site of the Church family. As in Ivory's case, Elijah had first given this land to the Church.[37]

The apparent discontinuity between the Shaker principle of joint interest and the actual practices at Harvard and Shirley is understandable when one considers the Shakers' preconversion background. The Shakers came directly out of a yeoman farmer tradition that valued land for both its physical and its symbolic characteristics and employed a land-tenure system that supported private ownership. Land, of course, was central to the rural economy and the main source of a farmer's livelihood. Yet the social and moral values attached to owning property, such as independence and social acceptability, were equally important to yeomen farmers and paved the way for their participation in society.[38] Land ownership was an important criterion in the election of officers in the military as well as the election of men to political positions, and farmers benefited from this situation. After the American Revolution, the number of yeoman farmers in the state legislatures increased dramatically from the prewar years.[39]

Thus, land ownership as a measure of independence and social credibility was deeply ingrained in rural New Englanders, and despite Meacham's well-intentioned ideals, many Believers continued to treat private property as an important element in social arrangements. The Believers of Harvard and Shirley were not purposefully subverting Shaker ideas, but filtering them through their own experience, implementing Shaker practices in a way that fit their own understanding of the proper relationship between people and property.

Another manifestation of the yeoman predilections of Shaker converts was the Believers' use of meticulous records. Record keeping was an important aspect of the yeoman farmer's life because it defined the boundaries of his interdependence. As Christopher Clark notes, New England farmers occasionally maintained double-entry account books in which they listed both their debits and credits. Most farmers, however, only kept track of what they had given to or done for others. Clark suggests that New England farmers may have found it offensive for someone to keep a running total of what was owed him by others because it put him in a position to call in his debts when it was advantageous to him.[40] Shaker records, however, reveal that the Believers used double-entry bookkeeping from the beginning, diligently recording when they settled with somebody and when somebody settled with them.

The Shakers not only maintained records of their business relations with the world but also kept track of debts within the society. Contrary to the idea of communal living, goods and services were not always freely given, either within one community or between two different communities. In 1801, for example, the Harvard Church paid David Dwinell, a Church family member, $1.27 to weave twenty yards of cloth. Ivory Wilds, the head of the Shirley North family, was in debt to the Harvard Shakers between 1801 and 1805 for a bitstock and bits, nails, a horse harness, a sieve, a dipper, an onion, a wooden wheel, and other items. He received credit for supplying the Harvard community with boards, rye, corn, bristle, "1 dog skin dresst" worth $1.00, white beans, and cash. One of the most blatant "noncommunal" transactions involved the Harvard Church's billing Simon Cooper for taking care of his widowed mother, Sarah Cooper, who was a Believer. In 1802 Simon Cooper was charged $4.50 for sugar and tea and $113.00 for "entertaining your mother from 23rd of March 1801 to this time [19 January 1802]." The Shakers credited him $66.39 for butter, rye, building a wall, and cash. Several years later the Shakers charged Cooper $118.49 for "entertaining" his mother from March 23, 1802, to January 1807. The Shakers then billed him $28.00 for boarding and nursing his mother from January 1 to April 9, 1807, the day that she died, adding a $3.00 charge for building her coffin and digging her grave. Simon Cooper received credit for the years 1805 to 1808 for providing the Church with veal, lamb, and the labor of his son, Jonathan.[41]

The charges made to Simon Cooper are puzzling. Sarah Cooper, then eighty-six years old, was admitted into the Harvard Church in March 1801, the date it began assessing charges, and she lived in the Square House until her death in 1807. As a covenanted Church member, her support should have been taken on by the society, not billed to her son. The Harvard Church family, however, probably justified the charges by arguing that Cooper, being elderly, could not work and earn her support. Furthermore, her husband had been a saddler, a low-paying occupation, and may well have left his wife only a small inheritance. Hence, she probably had little money to give to the Church.[42] The Shakers' insistence on charging for Cooper's care and their keeping records of these transactions reflect their notion of interdependence—somehow, Sarah Cooper had to carry her fair share of the family's expenses.

Sarah Cooper's story represents the ambiguities of life in the early Shaker movement as the Believers struggled to work out their religious convictions in practical terms. Yet, as the Shakers at Harvard and Shirley settled into their communities, they seem to have found a niche for themselves in the American landscape. William Bentley, the diarist who had visited the Shirley Shakers in the 1780s, made another visit to both Harvard and Shirley in 1795, intrigued by a group that had "advanced from such unformed state, to the more civilized condition of little Towns, & families."[43]

When he visited Shirley, with its population of around 180 residents, he found the buildings to be neat, tidy, and in good order. The Shirley Shakers, he was told, owned about three thousand acres of land and grew rye, corn, and flax. He did not meet the Shaker sisters because they "were busy at their Looms," but the ones who came to the window to wave to him "were modest, more free than we expected, & discovered obliging manners." He noted that the style of their clothing was similar to that of rural folk, the main difference being "the wide borders on their caps which hid the greater part of the face." Bentley left with a positive impression of Shirley. "It is said," he wrote, that "the services are too severe, which are exacted [from Believers]. But upon their countenances nothing could be seen which discovered discontent. In their general industry, & equal condition, there seemed no present cause for complaint. There were persons of all ages, & in the proportions usual in our Towns." Several days later Bentley took a tour of Harvard. He learned that the village owned about a thousand acres and numbered more than two hundred residents. Bentley saw a four-acre garden bursting with vegetables and visited the various industries of the village.[44]

Bentley's diary depicts Harvard and Shirley as two fledgling but thriving communities similar to neighboring non-Shaker towns. Bentley was impressed by the changes he observed from his first visit, when the Shakers lived in a less organized manner and were more aggressive about their religion. His description of the villages in 1795—sturdy and well-kept buildings, productive fields, a wide range of industries, contented residents, and a good balance in gender and age ratios—placed the Believers among the ranks of solid and upstanding citizens. He does comment on Shaker practices, such as the sisters' bonnets, celibacy, and the separation of the sexes, but he does not emphasize these differences over the generally "normal" conditions he found in the two villages.

Clearly, then, despite the Shakers' attempts to remove themselves from the world, they shared many beliefs and attitudes with their non-Shaker neighbors, which influenced their ideas of social organization and communalism. A close look at the Believers' preconversion background highlights these often overlooked similarities—their participation in the rural network of interdependence and their shared place on the religious continuum of rural New England. These similarities in no way minimize those aspects of Shaker life and thought that did separate the Believers from the world, but they do suggest that, from the beginning of the movement, the Shakers were less marginal to American society than scholarship has suggested. Both Believers and nonbelievers were seeking a place for themselves in a world turned upside-down by revolution; Shakerism was just one expression, albeit a radical one, of that search.

3

Constructing Community

WITH THE OFFICIAL GATHERING OF BELIEVERS under Rand and Kendall, Harvard and Shirley entered the formative period of their history. During these years the Believers faced the fundamental challenge of translating their ideas into a workable reality. In short, each village had to construct a sense of community and forge the bonds that would keep it united. Merely living together would not insure survival or give meaning to the Believers' actions. The group had to function as a family—defining its boundaries, providing a rationale for its actions and organization, and supplying an identity for its members.

The success of the Shakers in these early years depended largely on the quality of leadership that the Central Ministry appointed. Fortunately, Eleazer Rand and Hannah Kendall proved to be capable and popular leaders who gave the two villages the early stability they needed to survive. As the "parents" and first Ministry of Harvard and Shirley, Rand and Kendall divided their time between the two villages. Though Harvard was their primary residence, they made periodic, and sometimes lengthy, visits to Shirley, often in response to a crisis or problem. Such constant attention to the needs of the bishopric insured a strong foundation for future growth.

Although both Rand and Kendall played an important function in the establishment of the two villages, "Mother" Hannah, in particular, influenced the development of Harvard and Shirley more than any other single person. A competent and intelligent woman, she led the Shakers in addressing the temporal and spiritual issues which surrounded their newly gathered communities, including the nature of communal property, the merits of the spiritual as well as the biological family, the status and role of women in Shaker society, relationships with the outside world, and the problem of apostasy, the term the Shakers used to describe the overwhelming turnover of population they witnessed during this period.

When Eleazer Rand and Hannah Kendall came to Harvard and Shirley in 1791, each assumed a particular role. Rand adopted the stance of the "suffering servant," much as Ann Lee and William Lee had done in the early years of the gospel.[1] Given to extreme moods of elation and despair, Rand's all-consuming passion was the spiritual well-being of his "children." Although he must have played some role in the physical organization of the communities, he was usually described as a loner. One Shaker sister recalled Rand's frequent late-night walks along the street that ran through the Shaker village and his habit of prostrating himself on the ground as he prayed. Others remembered a special rock in the woods that he visited when he needed to pray and meditate in solitude. Rand, like Ann Lee and William Lee, suffered emotionally and physically in his anguish over Believers' souls, seemingly with the belief that his personal suffering vicariously saved the Believers in his care. He could also appear abrasive in his zeal for the gospel. Some who left characterized him as a tyrant who arbitrarily enforced Shaker rules. This description of Rand contradicts the Believers' assertion that he was a kind and loving man. Nonetheless, similar charges were not made against Hannah Kendall, and given Rand's extreme moods, he probably was overzealous at times in dealing with people.[2]

Hannah Kendall, on the other hand, was even-tempered and did not experience the emotional highs and lows that kept Rand in a constant state of anguish. She was clearly concerned about the spiritual welfare of her "flock," but she also involved herself in the daily lives of Believers and dealt with temporal as well as spiritual issues. Overall, she appears to have had a deeper understanding of human nature than did Eleazer Rand and was better able to accommodate her vision of Shakerism to the needs of the people for whom she was responsible.[3]

Kendall's ability to govern effectively was aided by her flexibility. She was a firm believer in leniency when dealing with people, and she treated the concerns of individuals on a case-by-case basis and with particular care. Even when sick and in pain, she thought of others. Close to the time of her own death, for example, she spoke with a group of brothers who were in leadership positions and exhorted them to be understanding when dealing with their charges. If a person were assigned a job in which he or she could not "find a gift," then the elders were to release that person and find him or her a more suitable task. Shaker leaders were respected because they possessed the power to make decisions and to require obedience, but Kendall urged leaders not to abuse this power and to be sensitive to the feelings of others.[4]

The first task that faced Rand and Kendall was the physical organization of the communities and the development of a sound economic base. The sparse village landscapes quickly changed as families planted gardens and built houses, barns, and workshops. Yet while the physical landscape grew, the population of the villages did not. After a large influx of members during the gathering period, the population of Harvard and Shirley decreased slightly, and they became two of the smallest Shaker villages then in existence. Of the eleven Shaker communities gathered by 1803, Harvard ranked eighth in size with 101 members, and Shirley, with 92 members, ranked ninth.[5]

Throughout the first third of the nineteenth century, both villages maintained a fairly static population. Exact statistics for the two communities are difficult to find, but in 1822 Shirley's North family reported 20 members and the South family, 33. A comparison with the 1803 statistics reveals that the population in the Shirley "out families" (that is, all families except the Church family) had remained nearly the same for nineteen years. Priscilla Brewer has calculated the population of Shirley to be 84 in 1820 and 69 in 1830, compared to the Harvard Ministry's 1833 figure of 97.[6]

Statistics for Harvard are even more sketchy. Thomas Hammond collected yearly statistics for the Harvard Church family, showing that from 1816 to 1837 membership fluctuated between 97 and 120. In 1822 there were 50 students at Harvard, indicating a large number of school-age children living there. Brewer's statistics reveal that the total population of Harvard decreased a bit, from 173 in 1820 to 167 in 1830. This second figure corroborates Believer Joseph Hammond's 1828 figure of 175 and the Harvard Ministry's 1833 figure of 169.[7]

The Shakers, however, were not disheartened by their lack of growth, and members continued to donate land to the villages, anticipating the need for physical expansion. In 1807 Seth Babbitt consecrated a ninety-acre farm to the Harvard community, which became the site of the East family, one of the gathering orders. In October 1810 the deacons from Harvard went to Shirley to supervise five Shaker brothers in deeding their land to the "joint interest of the Church." Such donations were important, providing for the Shakers' potential growth and giving the communities tangible wealth, useful in dealing with the world.[8]

Land and agriculture were central to the Shakers' livelihood, but manufacturing and trade were also integral components of their economy. From the beginning the Shakers engaged in trades such as tanning, weaving, and blacksmithing. Though the primary purpose of these occupations was to meet the needs of the Believers, the Shakers also sold their services and manufactured goods to the world. Not content to sell only the by-products of these internal industries, however, the Believers, within a few years of the gathering, began to develop money-making enterprises that linked them even more closely to the outside economy. The Harvard and Shirley Shakers, like other Massachusetts farmers, traveled extensively as they sought new and lucrative markets.[9] One of the earliest of these industries, headed by Oliver Burt, was the seed business at Shirley. In 1805 the Shakers sold twenty-five kinds of seeds, deriving a net income of $971.33. The next year Shirley seed sales yielded a net income of $1,134.88. As head of the industry, Burt conducted "seed journeys" throughout Massachusetts and neighboring states.[10]

Central to this trade network was the city of Boston. Shaker economic connections to that city began early, long before the advent of the railroads. Already by 1809 the Shirley Shakers were selling their seeds there, and in the following years a steady stream of Shaker goods made their way to the city.[11] Although Henry Binford does not include the villages of Harvard and Shirley (Shaker or non-Shaker) in his discussion of Boston's antebellum suburbs, the Shaker villages generally fit his definition of a suburb as a fringe community, located within twenty miles of Boston, that farmed and manufactured items specifically for the urban center. Food supply made up a large part of this trade. Providing beef, milk, and vegetables for urban residents became an important part of the outlying farmers' responsibility.[12]

Although located a few miles further distant from Boston than Binford's outer suburbs, the Shakers of Harvard and Shirley marketed their goods in Boston from early on. Their fruits, vegetables, manufactured items, and— after the railroads were built— milk all found a ready market in Boston. Unlike Binford's suburbanites, however, the Shakers never produced solely for the Boston market. Their trade networks extended north and south of Boston as well as into neighboring states. Thus, while profiting from their closeness to Boston, the Harvard and Shirley Shakers were not dependent on that city alone for their economic prosperity, integrating themselves instead into the larger economic network of the eastern United States.

The Believers' ties to the worldly economy were reflected in their early use of hired help. The Shakers at Harvard and Shirley seem never to have had enough male labor. As early as 1808 the Shirley Believers employed two outsiders to work on the "aged people's" house for cash wages. In some cases Believers worked out reciprocal relationships with nonbelievers. Between 1804 and 1808 Benjamin Cooper owed the Shakers for various items, including $5.58 for property taxes that the Shakers paid on his behalf. Cooper received credit for tending the Believers' pasture and watching their cattle, "entertainment from time to time," and "working out" two Believers' highway taxes. Isaac Whittemore of Ashburnham also tended Shaker pastures, mended fences, kept horses, and "entertained" for the Shakers, receiving an average of five dollars' credit for these activities. He, in turn, owed the Shakers for cotton and several debts that the Believers had paid for him.[13]

By creating a strong farming and manufacturing base and establishing good working relations with the world, the Believers enjoyed a period of general prosperity. By 1828 the Harvard Shaker village boasted a meetinghouse, six residences, an office, a school, ten workshops, a sawmill, a gristmill, a tannery, and seven barns. The Harvard Believers raised most of their own food; produced leather goods, "wooden ware," and high-quality cotton textiles for themselves and the world; and ran an herb and seed business. In 1831 they built a four-story barn—150 feet long and 45 feet wide—which newspapers hailed as "the largest on the Continent."[14]

While the Believers successfully organized the practical aspects of their economic situation, they were more troubled by the religious side of their economic arrangements. The Shakers adhered to the principle of joint interest, but they retained their ambivalence about private property, illustrated by Church members who kept money in private accounts. In 1812, for example, the Shirley Church family bought some land in Lancaster for six hundred dollars. Four hundred dollars came out of the communal fund; private individuals provided the remainder of the sum. Elijah Wilds donated one hundred dollars, and Ivory Wilds and Reuben Barrett each contributed fifty dollars; both Elijah and Ivory Wilds were members of the Church family, Elijah having entered in 1793 and Ivory in 1811. Parmilia (also spelled Pamela) Cooledge, who joined the Shirley Church in 1813, also retained a private cache of money. In 1815 she purchased two parcels of land in Lancaster for fifty-eight dollars and donated them to the Church. Eleven years later she gave the Church a horse valued at sixty dollars and fifty dollars in cash.[15]

Harvard Church sister Lucy Clark also retained a private store of money. In 1826 Clark made a monetary present to the Central Ministry. This startled its members because Clark was not supposed to have any private reserves. Taking the money was considered "out of order," but the Ministry finally accepted Clark's gift, arguing that she had acted from good intentions. The Central Ministry bent the rules in this case, but it made sure that the Harvard Ministry understood that Clark had acted contrary to order.[16]

Another issue with which the Shakers of Harvard and Shirley struggled during these formative years was the role of the family, both biological and spiritual, in their societies. The idea of using the family as an organizing principle of a community was not unique to the Shakers. As Amanda Porterfield has argued, antebellum communitarianism organized around the concept of the family was an important way in which nineteenth-century Americans faced the social upheaval caused by economic and political growth. Living communally, whether in a Shaker village or as a student at Mount Holyoke College, helped Americans form an identity that grounded them within a constantly changing world. "At Mount Holyoke and elsewhere," she argues, "the revitalization of an older style of social existence based on face-to-face consensus and authority made enthusiasm for industrial society possible."[17] This was certainly true at Harvard and Shirley, where the imperatives of communal living sometimes clashed with the Believers' eagerness to engage in the burgeoning market capitalist system, an engagement that both benefited and hurt the Shakers, as later chapters of this book will show.

The spiritual family was the working unit of a Shaker village. Just as in society at large, each Shaker family was an autonomous unit and maintained businesslike relations with the other families in the communities. Despite the communal basis of the villages, items from one family were purchased with cash by another. Asa Brocklebank of the Shirley Church kept track of the seeds that he bought for his family from other Shakers in 1808. That year he bought $24.66 worth of seeds from Ivory Wilds, head of the Shirley North family, and $5.00 worth of onion seeds from Moses Haywood. Haywood was a Believer who owned and lived on a farm contiguous with the Shirley Shakers until 1810, when he moved to the Shaker village and consecrated his farm to the Church.[18]

Moses Haywood's situation suggests that the incorporation of Believers into the villages proper was a gradual process. During the formative period there were numerous out families such as Moses Haywood's, people who adopted the celibate Shaker lifestyle but continued living in their private homes. This arrangement was a matter of economics as well as personal choice, for initially the communities did not seem able to support all Believers. Certainly the worth of these people as good Shakers was not questioned. Eleazer Rand once commented, "We cannot all live together; There are some that are not gathered into Church relations that are as good as those that are, & have as good faith."[19]

Those Shakers who did gather into families were generally organized according to "spiritual" age, though elderly Shakers lived in separate residences. Hannah Kendall was particularly concerned about those Believers who were chronologically and spiritually young. Initially, the young Believers were gathered primarily into the Church family, but Kendall felt that they needed their own order where they could receive the care and attention that might keep them in the Shaker faith. To that end, Kendall established a vague intermediary order in 1810. In 1813 she oversaw the purchase of a 164-acre farm and moved the intermediary order there. This site became the South family, the official gathering order for those first setting out to become Shakers. At first biological families managed the order. When the farm was purchased, Seth Blanchard's family moved there to live as managers. The next year Jonathan Chandler's and Benjamin Winchester's families joined the Blanchards, and Jonathan Chandler became head caretaker in 1815 when Seth Blanchard moved to the Church. The Ministry finally appointed official elders for the South family, a step that made the family truly autonomous, in 1822, six years after Kendall's death.[20]

Using biological families to manage the gathering order may have been a necessary expedient in the absence of qualified leaders, but it was more likely a strategy employed by Rand and Kendall to ease Believers into living in spiritual families. Accustomed to a certain amount of privacy, Shakers lived and worked with people of all personalities on a daily basis; taught to think of physical attraction between men and women as normal and desirable, Believers were now required to view such unions as sinful. Difficult as living in this manner may have been, Hannah Kendall assured the Harvard Shakers that life in spiritual families was beneficial to them because it tested their spirits, showed them their weaknesses, and taught them to put others' needs before their own.[21]

Despite the emphasis placed on spiritual families and renunciation of natural families—the early Shaker leader James Whittaker told his biological family that they were "a stink in my nostrils"—the Harvard and Shirley Believers maintained relationships with their biological families through approved visitations, setting a pattern that would continue until the villages disbanded. On a Sunday afternoon in October 1815, for example, members of the Babbitt and Blanchard families living at Harvard (the families were related) met in the Church office after a public meeting to visit with Joseph Blanchard, a nonbeliever and the uncle of Grove Blanchard.[22]

The ambiguous role of the biological family at Harvard and Shirley raises the issue of Rand's and Kendall's strategy for Shaker social organization. Sociologist Rosabeth Moss Kanter has identified six "commitment mechanisms"—sacrifice, investment, renunciation, communion, mortification, and transcendence—used by nineteenth-century communal groups to order and maintain their existence. She also examines the "concrete organizational strategies" used by these groups to enforce appropriate behavior.[23] The Shakers implemented all six of Kanter's mechanisms and used most of the "concrete organizational strategies" that she has identified, but in some cases they tailored these strategies to the needs of their villages, especially where the renunciation of family was concerned.

Rand's and Kendall's emphasis on the biological family may have resulted from their personal family experiences as well as from the demographics of the two villages. Kendall was raised in a loving family, and her conversion to Shakerism took place as a family event. Similarly, although Rand's early life was not very stable, he seems to have settled in as a member of the family after he began working for Zaccheus Stevens, converting to Shakerism when the Stevens family did and later moving with them to Niskeyuna. Furthermore, the demographics at Harvard and Shirley, with a majority of the Shakers having at least one other family member in the communities, reinforced the importance of natural relations. Given the conversion experiences of Rand and Kendall and the high value that rural New Englanders placed on the family, it is not unlikely that the Ministry saw encouraging commitment to spiritual families while at the same time reinforcing the positive qualities of biological families as more productive than an outright condemnation of natural family ties.

Biological families continued to play an important role in Shaker villages after the deaths of Rand and Kendall. Journals from the 1820s and 1830s record constant visiting between Shakers and their nonbelieving relatives, many of whom spent the weekend so they could attend the public Sabbath meeting. A relatively large number of Shakers were also allowed to leave the villages to visit relatives in their homes.[24]

The Ministry does not record why it allowed such frequent visiting. Contact with unbelieving relatives, particularly outside of the Shaker village, could lead Believers to abandon their faith and gave relatives an opportunity to restrain Shakers from returning. Yet the sheer number of visits, both in and out of the Shaker communities, indicates that the practice was common. The Ministry may have justified the visits as a way of easing people into Shaker life, gradually severing the cords that tied them to the world. They may also have construed the visits as "missionary work." If Shakers could be drawn to the world through contacts with nonbelieving relatives, then worldly relations could be drawn to Believers through their Shaker relatives. A perusal of the Shirley North family journal reveals the steady flow of visiting between the Shakers of that family (many of whom were related) and their friends and relatives in the town of Spencer, Massachusetts, between the years 1822 and 1834. This network of family and friends influenced several people, such as Chloe Loring, who had two sisters living among Believers, to join the Shakers.[25]

The biological family also served important functions within the community, in some cases acting as a stronger deterrent to leaving than any plea made by the leadership. When Daniel Myrick wanted to quit the Shakers, his elders informed Myrick's biological father, who then gathered ten or eleven of Myrick's relatives to "labor" with him until he agreed to stay. The Ministry was grateful because it considered Myrick "a prize if he can be saved." The conversion of entire biological families also built up the ranks quickly and, if the Shakers were lucky, provided a large pool of capable leaders. Such was the case with the Myrick family—two parents and eleven children, ranging in age from twenty-three years to twenty months—who came to Harvard after active Shaker proselytizing on Cape Cod. Most of them remained dedicated Believers and filled many leadership roles in the Harvard-Shirley bishopric.[26]

For every Shaker who remained a Believer, however, there were many who could not adjust to communal living. As early as 1795 the Shakers began to notice waves of apostasy. One of the leading instigators in spreading disaffection among the Believers at Harvard was Jeremiah Willard, a seemingly unlikely candidate. The Willards had been among the first people at Harvard to follow Ann Lee. The Shakers trusted Jeremiah Willard, appointing him as a Church trustee or deacon and as an elder in 1791, but by 1796 relations between Willard and the Shakers had soured. The Believers disapproved of his practice of choosing only young and able-bodied people to live in his family. From a practical point of view, his decision made sense. Willard wanted members who could work and support the family; admitting old or sickly people would only strain the family's economy. But Believers saw Willard's actions as contrary to Shaker teaching. He finally left the Believers in 1796, but not before spreading "heresy" among the young and vulnerable—perhaps one reason why so many young adults left the Shakers during this time. Willard's consequent life was not happy; according to the Shakers, he spent his final years as "a drunken sot."27

Willard left the Shakers because he was not willing to take orders or subordinate his will to the good of the community. Others left because they wanted to marry. Abigail, Olive, and Anna Wilds, daughters of Elijah Wilds, head of the Shirley Church family, left the Shakers to marry Benjamin Willard, Phineas Ames, and Flavel Coolledge, all of whom had also been Believers at one time. Many, like Phebe Whitney, gave no reason for leaving, but judging from her subsequent actions, she probably left the Shakers because she was profoundly confused or depressed. Less than a month after her departure, her father, Samuel Whitney, also a Shaker, was informed that Phebe had committed suicide. The Shakers sent Moses Haywood to Boston with twenty-four dollars to reimburse the man who had paid for her funeral.28

The defection of so many people, especially young and healthy ones, created both a spiritual and an economic crisis for Believers. The Shakers made financial settlements with every person who left the community, a practice that significantly hurt their economy. On October 29, 1794, the deacons "settled" with Aaron Williams, Jr., for his labor during the two years and four months that he lived there, and for the pair of steers, six geese, six fowls, and various other items that he brought into the Church. They also let him keep all the clothes made for him during the time he lived at Harvard as well as other items acquired from the Believers, including two pairs of shoes, two handkerchiefs, and a pair of oxen. Furthermore, the deacons did not charge Williams for the taxes they paid for him during the time he lived with the Shakers. The total value of Williams's settlement came to £22. On June 2, 1795, the Shakers "settled" with Martha Prescott, reimbursing her for the grain, a cow, and three yearlings that she brought into the Church and paying her £15 for her labor. As one Believer put it, "In the time of the apostasy . . . it seemed as though those who turned away would strip the Church of the little property that was left."[29]

If not handled carefully, disgruntled former Shakers could cause major damage, illustrated by an act of vandalism that occurred at Shirley in 1802. On the night of Friday, March 3, several former Shakers, including Peter Perham, Eleazer Robbins, and William Blanchard, all of whom had worked on the meetinghouse during its construction, broke into that building. The Shakers found them the next morning, barricaded in the upper rooms where the Ministry resided when at Shirley. The intruders' behavior—drinking, damaging furniture, spreading cooking grease everywhere, crossdressing in the sisters' clothing, and "many more things too obscene to mention"—not only damaged physical property but also defiled sacred space. The men were arrested on Tuesday morning and sent to Concord on Wednesday, where the court acquitted them; the Shakers attributed this acquittal to "treachery." Perham and Robbins, in turn, brought a suit against the Shakers that cost the Believers much time and money. The case went to the Superior Court, and the Shakers won.[30]

The mockery of sacred Shaker institutions exhibited by the Shirley apostates was, perhaps, more damaging to Believers than the burden imposed by financial settlements. It was important for those who remained with the Shakers not to lose faith in themselves or their leaders. The leaders responded by addressing apostasy in theological terms, urging the Believers to seek spiritual renewal in the fires of tribulation brought on by apostasy. Redemption was possible, however, only if the Believers maintained a constant vigil and removed the impurities and imperfections from society when they found them. Despite the immediate pain this might cause, the result would be a purer, stronger church.[31]

The theme of purging was important for Believers because it provided a framework in which to understand the apostasy problem and to justify a continued commitment to Shakerism. The problem was not with Shakerism itself, but with the undesirable people who could not fit themselves into that movement. This was a very important point to remember when many people left within a short period of time. After one such wave, particularly distressing because it involved many young people, the Believers tempered the sting of these desertions by claiming that Hannah Kendall had foreseen this "time of apostasy" in a dream: "They [youth and children] all appear beautiful now but the time will come that there must be a purging & then it will be known who are believers & who are not." The Believers used Kendall's prophecy to explain their suffering, not as a random event, but as part of a larger plan ordained by God for their benefit.[32]

Harvard and Shirley were not alone during these years. Several villages, including New Lebanon and Hancock, also experienced an exodus of Believers, particularly young males. In fact, 1796 was known as the year of the "great apostasy" at New Lebanon. A major reason for the defection of these men was their refusal to place themselves under the leadership of a woman, namely Lucy Wright, who became the head of the Central Ministry after Joseph Meacham's death. Rather than submit to "petticoat government," these men left the Shakers.[33] It is possible that some of the men who left Harvard and Shirley were angry about the prominent role of women there, but if so, they left no record of their feelings. On the contrary, the brothers at Harvard and Shirley gave every indication that they approved of Hannah Kendall as a strong leader.

Whatever the motivation for apostasy, by the first decade of the nineteenth century the number of departures had increased to an alarming degree, and Believers everywhere faced their first major crisis since the founding of the communities. Apostasy challenged the fundamental truth of Shakerism. In a classic religious response to the upheaval, the Shakers experienced a revival in late 1807 and early 1808, seeking the renewal promised to them after purging the unrepentant from their societies. The revival "gift" first appeared at New Lebanon, instituted by Lucy Wright so that the youth and children there could experience the same powerful work of the spirit as the Believers had when Ann Lee was alive.[34]

After the revival was under way at New Lebanon, Wright sent a letter to Harvard and Shirley describing the gift and exhorting the Ministry "to wake up to God and come out of our lethergy state." Wright did not, however, send the gift of revival directly to all the Shaker communities. In late January 1808 a Harvard Shaker brother went to Canterbury, New Hampshire, to deliver the gift of revival to that village. The Canterbury Shakers would, in turn, send the gift to the Shakers at Alfred, Maine.[35]

The revival, which began at Harvard in December of 1807, stirred the soul of Eleazer Rand, who "felt like Habbackuk[.] [W]hen I heard [of the work of God,] my Belly trembled & my lips quivered at the voice." The Shakers began "speaking in tongues, walking the floor, leaping & turning," behavior that had largely ceased after the gathering of the Church. Admonished for their faults, Believers were moved to increased repentance and confession of sins. The revival continued into 1808 and lasted about six weeks. Meetings were often spontaneous. A few Believers, meeting together to sing a song or two, would gradually be joined by other Shakers until "it was easy to feel a flow of the spirit." The group would continue to sing and dance for several hours, disrupting the Shakers' daily routine. As Rand wrote to Lucy Wright, activities such as eating and sleeping "became of but little use for a number of days."[36]

The revival temporarily raised the spirits of Believers, even Eleazer Rand, but he died soon after at the age of forty-five from what many Shakers believed was despair over the defection of so many members. Having spent the better part of his life not only as a Shaker but also as a leader in the movement, traveling with Ann Lee and physically suffering for his faith, he no doubt was disheartened to see his hard work threatened by apostates, some of whom were vociferous in their attacks on Rand after they left the Shakers. Worn out by the responsibility of gathering and maintaining two Shaker communities, he was ill and feeble in the final year of his life. He attended his last worship meeting on January 29, 1808, described by those who were there as weak, frail, and "suffering for the increase of the gospel." He died peacefully on November 9, 1808, resting hopefully on his prediction that the Shakers would one day gather many new members.[37]

Rand, though often a loner, was an important figure in the early history of Harvard and Shirley, helping in his own way to forge the bonds of community. He provided the Believers with a religious and uniquely Shaker foundation for their villages. When that foundation was threatened, he oversaw the purification of Shaker society. Rand, then, supplied the moral and spiritual dimensions of social construction. Hannah Kendall focused on the more tangible aspects of community formation, although she was also concerned with moral and spiritual issues. Her impact was felt in the decisions made concerning leadership strategies, economic arrangements, the role of the biological family, and provisions for young Believers. Thus, she, too, played a pivotal role in forging the bonds of community at Harvard and Shirley.

4

The Boundaries of Gender

WHEN ELEAZER RAND DIED IN 1808, Hannah Kendall was the sole "parent" of the bishopric. Although John Warner became Ministry elder, he had none of Kendall's authority, and he remained subordinate to her. Kendall was, indeed, a strong woman, and she presided as the matriarch of Harvard and Shirley until her own death in 1816. Overseeing the final fires in which the bonds of community were forged, she brought the villages to a level of social and economic stability that secured their survival after her death. Just as important was her position as male and female leader in one, an idea grounded in Shaker theology and notions of androgyny. Her model of leadership combined with celibacy to foster an environment in which the boundaries of gender were redefined. All Believers benefited from this system, but the sisters were most dramatically affected.

Shaker ideas on celibacy and androgyny offered a critique of the traditional social order that opened the way for a new interpretation of gender roles. This does not mean that the Harvard and Shirley Shakers brought a "clean slate" to their endeavor. Certain images were ingrained in their consciousness. The view of woman as temptress or seducer, for example, an image deeply embedded in Christianity,[1] was also found in Shakerism. Even Ann Lee could not escape this pernicious view of female nature. She once told a woman who had come to visit her at Harvard, "Ruth, go home, and set your house in order; take up your cross against the works of the flesh, and lay no temptations before Joseph [her husband]: for no one will turn from the way of God, but for their lusts."[2] Eleazer Rand reiterated this theme of the female temptress, though he also held a low view of the male sexual appetite. During a worship meeting Rand commanded the sisters:

"[P]rize your privilege in this day of Christ's manifestation in the female and be thankful that you are delivered from bondage to the filthy lusts of men." He asked the men to repeat the following words, "The Sisters are pure in their faith, and we will always keep them so." Then the women repeated, "The Brethren are pure in their faith, and we will lay no temptations before them."[3] Hannah Kendall emphasized this second point when she said "that it was a great sin for the Sisters, to lay any temptation before the Brethren, and the anguish that . . . souls would have to feel, who did it was past all discription." On another occasion, Kendall went into the sisters' workshop and "reproved [the young women] severely" for making unnecessary trips between buildings and for roaming the fields in their leisure time. She feared that unescorted walking provided the sisters with an opportunity "to tempt and allure" the young men.[4]

Kendall's concern for the women in her care could cause her to deal brusquely with them, but her goal was always to elevate female status and counteract distorted images of women. Kendall refused, for example, to accept the view of women as weak and infirm creatures. In a harsh rebuke aimed at the sisters during a meeting in which "she felt a gift to reprove old infirmities & bodily weakness," Kendall warned the women, especially the younger ones, to stop complaining about their illnesses. Believers, she said, should "walk about lively, & go about [their] work with a quick step. . . . [D]ragging along as though [they] had hardly life enough to crawl . . . [was] not the way to keep the way of God & honor the gospel."[5]

Kendall's efforts to change female behavior were aided by an important aspect of the Shaker system—celibacy. Celibacy affected both sexes, but its impact was more pronounced for women. As Judith Hoch-Smith and Anita Spring have observed, in the realm of religion, women, unlike men, have been defined primarily by their "sexual and reproductive status." Thus, "women are strikingly one-dimensional characters in mythology and ritual action."[6] A change in sexual relations, then, carries greater ramifications for women because it changes the basis of their identity in a more fundamental and dramatic way.

The effect of celibacy on Shaker women has been a source of debate for scholars, who line up on opposite sides of the issue. Sally Kitch, for example, believes that celibacy empowered Shaker sisters. In the Shaker interpretation of Genesis, she argues, Eve is no longer seen as the cause of humankind's fall. Rather, women become victims of the fall, spending their lives in subjection to their husbands as the result of God's "curse" upon Eve. The Shakers identified this subjection as the sexual act between husbands and wives, which they considered sinful. Celibacy, then, not only removed a woman's sin but also, by eliminating her victimization, gave her "redemptive power." Celibacy gave Shaker women a choice about how to order their lives and empowered them to make decisions about their sexuality.[7]

Louis Kern, on the other hand, argues that celibacy did not empower Shaker women. Although it protected them from the dangers of childbirth and gave them some "spiritual power" in their communities, in the end it only strengthened traditional male and female roles and left Shaker women with less power than their worldly counterparts. Shaker brothers retained "masculine control of the threatening power of sexuality," while Shaker sisters lost their "moral and social power based on parturition, child rearing, and domesticity."[8]

It is important to point out that Kitch and Kern are discussing Shakerism in the mid- to late nineteenth century. Their conclusions, then, cannot be applied to the earlier period of the Believers' history without a substantial analysis of women's position in Shaker society during that time. This analysis must take into account the cultural, social, and economic factors that affected women at Harvard and Shirley in the first third of the nineteenth century. A close consideration of these factors reveals that female empowerment, though greatly aided by celibacy—which granted the sisters access to social roles other than wife and mother—was rooted in more than sexual abstinence. Complete female empowerment was effected not only by the "deconstruction" of traditional female roles but also by the "reconstruction" of a new notion of gender based on the "androgynous ideal."

The Shakers were certainly not the first to posit a theory of androgyny. The belief in androgyny as wholeness or a perfect state of being is common to many cultures throughout time. Groups as diverse as the ancient Greeks, Gnostics, Jews, and eighteenth-century French reformers shared similar notions, though the origins and ramifications of those beliefs differed greatly.[9] In the 1970s feminists began to seek out these transhistorical concepts of androgyny as they looked for models of human nature that empowered women, and a debate ensued over the liberating or oppressive nature of androgyny. On the one hand, some feminists of the time, most notably Mary Daly, argued that male attributes were still the baseline against which all behavior was measured and rejected the notion of androgyny because it refused to acknowledge female characteristics as important.[10] On the other hand, because the theory of androgyny encouraged a broad spectrum of behavior in individual humans, other feminists viewed it positively. Carolyn Heilbrun wrote that androgyny could "liberate the individual from the confines of the appropriate," and Sandra Bem argued that with the abolition of "rigid sex-role differentiation . . . perhaps the androgynous person will come to define a more human standard of psychological health."[11]

Recent historical work has resurrected the notion of androgyny, not to debate its viability as a model for today's society, but to use it as an analytical tool for examining the construction of gender in previous periods. Caroline Walker Bynum's influential work reveals how medieval Christianity feminized Christ's body and the impact this had on female behavior and spirituality, while Teresa Shaw's more recent work highlights the emphasis that the early Christian church placed on fasting as a way for women ascetics to redeem their bodies by making them "masculine."[12] B. J. Gibbons elucidates the androgynous understanding of Adam's creation in the writings of the early seventeenth-century mystic Jacob Boehme and its impact on the religious experiences of men and women.[13] And a recent proliferation of work in American gender studies has revealed that Puritan divines, "founding fathers," and nineteenth-century men all used androgynous language to delimit primarily male activity, incorporating traditional female attributes into appropriate male behavior.[14] With the exception of Shaw's work, these studies represent examples of androgyny that encourage men to adopt female traits but that do not sanction women acting as men. What makes the Shaker case important is that the androgynous ideal was extended to women. Androgynous behavioral norms operated differently for the brothers and sisters at Harvard and Shirley, but both groups benefited from an expanded notion of personhood. In the spiritual sphere, the prevalence of a "gendered spirituality" that encouraged both brothers and sisters to become "spiritual mothers" allowed men to exercise feminine traits, as I will discuss. But in the temporal world, the communal nature of Shaker society erased the division of public and private spheres, forcing women's work and actions into the public realm to be evaluated on a par with male activity, a phenomenon discussed at length in the next chapter.

Shaker theology contains the concept of androgyny in its most basic form, as male and female in one body or entity.[15] In *The Testimony of Christ's Second Appearing*, published in 1808, Benjamin Seth Youngs posits the idea of androgyny when writing that man (Adam) was initially formed of two parts, male and female, and that woman (Eve) was created by the removal of the female portion of the man. This duality of human nature was a reflection of the duality of the godhead, which contained both a male/Father and a female/Mother principle. Maleness and femaleness were not separate entities but attributes of one God. As Shaker theologians Calvin Green and Seth Wells later expressed it, "[T]he manifestation of Father and Mother in the Deity, being spiritual, does not imply two *Persons*, but two *Incomprehensibles*, of one substance, from which proceed all Divine power and life."[16]

Adam's androgyny is clearly articulated in several hymns found in the Shakers' first hymnal, the 1813 *Millennial Praises*. In "Old Adam Disturbed," the hymnist writes, "As he [Adam] was male and female, / The man must be the head, / And by his wholesome counsel, / The woman must be led." In 'The Everlasting Parents," the writer reveals that the godhead, which was both male and female, was the prototype for Adam. "Man was at first created / Upon this blessed scale, / In Adam were united / The female and the male." The author goes on to suggest that androgyny was the first, and perfect, state of humankind, altered only after Adam and Eve sinned. "When Adam had transgressed, / His union soon was gone, / And now the male and female / No more continue one." Theoretically, androgyny was the ideal state to which the Shakers aspired in their recreation of Paradise.[17]

Early male Shaker theologians, however, did not necessarily equate androgyny with equality as the hymn "Old Adam Disturbed" makes clear. Eve was subject to the headship of Adam because, as Youngs argues, man was formed first and woman was extracted from him; thus, man was "first in the order and government" over woman.[18] This male-oriented interpretation of androgyny would seem to undermine the liberating possibilities for women of the androgynous ideal, but such a harsh view of gender relations was tempered when it was translated into the reality of Shaker life at Harvard and Shirley. A close reading of Shaker texts and Shaker behavior at these villages indicates that the brothers and sisters there were encouraged to develop the many sides of their personalities, not merely those associated with their biological sex.

The androgynous ideal was liberating for these Believers because it fostered the view that celibacy was a "normal" lifestyle. As George Tavard has argued, when men and women are conceived of as "identically human" in every respect except sexual characteristics, and when masculinity and femininity are understood as two dimensions of every human being, varying in balance and degree from person to person, "then, celibacy is not an anomaly or an extraordinary vocation, for personal fulfillment does not demand partnership with someone of the other sex." As individuals complete in themselves, men and women "stand to each other in a position, not of complementarity, but of *supplementarity*. Each brings to the other a supplement of humanity, a surplus, which enriches each." Celibacy, then, becomes as "normal" a lifestyle choice as marriage.[19]

Tavard is not writing specifically about the Shakers and is addressing concerns of the contemporary world, but his observations hold true for the Believers. Each individual Shaker was like the original Adam—a reflection of divine duality, of the male and female godhead. Sin, however, had corrupted this perfect original state and spawned a wide spectrum of individuals who possessed a varied combination of male and female traits. Shaker families, in their attempt to recreate a perfect and whole community, became places that fostered the complementary balancing of individuals in various stages of androgyny.

Clearly, community was important to the Believers' endeavor, but the individual was not lost in Shakerism. Within a communal setting, each person was on an individual trek to God, and the role that the individual played in the group and the benefits he or she derived were constantly reiterated. Dance, for example, was an efficacious mode of communal worship, the Shakers argued, because "each individual may participate in the united devotions of the whole body, and mutually contribute to the strength, and share in the harmony of all." Furthermore, the Shaker concept of church as a union of Believers sharing the same faith, motives, and interests, "will bring into operation every individual talent for the general good of the whole body. . . . In this united capacity, the strength of the whole body becomes the strength of each member; and being united in the one Spirit of Christ, they have a greater privilege to serve God than they possibly could have in a separate capacity."[20]

The community was best served when individuals contributed their talents and abilities to the group endeavor. Salvation was an individual matter, but the Shaker family supported each person's quest for salvation and took individuals out of themselves to open to them an experience of the divine that they could not achieve alone. Supplementarity and complementarity, then, combined in a sometimes uneasy tension to encourage a wide range of behavior in both men and women.

The central model of androgyny for the Shakers was Ann Lee. Although many scholars emphasize her role as mother,[21] which was certainly central to her identity, often overlooked are the many times when she ventured into male roles. In addition to adopting the typical female roles of spiritual mother, spiritual housewife, daughter, and bride of Christ (providing a female or "gynocentric" orientation to the early movement), Lee also took on the male roles of apostle, public speaker (though she was reluctant to do so), teacher of both men and women, spiritual judge, community organizer, and maker of economic policy.[22] Her challenge of traditional roles led to several stories in the 1816 *Testimonies* that reflect the ambiguity surrounding her gender roles as well as her actual sex. After Ann Lee first opened her message in America, Joseph Meacham, who soon became a devoted follower, challenged her on the propriety of her public speaking and visible leadership role in light of Paul's injunction against women speaking in church. Ann Lee answered that in both the biological and the spiritual families "the right of government belongs to the woman" when her husband or male head is absent. Thus, Lee justified her position in the Shaker movement by claiming her designated place as Jesus' partner on earth.[23]

Twice while Ann Lee was on her missionary journey through New England, mobs attacked her and questioned her actual sex. In 1781 a mob attacked the house where she was staying in Petersham, Massachusetts, "seized her by her feet, and inhumanly dragged her, feet foremost, out of the house, and threw her into a sleigh." They ripped her clothes "in a shameful manner. Their pretense was to find out whether she was a woman or not." In 1782 a mob in Ashfield, Massachusetts, set out to discover if Lee was "a British emissary, dressed in women's habit" who had been "cropped and branded, and had her tongue bored through for blasphemy." Lee quickly dispelled this second rumor by showing the mob her ears and tongue, but the leaders of the group were still not satisfied as to her true sex. Finally, two women "appointed, as a jury, to examine her" presumably stripped Lee and ascertained that she was, in fact, a woman.[24]

Such examples of androgyny and gender/sexual ambiguity were available to any Shaker who read or heard the stories of Ann Lee's life, but the "parenthood" of Eleazer Rand and Hannah Kendall provided a more immediate example of androgyny for the Believers of Harvard and Shirley. According to Shaker testimony, Rand and Kendall often exhibited characteristics associated with their opposite sex. Although Rand was the "Father" of the bishopric, his excessive emotional states, his preoccupation with religion and sometimes overzealous piety, and his almost constant condition of suffering are stereotypical traits often associated with women. Conversely, Kendall had a much stronger personality than Rand and closely resembled Ann Lee in the various roles she played. This is not surprising given that Kendall spent several of her early adult years with Lee, whom she admired. Kendall possessed "mothering" attributes, that is, she was concerned about the spiritual well-being of her "children" and was a nurturer, but she also participated in the temporal running of the villages to a much greater degree than Rand. She understood agriculture and business, was a consummate politician, and knew when to bend the rules to accommodate human nature, traits society often associated with the male sphere.

The androgynous ideal reached its apex after Eleazer Rand's death when Hannah Kendall became the matriarch of the society, as Lucy Wright had become head of the Central Ministry after Joseph Meacham's death. The Believers at Harvard and Shirley felt that the "first gift rested in Mother Hannah" in whom they "found the full gift of the Ministry, Father and Mother in one."[25] Giving up biological motherhood, Kendall expanded her influence and power by adopting the dual role of spiritual mother and father. Celibacy within the structure of Shakerism allowed Kendall to develop and exercise both her male and female attributes, making her an important role model for the Believers of Harvard and Shirley.

Hannah Kendall was a capable and popular leader, and her followers did not resist her leadership, willingly trusting her decisions in everything from agriculture to spiritual guidance. One incident involved Kendall asking the brothers to clear an overgrown field and plant it with rye. Levi Warner doubted the wisdom of Kendall's plan, fearing that the job would overtax their few farmhands, but the rest of the men convinced Warner to comply with Kendall's request. Later, he testified that he was glad that he had, for they harvested a bountiful supply of rye that year.[26] Whether this story was true or apocryphal, the moral lesson was clear: "Mother" knew best.

The men's willingness to follow Hannah Kendall's suggestion may have been influenced by her motherly concern for their physical well-being. In accord with the hands-on approach that she used in running the communities, she sometimes cooked food herself and took it to the brothers when they were working in the fields. She also insured that the men were well fed on days when they performed heavy physical labor, instructing the kitchen sisters to give the brothers larger helpings of food during these times, even though the early years were lean ones for the Shakers. In 1794 a frost killed most of the Shirley Shakers' fruit and English grain, leaving them very low on supplies. Harvard, too, struggled with food shortages. One Shaker sister noted that frequently the cooks barely had enough flour for a pie crust, yet Kendall urged the sisters not to serve "skimpy" portions of food, afraid that small servings would make people feel cheated of their rightful share.27 Kendall's philosophy was to take care of the Believers' needs whatever the cost, precisely what rural women everywhere were expected to do during the busy harvesting seasons when they engaged in a constant round of meal preparation and cleanup.28 Thus, Kendall's own involvement in food preparation and distribution was an important part of her role both as "mother" and farm manager.

Hannah Kendall was an imposing presence at Harvard and Shirley. She served as a link to Ann Lee's model of androgyny and a bridge to future androgynous models. Through her position as "Father and Mother in one," she both directly and indirectly influenced the development of gender roles among the Believers in her care. The pervasiveness of the Shakers' reconstruction of gender is attested to by the continued crossing of gender lines that occurred among the Harvard and Shirley Shakers long after Kendall's death, especially in the area of Shaker spirituality. Robley Whitson has argued that "because the Shaker tradition is centered directly in religious experience . . . concentration on spirituality is probably the most effective point of entry into the Shaker world."29 If Whitson is correct, as I think he is, then examining the gendered nature of Shaker spirituality at Harvard and Shirley can tell us much about the larger place of men and women in these two communities.

Shaker spirituality in general centered on the concept of "spiritual motherhood." The life of "Mother" Ann Lee was the basis for this ideal, but over time a broader concept of spirituality evolved that moved beyond Lee's life to encompass a system that made experience, feeling, and interpersonal relationships—traditionally female traits—the yardstick for measuring spiritual relations. The Shaker family was the arena in which this spirituality was lived out. All Shakers were to nurture and care for each other while working toward a state of true dependence on their spiritual "parents."[30] Dependence and submission were qualities, especially in Shaker men, that contravened the spirit of male independence prized by American society.[31] Yet Shaker brothers at Harvard and Shirley often made reference to their feelings of submission to their "gospel Parents." In a series of testimonies taken down in 1826, Shaker brothers who had been with the movement from its founding stressed the importance in their own lives of obedience to "Mother [Ann] and the Elders" and to the "gospel" that they taught. Abijah Worster, a beloved Shaker brother at Harvard, wrote that after he met Ann Lee and the other Shaker leaders he "laboured to be obedient, and Subject as a Child, and I soon found, that God owned me in my obedience; By Blessing me with increas [sic] in Strength, against the Power of Evil." Nathan Willard, John Robinson, and Elijah Wilds also testified to their obedience to "Mother's gospel" and the power of that obedience to save them from sin.[32]

Because Shaker spirituality privileged female characteristics and upheld them as normative for spiritual relations, Shaker sisters as well as Shaker brothers could offer theological insights that were valued by all Believers. Admittedly, women's theological works took a different form than male works. All of the major theological treatises published by the Shakers were written by men until the late nineteenth century. For most of their history, Shaker women did not venture into the public sphere of the temporal intellectual world. But within the villages of Harvard and Shirley, women's writing took on special importance as an embodiment of the gendered nature of Shaker spirituality.

The best example of Shaker spirituality and female creativity coming together to foster theological reflection is the spiritual and literary relationship between a niece and her aunt—Eunice Bathrick and Eunice Wyeth—both Harvard Shakers. A story that spans a century, from Eunice Wyeth's conversion to Shakerism in the 1780s to Eunice Bathrick's death in 1883, Wyeth's experiences and Bathrick's retelling of those experiences offered several generations of Believers two levels of spiritual insight and reflection.

Eunice Wyeth's story begins in the 1780s, when she "embraced the gospel" after meeting Ann Lee. Eventually she convinced her husband Joseph to convert as well, and when the Harvard Shakers gathered in 1791, Eunice, Joseph, and two of their daughters joined them. Never as committed as Eunice, Joseph soon took the children and left the Believers, returning to their private residence, which was located nearby. When the oldest girl moved out to get married, Joseph was left alone with his sixteen-year-old daughter, a "cripple" who required constant care. Unable to cope with the demands of running a home and raising a disabled child, he pleaded with Eunice to move back and resume these responsibilities, promising not to "violate her faith." The Harvard elders consented to this arrangement and sent a very unhappy Eunice back to her husband. For the next twelve years she lived with Joseph, unable to attend Shaker meetings. During the 1807 revival she received the "privilege" of worshiping again with the Believers. Unfortunately for Eunice, her widowed daughter, a vocal opponent of Shakerism, had moved back home. The Ministry, unwilling to have Shaker songs and ideas ridiculed by this woman, forbade Eunice to learn (so she could not sing at home) the inspired hymns received in the meetings. Deeply grieved by this turn of events, Eunice sought comfort in prayer and soon became filled with a "poetic spirit"; during the night she claimed to "see" hymns written in gold letters hung from the ceiling. When she lit her lamp, the words disappeared, but she was able to write them down because they were "engraved" in her soul. This "gift" of the poetic spirit marked the beginning of her career as a hymn writer.[33]

In 1808 Joseph "embraced the gospel" a second time, but the Wyeths remained in their own home because the Ministry did not believe that Joseph was prepared for life within a Shaker community. Only after seventeen years had passed were the Wyeths allowed to move to the Square House, and Eunice achieved what she had desired for most of her life. She lived with the Shakers for only four and a half years, however, before dying of consumption at the age of seventy-four.[34]

Eunice Wyeth was a remarkable woman whose career as a hymn writer was fostered by the leadership of the Harvard and Shirley Shakers. Both her output and her dedication were legendary. Only relinquishing her pen when death forced her hand—"she finished her poetical gift while on her Deathbed"—Wyeth composed about six hundred songs during her lifetime according to the Harvard Ministry. Many of these hymns were well known among the Shakers and appeared in a variety of manuscript collections.[35]

What is intriguing about Wyeth's work, however, is not simply the number of hymns produced but the theological function that Wyeth's hymns played within the Shaker community. Daniel Patterson has argued that gender-specific roles in Shakerism extended into the area of music.

Men, as the writers of theology, typically wrote doctrinal hymns; women generally "received" gift songs which expressed praise and thanksgiving and were rooted in personal religious experience.[36] Though Patterson does not elaborate on these observations, it is clear that his analysis is based on the idea that gender divisions in music paralleled the traditional notion that men were rational and active creatures while women were emotional and passive. Thus, women's creative energies were channeled into songs that were experiential rather than theological.

Wyeth's work, however, is instructive because it falls between the categories of hymns and gift songs. The Shakers identified Wyeth's songs as hymns, an important point because hymns were used to disseminate correct doctrine. Yet Wyeth claimed to receive the hymns in vision, and the songs were rooted in her own experience, making them similar to gift songs. Although this labeling of Wyeth's hymns as both doctrinal and experiential may seem contradictory, in fact, Wyeth's songs were squarely in line with the Shaker concept of gendered spirituality. Because the Shakers valued experience and feeling as appropriate categories of knowing, Wyeth's hymns were fully accepted as a window onto the subject of the human-divine relationship. The legitimacy of Wyeth's experience is even more pronounced if one considers that she lived very little of her life in an actual Shaker family. Despite her struggles, Believers judged her personal experience of Shakerism, gained largely through visions, as legitimate. Thus, Wyeth was able to participate in the larger Shaker community through her personal and visionary experience of Shakerism within her biological family.

Eunice Wyeth's story might have been lost to modern historians had it not been preserved through the efforts of her niece, Eunice Bathrick. Bathrick, too, was a Harvard Shaker and a prolific writer in her own right during the second half of the nineteenth century. Living out the concept of spiritual motherhood first embodied in Ann Lee, then in Hannah Kendall, "Mother" Eunice (as Bathrick was called near the end of her life) acted as spiritual guide and counselor to the rising generation of Shaker sisters. Part of her legacy was the compilation of Wyeth's hymns, prefaced with a biography of Wyeth. This biography is important because it reveals Bathrick's concept of Shaker spirituality as reflected in the life of her aunt and serves as a bridge to link the early "mothers" of the Harvard and Shirley communities with those of the later period.

Bathrick offered her readers a carefully constructed story of Eunice Wyeth's life. What emerges from this biography is a picture of an exceptional woman who replaced Hannah Kendall as the androgynous role model for the Believers after Kendall's death. Wyeth resembled the ideal woman in her meekness, humility, and obedience to the Ministry. Yet Bathrick also portrays Wyeth as strong, stoic, and decisive, traits associated with men. Bathrick highlights these particular traits by using Wyeth's husband, a man who had trouble committing himself to Shakerism and who fell apart when faced with taking care of a handicapped daughter, as a foil. She further marks the difference between Eunice and Joseph by citing Hannah Kendall's prediction that Eunice would ultimately have to "save" Joseph because he was too weak to follow "the Shaker way" on his own. Joseph's eventual return to the fold seemed to prove the truth of Kendall's words.[37]

Like Hannah Kendall, Eunice Wyeth found empowerment within Shakerism, even in the midst of personal sorrow. Her discovery of her literary talent and the Believers' constant encouragement of her abilities opened a new world to Wyeth and enabled her to pass her experience on to others in the form of hymns. Unlike Kendall, however, Wyeth developed her talents largely while functioning as a traditional, albeit celibate, wife and mother. Celibacy did not free Wyeth from caring for a husband and children or running a household, but because of this she functioned as an especially powerful symbol. She was able not only to fulfill her traditional female roles but also to develop other sides to her character. In this respect she was not unlike Hannah Kendall, who, while functioning as a "mother," adopted many other roles as well.

Moreover, Bathrick's role in the preservation of Wyeth's story, and her own position as "Mother" to the younger generation of sisters at the end of the nineteenth century, brought the issues of Wyeth's life full circle.[38] Bathrick's own experiences of Shakerism, gained over a long life, gave her the authority to offer her theological reflections on Shakerism in the form of a biography of her aunt. Bathrick, then, became the next link in the chain of "mothers" at Harvard and Shirley.

As the lives of Hannah Kendall, Eunice Wyeth, and Eunice Bathrick show, Shakerism as practiced at Harvard and Shirley empowered women and allowed them to move beyond socially constructed boundaries of gender. The notion of gendered spirituality, combined with Shaker leaders who openly encouraged sisters to develop their talents, created an environment in which all Believers were able to strive for the androgynous ideal.

5

Labor and Gender

THE BELIEVERS' INDUSTRIOUSNESS has become legendary, popularized for today's reader by books such as Edward Deming Andrews's and
Faith Andrews's *Work and Worship: The Economic Order of the Shakers.*[1] Although
the Andrews offer a romanticized view of Shaker labor, their thesis that
work was central to Shakerism is valid. Yet the issue of work in Shaker communities often receives only one-sided attention. When assessing labor
among the Believers, scholars typically point out that the Shakers divided
labor along gender lines, reflecting the nineteenth-century division of society into public (male) and private (female) spheres.[2] Implicit in this discussion is a criticism of the Believers for not doing away with gendered labor.
The assumption behind this critique is that the model of separate spheres
devalued the sisters' work just as it did that of non-Shaker women. Karen
Nickless and Pamela Nickless, for example, claim "that at least until 1864
the Brothers' work [at New Lebanon] was considered the Family's work"
and postulate that the Shakers prized men's labor more than women's. They
base their argument on the fact that the financial records for that community rarely list the sisters' contributions separately or cite a monetary value
for their work.[3]

Certainly, labor was usually divided along gender lines among the Believers, but this fact alone is an insufficient basis for drawing conclusions
about their view of women's work. Many other aspects of Shaker life—the
rural nature of their work, their positive view of physical labor, their emphasis on skilled work, their views on gender, and the conflation of the public and private spheres in their communities—affected labor practices
among the Believers. It is also important to consider the larger historical
context of the changing nature of women's work in American society. Only

by evaluating all of these factors can we better understand the role that women played in the Shaker economy.

The model most often used to explain the evolution of women's work in America is based on the ideology of separate spheres (also called the Cult of Domesticity). This paradigm assumes a "golden age" of women's work during the colonial period and traces the steady decline in the status of women's labor until the Industrial Revolution forced women's activities into a separate, degraded sphere of their own.

During the early colonial period the family was the focus of economic life. Together, men and women secured their livelihood in a barter economy. Because domestic skill was integral to the maintenance of the household, it had economic value and achieved what Jeanne Boydston calls "cultural visibility."[4] As early as the late seventeenth century, however, this seemingly idyllic situation began to crumble as market forces collided with traditional patterns of labor, leading to a decline in bartering and an increasing dependence on cash. This economic shift, argues Boydston, led to "the emergence of essentially commercial habits of mind [that] . . . heightened the association of *men* with the symbols of economic activity and profoundly weakened the ability of women to lay claim to the status of 'workers.' "[5] In other words, women's work, because it remained unpaid, was losing its "cultural visibility."

With the rise of industrialization in the nineteenth century and the concomitant growth of the corporate world and white collar jobs, the degradation of women's work was complete. Women were relegated to a domestic sphere that was completely removed from, yet totally dependent on, the public world of men. Ideally, a man would earn enough through a skilled occupation to support his family, while his wife stayed home, raised the children, and performed unpaid and "unskilled" housework. Although essential to the smooth running of the home, women's domestic contributions were devoid of any connection to finances and hence regarded as trivial and less important than the wage-earning work of men. Their power in the family, if they had any at all, was moral rather than economic.[6]

Ironically, the domestic ideal of separate spheres—based on high wages and skilled work—operated among the working class as well as the middle and upper classes. Male laborers, like their economically advantaged counterparts, wanted their wives at home, and they repeatedly fought for a "living" or "family" wage that would allow them to support their families on one income. Workers rarely won their demands, however, and working-class women, married or single, had no choice but to contribute to the family income through their labor.[7]

These women were caught in a bind. Unable to live up to the demands of middle-class America, they were branded as moral degenerates and bad mothers because they worked outside the home.[8] Yet they received little support, in the end, from male workers of their own class. Native-born, white, working-class men were very conscious of the difference between skilled and unskilled labor. With the support of labor unions, they reserved the more prestigious and higher-paying skilled jobs for themselves and drove women, immigrants, and other "undesirables" into low-paying unskilled positions.[9] Consequently, even among the working class, women's labor came to be categorized as unskilled, physical, and less valuable than men's.

The arguments summarized thus far support the idea that by the mid-nineteenth century, separate-spheres ideology played a role in trivializing women's skills, defining work solely in economic terms, and relegating women to a secondary status. As useful as these observations may be for explaining the degradation of women's work in middle-class families, recent scholarship has revealed a picture of female life and labor that is more complex than the Cult of Domesticity would suggest.

One group overlooked in earlier discussions of separate spheres, but given their due in current scholarship, is rural women. A close examination of their lives modifies significantly the idea that rending society into two distinct spheres was the norm in antebellum America. In fact, Joan Jensen, a pioneer scholar of rural women's history, has shown that separate-spheres ideology was only sporadically implemented in the nineteenth-century countryside. "Rural women," she writes, "seldom adopted full-blown theories of domestic power that emphasized the home as an exclusive sphere for women, for both women and men were present on the farm, and women worked in the barnyard and the field as well as in the home." Moreover, models of "rural domesticity" ranged from one extreme to the other. John Mack Faragher argues that midwestern farms were almost completely segregated by sex. Consequently, he found that farm wives who moved west with their husbands preferred to maintain strict gender boundaries on the overland trail as well as in the new frontier settlements because they believed that their status was directly linked to their domestic role. But in two different studies, Sally McMurry's penetrating analysis of farmhouse blue-prints and dairy farms reveals that through the first half of the nineteenth century the farm kitchen and cheese shop remained centers of production where women made valuable economic contributions to the family. Only in the second half of the century were women edged out of the farm econ-omy as wealthier families began to emphasize rigid gender roles (reflected in smaller kitchens and the appearance of rooms for hired help) and as mechanization and the rise of factories turned cheesemaking into a male occupation.[10]

Karen Hansen provides an even more direct challenge to the model of separate spheres. When she looked at working-class and farming men and women, both black and white, in antebellum New England, she found that they did not live in strictly separate worlds. Although they sometimes prac-ticed a gendered division of labor, there were also many times when men and women "mix[ed] in social situations." Hansen, accordingly, introduced the concept of "the social" as a "mediating category" between public and private. The social "embraces activities that transcend individual house-holds and operate independent of the state, such as visiting, gossiping, churchgoing, attending lectures, joining political movements, baby-sitting a neighbor's child, and shopping."[11] Admittedly, Hansen's work addresses more than the division of labor between men and women, but what is im-portant for this discussion is her modification of the separate-spheres model to explain the behavior of the people she studied.

Indeed, the work of Jensen, McMurry, and Hansen forces us to rethink the separate-spheres interpretation of men's and women's labor. I am not suggesting that we throw out the paradigm completely. In fact, the Cult of Domesticity argument works quite well when we look at urban, middle-class settings. But not every situation warrants an application of the sepa-rate-spheres model. Issues such as class, geography, and religion influence people's valuation of work. Thus, we need to be aware of many factors be-sides the way in which labor is divided when we analyze the role of work in a given society.

For Shaker scholars, this means that it is time to move beyond simply berating the Believers for using a gendered division of labor. We must use the expanding body of literature on women and work and evaluate the Shaker system within the larger historical framework of labor in eigh-teenth- and nineteenth-century America. Then we can make a reasoned assessment of the role that women played in the economy of Harvard and Shirley.

We can begin by contrasting Shaker attitudes toward work with those underlying the separate-spheres model. Perhaps the most striking difference is the Believers' high regard for physical labor. Instead of viewing manual work as a mark of low status, the Believers accepted it as an integral part of community building. In fact, they shunned "book learning" and made sure that even community leaders engaged in some form of physical labor. To do one's assigned task, and to do it well, was the yardstick by which the Believers measured success. For this reason, they did not devalue women's work merely because it was physical; both Shaker men and women were expected to engage in manual labor and spent many hours each day in physically demanding occupations. Typical chores performed by the brothers included planting, weeding, harvesting, digging canals, composting, and haying. The sisters cooked, cleaned, washed and ironed laundry, milked cows, boiled cider, picked and processed fruit, whitewashed, and made soap, candles, and baskets.[12]

Affecting the Believers' attitude toward work was also the rural nature of Shaker life. Although the Believers, as I show throughout this book, were savvy businesspeople, well connected to the markets and economic networks of America, they always remained an agricultural people. And, just like the farm families in Jensen's study, the Shaker family treated men's and women's work as equally valuable and necessary for the maintenance of the community. In the yearly agricultural cycle every act, from planting seeds to processing food, contributed to the survival of the group.

Nevertheless, the Shakers did not believe that physical tasks had to be burdensome for either men or women. Productive labor, not drudgery, was their goal, and they willingly invented and adopted labor-saving devices when possible. Revolving ovens, clothespins, circular saws, apple-corers, washing machines, silk-reeling machines, revolving timber planes, even steam-powered centrifugal clothes dryers made daily life easier for the Shakers.[13]

The Believers' views on labor, then, had a significant impact on the sisters' work at Harvard and Shirley. One of the main reasons for the degradation of women's work under the separate-spheres model was its categorization as menial, unskilled, and unpaid. These concepts simply did not apply to the work of the Believers. No job was considered too lowly, no Believer received a wage for his or her labor, and technology was used as often as possible to lighten everyone's workloads. Thus, the "cultural visibility" of women's work did not decrease within Shaker villages, even though jobs continued to be divided along gender lines. The dichotomizing of work into "valuable" skilled work and "nonvaluable" housework never happened.[14]

Another important feature of the Believers' labor system was their practice of job rotation. Men traded farming duties and women rotated posts in the kitchen and laundry so that these physically demanding and monotonous tasks would not become the lot of only a handful of Believers. Individuals still complained about these chores in their journals, but the Shakers were generally happy with the system because they were assigned specific duties and were not responsible for all facets of a given industry. Kitchen sisters at Harvard, for example, were divided into three groups of two women assigned to the cook room, the sink room, and the dining room. Each sister within a group was given certain tasks—one sister made all the soups and meat entrees; another, with some help, baked all the pies and cakes; and a third was responsible for boiling the potatoes for meals—so that there was some room for a woman to use her particular culinary skills. The sisters, however, were also expected to help each other if this help did not interfere with their assigned tasks. To encourage the participation of "sickly" sisters in the daily routine, leaders put them in charge of brewing tea for meals or making sure that butter and cheese were on the tables, tasks that were "not so hard as the other places." All kitchen sisters helped set and clear tables and wash dishes to foster cooperation among them. "In these and many other cases it will be found that a spirit of meekness and condescention will be necessary in order to keep that degree of love and good feelings which will make the work go easy."[15]

Scholars tend to take for granted that sharing onerous tasks and rotating jobs were built into the Shaker system. Yet this arrangement provided enormous benefits for all Believers, especially the sisters, whose worldly counterparts faced long hours of backbreaking work on a daily basis. According to Ruth Schwartz Cowan, even the introduction of labor-saving devices in the late eighteenth century did little to help women because these devices simply "reorganized the work processes of housework" instead of eliminating the work. In fact, industrialization, by pulling men and children out of the home, actually increased the workload of women.[16] Farm wives, too, worked long days engaged in a variety of occupations. Farm journals of the nineteenth century featured stories and poems written by farm wives in which they complained of their never-ending round of chores and expressed their fears that "menial labor [led] to physical breakdown." Moreover, rural women's workload increased between 1750 and 1850 as a result of their increased responsibility for household production and "increased household consumption."[17]

Compared to other nineteenth-century women, then, Shaker sisters were fortunate in the limited amount of time they had to spend on the "dirty work" of the community. But equally beneficial to them was the Shakers' recognition that skilled work was also important, not just for the family economy but for the mental stimulation and companionship it provided Believers, especially women. Skilled work was often done in groups, and Shaker sisters developed an extensive network of friendships within and between villages. This feature of Shaker life should not be taken lightly. As Karen Hansen has argued, the "sociability dimension" of labor was important, especially for isolated farm wives who often made special arrangements to work together.[18] For Shaker women, communal work was a normal part of their routine, enabling them to develop relationships with sisters outside their own family and to pass on useful skills to future generations. Sylvia Atherton learned how to cut and sew leather gloves from two of her Shirley sisters, then went to Harvard to learn the art of weaving sieves. Tabitha Babbitt visited the Shirley South family to teach the sisters how to "bottom" chairs, while Sally Loomis taught others how to weave palm-leaf hats.[19]

The camaraderie among Shaker women and the stability of their lives contrast sharply with the disruptions experienced by non-Shaker working women. Although female laborers valued their friendships, those who worked in factories moved frequently from job to job in the volatile labor market of the early Republic and had a difficult time maintaining ties to family and friends. Moreover, single women living in unfamiliar towns were vulnerable to the advances of unscrupulous men. The tragic case of Sarah Cornell, a young factory girl who was seduced and then murdered by her minister in Fall River, Massachusetts, highlights the precarious lot of the working woman.[20]

Freed from the dangers of life in a factory town, armed with a variety of skilled trades, and esteemed by their communities, the sisters of Harvard and Shirley made a significant economic contribution to their villages. A Harvard Church family account book for the years 1825–1836 verifies the importance of women's work to that family. The ledger records the money spent and income earned each month, indicating the prices of items sold. Although the entries do not explicitly state if the income was earned by the brothers or the sisters, the kinds of products sold provide a rough estimate of the percentage value of each sex's labor because certain items were made by men and others by women. The items producing the largest income were seeds and leather. Tanning was an exclusively male occupation, but the seed industry, which was the single largest producer of income, employed both men and women.[21]

Money derived from the sale of seeds and leather was augmented by the sale of a variety of other items. Some products, such as sieves, were a joint industry; men made the wooden rims, women wove the bottoms. The herb industry, too, involved the labor of men and women. But sisters also contributed items made solely by themselves—mats, hats, fans, knitting and sewing work, textiles, and fancy work items such as emery balls—and the income from these sales was not inconsequential. For months in which seed sales were high, such as January, the total proportion of women's work in the monthly income was less, though not insignificant. In January 1829 the total family income was $1,069; of that, $729 (68 percent) came from seed sales, and the rest came from the sale of various other items. The sisters contributed $65 through the sale of frocking, knitting work, mats, and forty yards of cloth, which equaled 19 percent of nonseed income for the month. If one adds to this figure $45, which was approximately half of the sieve sales (since women produced half of each sieve), then women contributed 32 percent to nonseed income, or 10 percent of the total monthly income. And if one considers that women also contributed some percentage of labor to the seed industry, then their total contribution for January increases even more.[22]

During the summer months, however, when seed sales were low or nonexistent, women's work was crucial to the family income. In May 1829, women contributed $83.00, or 45 percent of the total income of $184.00, by "entertaining" company (valued at $1.50) and selling straw hats, fans, sieves, and emery balls. The next month, when the total income was $209.00 with no seed sales, women contributed 48 percent of the income with the sale of 350 straw hats (worth $59.90), emery balls, sieves, mats, and fans totaling $100.00. In July 1830 the sisters contributed about $58.00, or 54 percent, of the $107.00 brought in that month with the sale of mats, hats, cider, sieves, and rosewater.[23]

Shaker women's contributions to the economy were not limited to the items they manufactured. Shaker sisters were also talented saleswomen. Although "peddling trips" were the province of male deacons who could cover hundreds of miles over the course of several weeks, the Harvard and Shirley sisters engaged in local trade, selling products of their own making. In July 1828 two women from the Shirley South family walked to the local dry goods store and sold the proprietor three hats, two dozen fans, and some thread. In August, two sisters and a brother made a trip to the same dry goods store and two textile factories, selling six fans. In October, two sisters and two brothers went to Fitchburg where they sold a dozen mats and several pairs of socks and stockings and purchased a peppermill. Lucy McIntosh, identified as a Harvard Church family trustee (generally a male position), rather than as the more usual office sister, was a particularly competent saleswoman. In May 1831 the Church family account book shows that of the $574.90 earned that month, $111.79 came from the sale of "sundry" items by McIntosh.[24]

Given the sisters' contributions to the economy, one would expect the women to take pride in their accomplishments, and records indicate that they did. On December 15, 1828, a female journal keeper calculated the value of all the articles purchased by the Shirley South family since April 16, proudly concluding that $132.00 of the money used in those purchases came from the sale of the sisters' work. Women's financial contributions even led to a certain level of independence. In 1835 the Ministry decided that the Harvard North family sisters were to buy half the materials used to weave sieve bottoms and receive half the completed sieves to sell. They could keep the profits, but they were then required to buy their own dress material.[25]

The relative financial freedom of the sisters is even more apparent if we compare their economic situation with that of other rural women. By the first half of the nineteenth century the New England countryside was clearly evolving to a market-based economy. Farm women participated in that process, many of them as braiders of palm-leaf hats, the most popular form of rural outwork for women well into the 1850s. Typically a farm wife or her daughters braided the hats for a local store, earning credit from the shopkeeper. Often, however, the store accounts were in the husband's name, so that wives had little control over how the money was spent. Like their non-Shaker counterparts, Shaker women also contributed to the family economy by participating in transitional rural work. In fact, braiding and selling palm-leaf hats and bonnets was a major industry among the Shaker sisters until the Civil War closed down their markets.[26] But because their income was communal rather than a husband's property, they had more input into the eventual use of the money they earned.

Clearly, Shaker women were important financial contributors to their families, but a full assessment of the value of women's work must take into account the nonmonetary side of their labor. Women's work possessed significance for the sisters beyond its economic value because of the unique structure of Shaker society. As Karen Hansen has pointed out, the public sphere/private sphere dichotomy does not always explain adequately the reality of people's lives.[27] But although she added an intermediary third sphere to analyze the working people she studied, to understand the value of Shaker labor we must move in the opposite direction and eliminate the notion of spheres altogether. For the Shakers there was no such thing as a division between public and private within the Shaker village (though they differentiated between themselves and the outside world). Women's domestic duties—cooking, cleaning, sewing, and washing—were an integral part of the Shaker community and thus functioned as public events. How well one cooked or sewed was not an individual matter. Thus seemingly mundane domestic affairs held symbolic importance for Shaker sisters and were recorded in women's journals.

Perhaps one of the most important of these symbolic activities was cap making. One diarist noted that in March 1827 the Shirley South family sisters started a new trend by making "meeting bonnets" from white cambric, and another diarist recorded that they began wearing these bonnets in May. These caps were more than mere items of clothing; they were important symbols of belonging, identifiable badges of Shakerism, and the Believers recorded the day when a sister first wore her bonnet to meeting. One woman's journal noted that on December 2, 1827, Martha Prouty wore a cap to meeting, a sign that she had opened her mind and confessed her sins. Even men acknowledged this symbolic event in their journals. Joseph Hammond recorded that on April 6, 1826, Cynthia and Mary Pratt, wearing their caps and handkerchiefs, "united" with Believers in a worship meeting. Jane Freeman Crosthwaite has suggested that the many caps which Shaker women made (and journals reveal that sisters produced a phenomenal number) can be viewed as both "portable work" and "personal gifts" from the Shaker leadership to Shaker sisters. Female leaders who traveled frequently could take their cap making with them and present the finished product to other sisters, thereby strengthening the bonds of friendship and sisterhood.[28] Most caps, however, were made not by the female leadership but by the family sisters, and the sense of belonging and connectedness symbolized by the bonnets they produced established important ties within the family.

Shaker brothers also came to appreciate the symbolic aspects of women's work, including their continual round of domestic chores. During an end-of-the-year worship meeting in 1856, the Shirley brothers, knowing that the sisters' "manifold labors / From us some tribute demands," read aloud a lengthy poem of praise to the women. In the poem the brothers recounted the many tasks that the women did for them, such as preparing and serving food (the brothers estimated that the sisters provided 1,095 meals a year), housekeeping, and washing and mending the men's clothes. The brothers appreciated the physical demands of women's work, but they also noted its spiritual side. "[H]oliness seems to be spoken / By things in a well order'd Room, / Where the floor or carpet gives token / Of a close acquaintance with broom. / There is no conflicting oppinions, / This statement each brother attests: / All over the Sister's Dominions / The spirit of cleanliness rests."[29]

Another area in which women's work became public work was their labor in the physician's order. As healers and nurturers, the women of Harvard and Shirley provided nursing care for their fellow Believers. Often, however, these same women also acted as physicians. Sarah Jewett, assisted by Tabitha Babbitt, served as Harvard's first physician from 1791 to 1810, at which time she was replaced by Salome Barrett. Though the rule was to have two males and two females in the physician's order, no man was appointed at Harvard until 1816.[30]

The sisters made their biggest contribution to the practice of medicine at Harvard and Shirley by introducing the latest in sectarian treatments. The Shakers practiced an eclectic kind of medicine, utilizing both standard nineteenth-century heroic medicine and new sectarian medical discoveries. Male physicians, Shaker and non-Shaker, administered treatments associated with heroic medicine and performed tasks that were intrusive to the body. Believers Asa Brocklebank and Joseph Hammond, as well as outside physicians, were called in when a Shaker patient needed bleeding. Hammond also pulled teeth, lanced sores, and inserted setons (thread or horsehair inserted into a wound to induce infection and facilitate drainage). And Thomas Corbett, a Believer from Canterbury, New Hampshire, made several trips to Harvard to treat Lucy Hannum's cataract using a surgical procedure known as couching.[31] Female physicians, however, generally practiced a "gentler" kind of medicine, using herbal remedies and sectarian techniques that evolved as alternatives to the extreme and often fatal ministrations of heroic practitioners.[32]

One of the first important medical sects of the early nineteenth century, and the first to be introduced at Harvard and Shirley, was Thomsonianism, named after its founder, Samuel Thomson, a New Hampshire farmer. Thomson used his knowledge of folk remedies to develop a system of botanical medicine that became popular in the rural areas of New England and New York as well as in the South.[33]

The Harvard and Shirley Shakers were in the middle of Thomsonianism's domain, both geographically and intellectually, and several factors may have influenced their adoption of the system. Living in close proximity to Boston, where Thomson eventually set up an office and infirmary, they were in the path of circulars and periodicals that promoted his brand of medicine. As farmers, they were familiar with Thomson's use of plants and knowledge of folk medicine. The Believers may also have felt that Thomsonian treatments, because they were natural and used everyday plants, were less of an affront to Shaker faith than drugs or mechanical heroic practices. Finally, Thomsonianism appealed to the Shakers' bias against formal education. The only credential necessary to practice Thomsonian medicine was a "right" purchased from Thomson for twenty dollars. In return, the purchaser received a copy of Thomson's book on botanic medicine and the privilege of using the Thomsonian system on his or her family. Unlike traditional medical practitioners who excluded women from their ranks, Thomson sold his rights to women as well as men.[34] It is no surprise, then, that it was the Shaker sisters who embraced Thomsonianism and introduced it into their villages.

The practice of botanic medicine at Harvard and Shirley began in November 1827 when Roxalana Hill of Shirley went to Harvard and became "the first that was doctored in the New Manner, in Harvard." Elizabeth Myrick was the attending physician. That this "New Manner" was Thomsonianism is spelled out a few days later in a journal entry. On December 4, Myrick went to the Shirley Church to administer a Thomsonian treatment for Lucy Bodge, the first time the practice was used at Shirley. Myrick stayed two days and "doctored" both Bodge and Polly Ager.[35]

Often the gender of the person overseeing the Thomsonian treatments is not mentioned, but when the physician is named she is invariably female. Elizabeth Myrick, though perhaps the most prominent physician at Harvard and Shirley, was only one of several sectarian female physicians in that bishopric. Tabitha Babbitt, Eliza Myrick, and Lois Haywood also practiced Thomsonian medicine. The case of Elder Grove Blanchard illustrates the primacy of women in the medical field. From December 3, 1831, to January 9, 1832, he was at Shirley "taking a course of medicine." Haywood was the overseeing physician, though Joseph Hammond was Blanchard's primary attendant; a male attendant was probably considered more appropriate than a female in certain situations, such as when Blanchard took a lobelia enema which "had good effect." Lois Haywood, however, watched alone with Blanchard at times. When he was given two doses of lobelia on December 18, Hammond watched him until 3:00 A.M., and Haywood stayed with him the rest of the night.[36]

The position of sisters like Myrick and Haywood reflects the empowering aspects of Shakerism for women. Shed of familial responsibilities, these women fulfilled their female roles as nurturers and healers, but they did so not simply by following orders but by taking charge of an entire branch of medicine in their villages. These sisters were given the freedom to introduce and experiment with a new method of practicing medicine and to instruct others in it. Indeed, in all spheres of female labor Shaker women were given opportunities to expand their economic and intellectual horizons, and it is evident that the Shakers valued women's work in ways not illuminated by the standard view of gendered labor. The androgynous ideal, which encouraged women to step beyond their traditional boundaries of gender, allowed the Believers to value equally men's and women's labor and to acknowledge the sisters' contributions. In the temporal as well as the spiritual world, Shakerism bestowed power on the women who lived within its fold.

6

Creating an Identity

IN 1816, HANNAH KENDALL'S ROLE in the founding of Harvard and Shirley came to an end. After twenty-five years of intense emotional and physical effort, she began to prepare the Believers for life without their "mother." Seemingly aware of her imminent demise, Kendall announced four months before her death that after she died the Believers would be on their own and should "not even look for any parents after her." On August 18, at seven o'clock in the evening, "Blessed Mother" died, "the last pillar of our most sacred institution." These were, as one Believer noted, "Serious times." [1]

Kendall's death left a void in the Harvard and Shirley communities, and the Believers were "orphans" in a very real sense. Under Rand and Kendall the Believers had developed an identity and forged the bonds of community. Suffering together and covenanting to create a new society, these "first Believers" (first-generation Shakers) shared a united sense of purpose, but, concerned with the *establishment* of community, they had not looked ahead to its *maintenance*. With Kendall's death and the passing of the first generation, the bonds that the Shakers had forged were tried and tested. New leaders and new members introduced competing ideas into the societies, while contact between the Shakers and the world increased. In the midst of these challenges, the fundamental question for the Believers became, "What does it mean to be a Shaker?"

Upon Kendall's death, John Warner and Rachel Keep succeeded to the Ministry. Of the same generation as Kendall, Warner and Keep had lived in the Ministry's Order since 1794 and observed Rand's and Kendall's methods for running the villages. Keep died less than six years later, at the age of forty-eight, leaving Warner to take the leading role in the community.[2] Warner's position was significant, for he, in particular, represented the "old order" of Shakerism, promoting a sectarian view of the movement that emphasized strict separation from the world and obedience to Shaker rules. He modeled himself after Eleazer Rand in his behavior and his emotional concern for the Shakers' spiritual well-being. He once recounted a story about "walking the floor" on a Sunday morning, "laboring to know whether we were really owned and accepted of God or not; and while I was laboring, it appeared to me that I sensed as it were a great number of disembodied spirits, and they looked upon us and blessed us. . . . [T]his was a precious gift of God to me." By the end of his time in the Ministry, Warner had become a prophetic voice among Believers, emphasizing separation from the world, retention of Shaker practices, avoidance of doctors, and upright conduct in business.[3]

Warner's fears were not ungrounded. In the late 1820s the Shakers sensed that a general temporal and spiritual "disorder" had affected their communities. In 1829 the Central Ministry issued a circular epistle to all villages, warning them that the cause of their problems was complacency fed by their non-Shaker neighbors' social acceptance of the Believers. Shaker leaders worried that the Believers had not reached a "degree of internal order" strong enough to keep them "from the danger of losing the path of social and spiritual relation, as a consecrated people, bound together by an inseparable bond of union." The introduction of "many and various characters" into Shaker society, with their worldly ideas, challenged the homogeneity of the founding group. The Believers' only protection against the infiltration of these new ideas was to strengthen the bonds of their community through an ongoing examination of their early history and the teachings of Ann Lee.[4]

Perhaps the greatest sign of disorder among the Shakers was the haphazard enforcement of "joint interest." The reluctance of Church members at Harvard and Shirley to turn over all their property had remained a problem, and a year before the Central Ministry issued its epistle, Rufus Bishop had gone to Harvard and Shirley "to make the crooked straight." For a month Bishop worked closely with the Believers, rewriting their covenants and stressing the need for "church order." Both villages accepted his suggestions in "good faith and gospel simplicity," launching a campaign to encourage consecration of all private property.[5]

The Central Ministry was also concerned with economic matters of an external nature, as Believers everywhere were engaging in business with the world.[6] The pull of external economic forces was in constant tension with the internal demands of Shaker society, and despite the drive toward separatism, the Believers at Harvard and Shirley maintained their business contacts with the outside, a carry-over from their days as private farmers. Neither village had ever been totally self-supporting, and as soon as they were stabilized, the Shakers looked for income-producing industries to augment their economy. They manufactured a variety of products, such as brooms, sieves, textiles, foodstuffs, and baskets, which they sold on peddling trips through the adjoining countryside. But the seed and herb industries quickly became the cornerstones of Harvard and Shirley's market with the world.

The seed business was one of Shirley's oldest and most prosperous ventures. By 1806 the Shirley Shakers already had sixty-five steady customers, earning $1,835.18 in seed sales that year alone. Five years later Oliver Burt, head of the business at Shirley, listed nineteen kinds of seeds for sale. Harvard, too, engaged in the seed trade, and by the 1820s seed sales provided a major portion of the Church family's income. But even more lucrative for Harvard was the herb business. At first, Believers gathered herbs in the surrounding countryside, an occupation assigned to both men and women; later, they raised their own plants in extensive gardens. Although the first recorded sale of herbs at Harvard occurred in 1820, the industry began in earnest in 1829 when the Shakers purchased a water-powered mill that allowed them to process large quantities of dried herbs into powders. The business grew quickly from there.[7]

The Shakers at Harvard and Shirley did not express undue concern over their business contacts with the world. The decision to align themselves with outside markets was pragmatic—it was the only way to maintain a cash flow—and grounded in their experience as yeoman farmers. But their seeming ambivalence about relationships with the world held serious consequences for the Believers. The Shaker rhetoric of separatism implied an identity based on differentiation from the world. How much they adulterated that difference and modified Shaker principles would affect how they viewed themselves. The degree to which the Shakers did interact with the world in the first third of the nineteenth century attests to the fine line they constantly walked between the demands of their communities and the demands of the world.

The Believers' willingness to interact with people and ideas not origi-
nating within the Shaker community can also be seen in their interest in
matters of health care and diet reform. The Harvard and Shirley Shakers
were fascinated by their health. Not only did they visit their own physicians frequently but they also consulted world's doctors, as evidenced by
repeated references in Asa Brocklebank's and Joseph Hammond's series of
daybooks. The precedent for consulting worldly doctors, contrary to order
as it was, had been established under Hannah Kendall. John Warner tried
to limit the practice and complained about the Believers' overuse of physicians, both Shaker and non-Shaker. He believed that the Shakers should
"bear" their illnesses as a test of their faith rather than seek medical cures.
Yet his lamentations fell on deaf ears, as Shaker journals indicate that Believers made frequent use of the world's doctors, both traditional and nontraditional. In December 1826, for example, Cynthia Pratt, who suffered
from breast cancer, journeyed to Medway, Massachusetts, for the surgical
ministrations of Ruth Wheeler, a "cancer doctor." In November 1834 Mary
Babbitt and Susan Myrick took several ailing Shakers to see Dr. Gibson, a
"root doctor" in New Ipswich, New Hampshire. For the next two years Believers made many trips to Gibson, consuming with great zeal the pills and
powders that he prescribed.[8]

The Believers also displayed an avid interest in diet reform and began
experimenting in the late 1820s and the 1830s with temperance, vegetarianism, and Grahamism, movements popular with many Americans. At the
heart of these "isms" was the twofold belief that physical stimulation of the
body resulting from a diet of spicy food, meat, and alcohol increased a
person's sexual drive and that this "excessive sexuality" was bad for one's
moral and physical health. Sylvester Graham, a one-time minister and temperance advocate, solved this "problem" for many Americans by suggesting
that people could dampen physical desire through a diet of vegetables, cold
water, and "Graham" or whole wheat bread.[9]

The Shakers, for whom chastity was of paramount importance, eagerly
embraced an ideology that promised control of their passions, and many
Believers incorporated dietary changes into their daily life, with varied results. By 1828 the Harvard Ministry estimated that most of the Believers at
Harvard and Shirley had given up alcohol, but the injunction against drinking was repeated many times in ensuing years. Believers also experimented
with vegetarianism. In February 1834 the Shirley Church family gave up
animal flesh for six months. By November, a few Believers were ready for

"old-fashioned meat dinners," but most continued their vegetarian diet, though some added cheese to their menu. Grahamism was introduced into Harvard the next spring, and New Lebanon labeled the village a model of "abstemious living." In 1836 Grove Blanchard and William Wetherbee attended one of Sylvester Graham's lectures in Lowell and afterward discussed health issues with him for two hours. Three years later Graham spent several days at Shirley lecturing on diet reform.[10]

The Believers' readiness to adopt sectarian medical practices and diet reform, particularly evident under Grove Blanchard's leadership, suggests a willingness to accept ideas that originated outside of the Shaker community if such practices met the needs of Believers. In fact, the boundaries between Shaker villages and the world could be quite blurred, and leaders of the first generation such as John Warner worried about the consequences for their communities. Warner exhorted the Shakers to maintain practices that set them apart from the world, emphasizing the importance of using distinctive Shaker language and gestures. Though performing such practices in public apparently embarrassed some Shakers, Warner encouraged the Believers "not to be ashamed to own Christ before all men." In the spirit of Eleazer Rand, he told Believers that when they were "out among the world" they were "to use their own language, [yea or nay]; not to say yes & no, nor goodbye." If Believers were eating with the world's people, then the former must kneel before the meal, just as they did at home. Warner was also concerned about the Believers' reputation, and he insisted on honest business dealings. Because Shakers "were a people that professed to be the nearest to God of any people on earth . . . [they] ought to be upright & just with each other, and with the world of mankind." When the Ministry returned from a visit to New Lebanon in 1824, its members brought the gift "for believers not to hold their hands first to the world to shake hands, but let the world be first in holding out their hands if they want to shake hands with us. If we were very zealous to hold out our hands to them, it would show as though we were fond of getting their union."[11] In this "gift" the Believers succinctly stated the heart of their problem. How could the Shakers deal with worldly people, do business with them, exchange ideas with them, without creating the feeling that Believers were "fond of their union"?

John Warner's concern over the Believers' relationship with the world and a general laxity in obeying Shaker rules signaled an important transition at the end of his Ministry. As Warner and the Central Ministry predicted, changes in Shaker society and in the outside world made it necessary for the Believers to make a conscious choice concerning their sectarian position. Events in 1826 brought the issue to a head. That year, when the Harvard Shakers were taken to court for the abuse of fellow Believer Seth Babbitt, they faced the largest crisis of this transition period, forced to choose between maintaining their sectarian position or facilitating a more open policy toward the world. By the end of the trial, the Shakers had taken a stand; they would be Shakers, but they would do so in close relationship to the world.

The Babbitt "affair" began on July 25, 1825, when Harvard town officials formally charged nine Harvard Shaker brothers with the beating and abuse two years before of Seth Babbitt, a Believer diagnosed as insane. The trial was held in Worcester on April 21 and 22, 1826. Ten witnesses, seven of whom were former Shakers, testified that the Shaker brethren beat Seth Babbitt and chained him to the floor in an unheated room at the Square House. When this did not break Babbitt's spirit, the Believers moved Babbitt to another building and placed him in a cramped, windowless, cagelike enclosure permeated with an overpowering stench. Here they tied him up to prevent his escape. Shaker witnesses admitted to keeping Babbitt in chains, but only, they argued, because he was insane and dangerous; in fact, his entire personality had changed. Once a hard-working, even-tempered man, Babbitt had become a completely different person. He destroyed property, soiled his bedsheets and himself, swore profusely, was paranoid, and constantly threatened other Believers, including his wife, daughter, and sister. Given the situation, the Shakers felt that their "treatment towards him was not only lawful & right, but that it was [their] indispensable duty." Judge Putnam continued this line of argument. In his final address to the jury, Putnam pointed out that the issue was not whether the Shakers had restrained Babbitt, this point having been proven, but whether this restraint was warranted. If the jury believed that Babbitt was insane and dangerous, Putnam exhorted, they must acquit the Believers, because, in such a situation, the Believers were morally compelled to restrain Babbitt. After deliberating only five minutes, the jury found the Shaker brothers not guilty.[12]

After the trial, an unidentified Harvard Shaker wrote a detailed account of the Babbitt case to explain the Shakers' actions. Taken together with an account of the trial printed in the *Worcester Spy*, these documents provide insight into the Shakers' relationships with Seth Babbitt and with the world. Babbitt moved to the Harvard Shaker community with his wife and two daughters in 1793 and fourteen years later deeded his ninety-acre farm to the Church. Over the years he served the Shakers well, acting as both a deacon and a trustee for the Church family. In 1815 he asked to be released from his position as deacon for reasons of "age and decrepitude," but he retained his place as a trustee. Four years later, at the age of sixty-two, he suffered a "paralytic shock" that affected his speech, his mobility, and his mental abilities. Another "shock" the next year left him "insane" and violent, and he was restrained at his wife's behest. In November 1823 Babbitt promised to behave and was released from his restraints, but he soon resumed his violent behavior and was immediately bound again.[13]

News of the Shakers' treatment of Babbitt, heralded by several Shaker apostates, enraged the townspeople of Harvard, who had done business with Babbitt when he served as deacon and trustee. An official investigation conducted by five selectmen, two town residents, and two justices of the peace revealed a situation that was not good for the Shakers. The selectmen noted that Babbitt suffered "paroxysms" of violence, but they believed that these fits were not severe enough to justify the use of restraints. They also found what they considered to be evidence of cruelty and neglect. The report claimed that Shaker adolescents teased Babbitt until he exploded in anger and that during the winter months the Believers chained Babbitt to the floor in his room and left him unattended during the night. The selectmen attributed this callous treatment to the Shaker practice of renouncing all "natural attachments." The investigating committee suggested that Babbitt live with a non-Shaker family for a month to see if he continued to act "deranged," but the Shakers refused to comply.[14]

Seth Babbitt's case aroused both the anger of the town and the passions of the Shakers as they defended themselves against attacks of cruelty. The case also raises several troubling questions concerning the Shakers and Seth Babbitt. First, was Seth Babbitt really insane? According to all available testimony his "shocks," most likely strokes, impaired his mental abilities and led to violent fits. Whether or not Babbitt would be considered insane by today's clinical standards, the Shakers' diagnosis of his behavior was in line with early-nineteenth-century ideas about mental illness. Violent behavior, such as that displayed by Babbitt, was a key factor in diagnosing insanity because, as Norman Dain writes, it signaled the "loss of reason [which] was seen as the loss of the soul and of humanity and God's grace." Second, did the Shakers abuse Seth Babbitt? This is a difficult question to answer, for what today would be considered abusive treatment of the mentally ill was accepted practice at the time. Even during Babbitt's lifetime, few physicians in the United States knew or cared about European theories of mental illness and "moral management" that construed insanity as a curable disease and advocated placing patients in asylums and treating them humanely. Most Americans, medical and lay, still believed that mental illness was incurable and treated the afflicted as little better than animals. One doctor reported that the family of one of his "insane" patients had chained the patient to the floor and tied his arms to his body, apparently to prevent him from hurting himself or others; the doctor did not mention whether he found the family's treatment of the man offensive, an omission that leads one to conclude that he did not. The Believers' treatment of Seth Babbitt sounds strikingly similar. The Shakers never denied restraining Babbitt because they did not consider such treatment cruel or abusive. Even if the charges of beating and ignoring Babbitt were true, these actions, reprehensible as they are today, were considered standard practice in the care of the insane at that time.[15]

Despite the Believers' claim that they had done nothing wrong, the publicity generated by the trial brought to the public's attention matters the Shakers would have preferred to keep to themselves. The original accusers of the Shakers and most of the witnesses for the prosecution were Shaker apostates who could easily have been motivated by reasons that had nothing to do with Seth Babbitt. The townspeople, however, seemed genuinely enraged at the reports of abuse. They knew Seth Babbitt personally, had worked with him, and could not accept the Shakers' treatment of him, even if that treatment was typical of nineteenth-century medical practice. Underpinning this response was the Shakers' ambivalent relationship to the world. Although the Believers fostered many kinds of connections with the world, the town's general acceptance of the Shakers was still tinged with distrust, and accusations of abuse unearthed buried feelings against the Shakers. Furthermore, the townspeople probably saw Babbitt's treatment as a breach of faith, an insult to a man who had served the Shakers faithfully for years and had given them all of his property. The Shakers, who portrayed themselves as peaceful and loving people, showed the world that they were no more enlightened than the rest of society in their views on the mentally ill. They, too, were capable of abusive behavior and made no special room in their "heaven on earth" for people with mental incapacities.

The records are silent concerning the feelings of individual Shakers about the treatment of Seth Babbitt, but as a group they maintained that restraining Babbitt was their right and duty. In this the court agreed. Despite the hostility of town residents, men of influence sided with the Shakers. Dr. Amos Bancroft of Groton and Dr. Aaron Baird of Lunenburg both testified on the Shakers' behalf, and Judge Putnam (a well-connected and influential man who afterward became a good friend of the Believers) and the jury were openly on their side. In short, the Shakers were exonerated and portrayed as upstanding citizens falsely accused of base behavior.[16]

The Babbitt case was a turning point for the Believers. The Shakers had been involved in court cases before, but none had generated as much publicity as the Babbitt case. The Shakers at Harvard and Shirley were put on display to be judged by their peers, and they were found to be normal, decent people who behaved according to accepted social views. They were well served by the American legal and medical systems. Thrust into the limelight, the question for Believers was whether to embrace the acceptance they had been accorded by the outside world or to withdraw into themselves. They chose the former, and this changed the course of their history.

The decision to embrace the world's acceptance did not entail an abrupt rupture in Shaker life but led to a gradual yet constant accommodation to the people and ideas of the world. This change was accelerated, however, with the transfer of leadership from the first to the second generation of Believers. The trial of Seth Babbitt was the last major event during the Ministry of John Warner, and the danger of the Shakers' position probably weighed heavily on his mind. A little more than two years after the Babbitt case, Warner resigned his position as Ministry elder.

Warner did not announce his own resignation but arranged for Rufus Bishop to do so when he visited Harvard and Shirley in 1828. Warner had gone to New Lebanon with the rest of the Harvard Ministry on a routine visit and while there requested to be "released from a weight of care & Labour, which I was no[t] able to Endure," ostensibly because of advanced age and feeble health. When his resignation was announced at New Lebanon, it came as a surprise to everyone, including the other members of the Harvard Ministry. He remained at New Lebanon for several months after the others returned to Harvard. Rufus Bishop read Warner's letter of resignation to each family at Harvard and Shirley, which generated "considerable discussion" among surprised Believers. When Bishop left Harvard in August, he appointed Grove Blanchard as Warner's replacement.[17]

Warner's resignation was shrouded in secrecy, a tactic the Shakers often used when dealing with problems, suggesting that there may have been a conflict between Warner and other, perhaps more progressive, Believers at Harvard and Shirley. Warner was old and in bad health, but if these were his only reasons for resigning, and such reasons were legitimate, why keep his retirement a secret? Events after his resignation point further to some unspoken conflict surrounding Warner. He chose to return to Harvard to live after his resignation, a natural and reasonable choice, yet his decision seems to have generated some negative feelings. On October 25, 1828, the Harvard Ministry wrote to New Lebanon to reassure its members that the people at Harvard had gone out of their way to please Warner since his return, setting aside a room for him and assigning him a sister to do his housekeeping and cooking; they thought that Warner approved of the arrangements. On the same day, the Harvard Ministry wrote to South Union, Kentucky, explaining why it had taken seven months to respond to South Union's last letter. Warner's resignation came as a surprise, the Ministry noted, and the suddenness of the change caused "a series of feelings on all concerned." Though the arrangement seemed to be working, the underlying tone of the Ministry's letters was a grudging acceptance of Warner's decision to live at Harvard.[18]

With no detailed explanation of Warner's resignation in the records, one can only speculate on the conflict that may have surrounded him at Harvard. It is possible that the conflict was generational, centering on the future direction of the two villages. Warner was a first-generation Believer who had known Ann Lee, Eleazer Rand, and Hannah Kendall and suffered persecution in the early years. He was dedicated to the preservation of the gospel and was most often remembered for his exhortations to maintain Shaker principles and to remain separate from the world. Grove Blanchard, his replacement, was a second-generation Believer who joined the Harvard Church in 1812 at the age of fifteen, entered the Ministry's Order as elder brother in 1818, and became elder at age thirty-one.[19] Following the Babbitt case and Blanchard's appointment as elder, the Shakers began a more open relationship to the world with the introduction of sectarian medical practices and active proselytizing among the world's people. Perhaps it was precisely this new openness to the world that Warner opposed, creating conflict within the community.

Certainly Warner's resignation was a graphic reminder that the first generation of Believers was not only aging but also passing away. The deaths of important leaders of the early years, such as that of Elijah Wilds on March 14, 1829, created anxiety among the Shakers. On December 1, 1832, Salome Barrett died, and a Shaker sister remarked, "Our Beloved Mother Ann, has taken home another of her faithful first born children, one that bore the burden & heat of the day. . . . It brings a very solemn feeling to have one after another drop away of the first believers." The next year, after the death of Rebekah Proctor, the same sister remarked that "the *first* believers are fast going home & leaving us behind."[20]

Among other consequences, the deaths of these first-generation Believers constituted a loss of human connections to the Shaker past. With fewer people left who had known Ann Lee personally and who could recount the history of the early years of Shakerism, the Believers faced the possibility of losing that historical grounding for their identity which the Central Ministry deemed so important. By the early 1820s most of the "first parents," (the original founders of the communities) were dead. When Job Bishop of Canterbury, New Hampshire, visited Harvard in October 1823 he observed "that all called him Father. He said he owned it in this sense; that he had been called in the parent order, & he was the last that remained." To keep alive the memory of the early years, the Believers visited the sites of persecution where their first leaders had suffered. In 1829 a group of Harvard and Canterbury Believers stopped at the place where the mob had beaten James Whittaker and William Lee almost fifty years before. One member of the group was Bethiah Prescott Willard, the only Believer left who had actually been present at the attack, and she recounted how she had clung to Whittaker's back and taken the blows meant for him.[21]

Vivid accounts of persecution by the first Believers provided that "inseparable bond" which the Central Ministry warned the Shakers was so necessary for survival. The Shakers were well aware, however, that they would soon have to find other ways of linking their past with their future, and they did so by scrutinizing their troubles through the lens of theology. The deaths of the first Believers "would feel heavy to us," wrote the Harvard Ministry, "did we not believe that their blessing would continue with an increase upon all the faithful."[22] Just as they had interpreted the wave of apostasy in the early 1800s as a trial that would bring blessing to the people, so they found consolation in seeing the deaths of the first Believers as a spiritual battle. By enduring the trials and tribulation of loss, the Believers would be blessed spiritually. Their faith would be strengthened, and, in a real sense, so would their identity.

The Harvard and Shirley Shakers believed that this spiritual blessing would begin as spiritual growth within the communities. Internal growth was important because the Shakers believed that the world would not turn toward Shakerism until the Believers themselves were spiritually strong enough to meet the needs of the nonbelievers. The first step toward preaching the gospel to the world, then, was to revitalize Shaker communities. The Believers searched eagerly for signs of God's blessing, and in the mid-1830s they observed the signs of a "general awakening" in their villages as the Believers put their own spiritual house in order before welcoming the world's people. As the Harvard Ministry noted, "It is our feelings [sic] to labor to be prepared to meet the event of God's work as it comes to view." Beginning in February 1835 meetings were imbued with a "good portion and outpouring of the good spirit," and "the gift of repentance" took hold among the people. Expiatory meetings of conviction and repentance, held several times a week, continued into 1836.[23]

As the Shakers experienced a spiritual awakening, they began to look for the concomitant physical growth of their villages. Accordingly, the Shakers began a period of intense missionary activity from the mid-1820s through the 1830s in Cape Cod, southern Massachusetts, and parts of Rhode Island, Vermont, and New Hampshire. Both men and women served as missionaries and sometimes spent long periods of time away from home. In April 1826 the Ministry noted religious stirrings "in a line considerable distance on the Cape," and they sent Ebenezer Grosvenor and Eunice Bathrick there as missionaries. The pair left Harvard on July 30 and did not return until October 5. In 1827 Grosvenor and William Clark journeyed to New Hampshire and Vermont on a missionary tour; that same year Thomas McGooden conducted a three week "preaching tour" of Middleboro and Taunton, Massachusetts, and Pawtucket and Smithfield, Rhode Island. During this period, several individuals and numerous families joined the Harvard and Shirley Shakers.[24]

The Shakers were optimistic about numerical growth. In January 1831 the Harvard Ministry noted an "evident increase" in population, especially at Harvard, and cited a "gradual increase" at Shirley in May. Children and adolescents constituted an especially large group; in 1832 the Harvard Shakers conducted three different schools, two in the day and one in the evening, to accommodate the ninety-five students who lived there. The anticipated growth of the communities was part of the Ministry's justification for building a large, new office at Harvard. It had originally planned to construct a four-room building with one hall, but the elders, deacons, and "principle" brothers and sisters had talked it over and decided to build a larger office, modeled after the one at New Lebanon, with six rooms, two halls, and a loft. The Harvard Ministry conceded that given the community's small population, plans for such a large office probably seemed "extravagant," but the Ministry justified its actions by claiming that its plans were based on Harvard's future, not its present.[25]

Although the Shakers were encouraged by the spiritual growth they saw in their communities, they also experienced a series of apostasies in the summer and fall of 1836. For those who had their minds set on leaving there was little the Shakers could do—the Shakers tried to convince Mary Hatch to stay but finally had to let her "follow her own evil desires"—and a series of departures occurred in July. Some left of their own accord, but others were too disruptive to keep, and the Ministry initiated a purge. On July 26 the elders and Ministry, after much soul-searching, agreed "to send Sarah Winchester to her own company. . . . [S]he leaves the Society for the world and none to [sic] soon, her day is fully out and out, for we must have a pure Church."[26]

Troubles continued to mount; not only were people leaving the Shakers, but these apostates were then returning to cause problems for the Believers. Maryann Adams went to the world on July 30. Several days later, Sarah Winchester and her brother Hosea, also an apostate, returned to Harvard "to see and be seen" and to gather up Sarah's belongings. On October 6, Walter Adams left the Shakers, followed by Lucinda Orsment on the 8th. On the 13th, the Ministry returned to Harvard to find that Sarah Winchester and Maryann Adams were hanging about the village, trying to lure others into leaving. We are, wrote the elders, besieged by "much affliction with apostates and evil without and within."[27]

This general sense of beleaguerment capped a period of transition in the Believers' search for their identity. During her lifetime, Hannah Kendall established the guidelines by which the Believers were to live their daily lives. Her strong leadership abilities and her popularity gave her the power to create an identity for her people. Furthermore, those people were a largely homogeneous group bound by the ties of family and spiritual affection. With the death of Kendall, the bonds that the Shakers had forged were sorely tested. Society had changed. New people joined who had not been involved in the pioneering efforts of community formation. A younger generation, untouched by persecution and more interested in issues of secular reform, took over the positions of leadership. Despite the warnings of John Warner, the Believers chose the path of accommodation to the world.

7

The Era of Manifestations

THROUGHOUT THE MID-1830s the Shakers gradually moved toward an accommodation with the world, actively seeking converts and experimenting with worldly ideas. Then, in 1837, the internal demands of Shaker society diverted the attention of Believers everywhere as they experienced a spiritual revival known as the Era of Manifestations or Mother Ann's Work. For more than a decade the Believers turned inward, seeking spiritual and social renewal in ecstatic religious experience, characterized by visions of the spirits of Mother Ann, first Believers, and many others. The revival, however, was a two-edged sword. While strengthening the religious convictions of many, the spirit manifestations also divided villages and families, pitting those who believed against those who did not. In the end, the revival would be the ultimate test of the bonds the Harvard and Shirley Shakers had sustained for almost fifty years.

The Era of Manifestations began in August 1837 when several young girls at the Watervliet South family experienced a profusion of visions.[1] News of the event spread quickly among the Shaker villages, and by early October the Believers at Harvard reported "shaking" in their meetings, followed by visions a month or so later. In January 1838 the Harvard Ministry wrote to New Lebanon that "an uncommon outpouring of the spirit and power of God" had been present at Harvard and Shirley over the past three months. Some Believers were "much exercised in visions, and sometimes lay in trances from 4 to 12 hours." At one public meeting Thomas Clapp, a Shaker brother who fell into a trance during the service, never "woke up" and had to be transported home in a wagon. Such behavior alarmed the world's people, many of whom began to stay away from public meetings.[2]

Spirit activity occurred in spurts at Harvard and Shirley. The first wave of activity lasted until April 1838, manifested largely in meetings at the South and East families, the gathering orders at Harvard, but also in public Sabbath meetings. Caught up in the excitement, the Shakers lost all sense of time. Once, when Grove Blanchard went to the South family on business, he spent the entire day there listening to the visions of Edwin Myrick and Jane Durant. "Poor little Edwin Myrick (the Simpleton)" was a particularly prolific visionist who gave "pointed testimonies against sin" and had visions of Ann Lee. Anna Mayo, a fifty-four-year-old resident of the South family in 1838, also experienced visions during this early period.[3]

By July 1838 the visions had mostly ceased. However, they began again in October, this time in the Church as well as in the gathering families, and lasted until January 1839. On November 25 a number of young people began "turning" (spinning in place) in a public meeting, repeating the action four days later at the public Thanksgiving meeting. Visions also became a part of the Shaker daily routine. On November 30 Charlotte Priest of the Shirley Church family was "taken in vision" at the supper table. After seven hours her visions ended, and "she sang 46 new and heavenly songs." The next day she spent five more hours in vision at the breakfast table, and that evening in a family meeting she and Sophia Foster "were taken in visions and operations" until after midnight. In that time, Priest sang another sixty songs and Foster "danced some of them."[4]

Those "instruments" (receivers of visions) listed by name who were active in these first two waves of spiritual activity defy easy categorization. For the periods under consideration I have identified five named instruments at Shirley and twelve at Harvard, though many more unnamed Believers were also involved. Out of those seventeen identified instruments, ten were female and seven were male. Of the ten females, in 1838 eight were over eighteen years of age (Joanna Randall, S; Charlotte Priest, S; Lydia Persons, S; Anna Mayo, H; Minerva Hill, H; Sarah Pratt, H; Betsy Hall, H; Jemima Blanchard, H), one had turned thirteen (Sophia Foster, S), and one's age is unknown (Jane Durant, H). Of the seven males, two were elderly (Amos Buttrick, S; Abijah Worster, H), one was twenty-six (Joseph Parker, H), two were adolescent (Abial Crosby, H; Alfred Collier, H), and two were probably twelve or thirteen years old (Edwin Myrick, H; Thomas Clapp, H). Nine of the visionists lived in gathering families (though one of them was an office sister in a position of authority), seven lived in the Church family (one of whom was also an office sister), and one lived in an intermediate family. Blanchard, Buttrick, and Worcester were elderly first Believers.

This brief portrait of these earliest acknowledged instruments revises one of the major theories about the Era of Manifestations—that the revival was a "protest movement" [5] and a bid for power, achieved through divine inspiration, by young women on the fringes of authority. Marjorie Procter-Smith writes that "the ecstatic operations originated with, and retained their predominance among the 'peripheral' members of the Shakers' hierarchically ordered communities," and many other scholars have made the same argument. [6] The situation at Harvard and Shirley, however, only partially fits this generalization. Although the visions were originally centered largely in the gathering families, prepubescent girls were not the only instruments; in fact, three of the earliest instruments, Thomas Clapp, Edwin Myrick, and Anna Mayo, were decidedly not adolescent females. When writing about worship meetings, Shakers do indicate that at times a large number of youth and children were engaged in spirit activity, but the records do not leave the impression that they were the only ones who experienced visions.

Furthermore, very few of the named instruments were marginalized, if by that term is intended girls or female adolescents who lived in gathering families with no access to authority or power. Of the named instruments, almost as many males were active instruments as females. More than half of the instruments, 65 percent, were postadolescent, including a woman who turned nineteen in 1838. Furthermore, many of the named instruments had access to status or authority, either by living in the Church family, holding a leadership position, or being a first Believer, a revered position in the communities of Harvard and Shirley. The mixed nature of these early instruments does not minimize the significance of spirit activity in the gathering families nor the challenge to Shaker authority indicated by that activity, but it does suggest that this challenge was more broadly based than has been assumed and was not necessarily or primarily a reaction led by women.

Certainly the Shaker leadership recognized both male and female instruments from the beginning of the revival. Diane Sasson, in her work on the Era of Manifestations at Harvard, argues that the Ministry's appointment of official instruments for the spirits involved concerns both about gender and authority. She argues that power was weighted on the side of male Shakers and that male instruments were often appointed to control the course of the revival. Thus, she posits that William Leonard was especially privileged by the Harvard Ministry because he was a mature and intelligent Believer whose messages could steer the revival in an ordered direction. But his performance was often perfunctory, coming from the orders of his elders more than from personal inspiration. Minerva Hill, on the other hand, a prolific visionist who was less well positioned in the Shaker community, actually had more power as an instrument because her visions came from within.[7]

Although I would agree that power issues were central to the act of choosing instruments, I see the struggle for women to become recognized instruments as less pronounced than does Sasson, because there were numerous sisters throughout the revival whose messages were "privileged" by their Ministries.[8] Nevertheless, the important point to be taken from Sasson's work is that both women and men were active participants in the revival, and thus, the revival should not be construed as primarily a female phenomenon.

If the impetus for spirit activity at Harvard and Shirley was not a female challenge to authority, then how does one explain the outbreak of revival? Many authors attribute the revival to the Shakers' despair over apostasy, the deaths of the first Believers, a general loss of "order," and a growing sense of worldliness.[9] All of these factors most certainly contributed to the outbreak of revival at Harvard and Shirley, but the revival was ultimately not the result of despair. The Shakers maintained an optimistic belief that in spite of their problems, and perhaps because of them, God would bless them with spiritual and numerical growth; they had never lost their faith that one day the world would acknowledge the truth of Shakerism. For the Harvard and Shirley Believers, the cycles of repentance and purification of the mid-1830s, even the crisis of apostasy from 1834 to 1836, were ultimately positive signs of God's preparatory work among Believers, laying the foundation for a future increase. The Harvard and Shirley Shakers, waiting in joyful expectation, saw the events at Watervliet as a sign that the promised work was beginning. Their participation in the revival, then, was an attempt to deal with the developing crisis of a changing social structure while simultaneously acknowledging God's promise of growth and prosperity.

The more immediate stimulus that seems to have prompted each wave of activity at Harvard and Shirley was the death of a Believer. The first burst of spirit operations at the end of 1837 followed immediately upon the demise of a well-loved brother, Jesse Myrick, Jr., who died on November 22 at the age of twenty-six. That his death deeply affected Believers is clear from Ministry letters sent to New Lebanon. Myrick's final minutes were "truly a heart trying scene. He had . . . a faithful upright soul, seemingly fit to live and fit to die." He was seen in vision soon after he died and continued to be seen almost daily six months later. His death explains both the profuse visionary activity of Edwin Myrick, Jesse's natural brother, and the concentration of so much of the activity in the gathering families. Myrick had lived almost his entire life as a Shaker in the gathering order, and his loss was felt by those who remained. The second wave of spiritual activity followed a similar pattern, occurring after three sisters—Elizabeth Jewett and Maryann Hammond of Harvard and Anna Wheelock of Shirley—died around the last week of September 1838. Both Jewett and Wheelock were first Believers, and all three sisters were considered dedicated Shakers. Visionists reported that some of the departed sisters were acting as guides to the spirit world.[10]

The power of death to act as a stimulus for charismatic behavior was rooted in the Shaker belief in an easily accessible spirit world. The boundary between the physical and the spiritual worlds had always been blurred for the Shakers. Ann Lee claimed that she could communicate with angels and souls of the deceased, and this tradition continued among Believers. Now, as the generation that had known Ann Lee was passing away, the spirit world once again became a focal point of Shaker life. Death was often tragic, but when the deceased was a promising young Shaker or a revered first Believer, both the community's past, in the collective memory of the elderly, and its future, were threatened. Shaker society was in transition, moving from a period in which its history and identity were rooted in direct contact with Ann Lee and the struggle for survival to an unknown future devoid of personal connections to its founder and the commitment of early Believers. By suspending the limits of time and establishing connections with the spirits of the recently departed, as well as with Ann Lee, Hannah Kendall, and other important Shaker founders, the Believers created an "eternal now."

This "eternal now," or to use Victor Turner's phrase, "liminal" space, provided a niche of security for the Shakers as they confronted their future.

According to Turner, a person (or a society, I would argue) passing from one life phase to another goes through a middle period known as the "liminal phase." Unlike the highly structured phases that precede and succeed it, the liminal phase is free of rigid social conventions. Thus, an immediate "communitas" develops wherein people relate to each other directly without the mediating influence of rules and social mores. "Communitas is of the now; structure is rooted in the past and extends into the future through language, law, and custom." Liminality, then, exposes the "essential and generic human bond, without which there could be *no* society."[11] The Shakers created the immediacy of communitas through direct contact with the spirit world. Impelled to action by conflicting emotions of optimism and despair, the Shakers tested the bonds of their community, searching for the "essential and generic" bond of their society in the spirit world.

In February 1839 spirit activity took a new, and divisive, turn as gathering family instruments assumed the power to purge the communities of disbelieving Shakers. During a union meeting in the Shirley South family, several instruments "exposed" the sinners in their midst, causing many to confess and repent. The next day, East family visionists revealed the sins of members there; "W. Clapp they wholly cut off—a solemn meeting especially to poor William." Clapp, who did not want to leave the Shakers, had to beg for permission to stay. Purging continued in the public Sabbath meeting. Abial Crosby of the South family announced that many Believers in the Church family were hiding sin in their lives and threatened to expose them publicly if they did not confess, creating an awkward situation indeed. The Ministry asked the Church family elders to speak privately with the accused members, but at the next public Sabbath meeting, instruments Abial Crosby and Minerva Hill revealed the names of several sinful Church members in front of worldly spectators, no doubt embarrassing the accused Shakers and the Church.[12]

Another dimension was added to the revival during this time when Believers began exchanging "spiritual gifts." These gifts, which were invisible, could come from living Shakers or from instruments chosen to speak for departed Believers and included items such as gold chains, pearls, trumpets, flowers, birds, food, and wine. When Believers received these gifts they acted out in pantomime the use of the items, pretending, for example, to drink a glass of wine or blow a trumpet. Some spiritual gifts, like gold breastplates, gold rings, or items studded with precious jewels, were very "unshaker" and clearly would have been prohibited in Shaker villages had they been real items. The Era of Manifestations, however, stretched the bounds of acceptable behavior among Believers. Though taught to eschew private ownership and forbidden to keep purely ornamental and superfluous items, Shakers became very possessive of their spiritual gifts. Individuals kept special books in which they listed the gifts they received.[13] Believers who performed certain tasks on earth even received distinctive spiritual clothing, adorned with gold, pearls, and jewels, to wear when they entered the spirit world precisely so that they would stand out.[14]

In 1841 Harvard and Shirley entered the most intense phase of the Era of Manifestations. For the next several years the Believers spent an inordinate amount of time in spirit activity and exhibited some of the most extreme behavior of the revival. This burst of activity followed the death of Abijah Worster of Harvard, who died on January 10, 1841, at the age of ninety-five. A devout and well-loved first Believer and "a father and a friend to the young," his death was a great loss to the community. Fortunately for the bereaved Shakers, Worster was with them in spirit, if not in body. Only a few hours after his death, Hannah Kendall's spirit informed the Believers that Worster's spirit would be "wintering" with them. The next day instruments saw Worster at his own funeral along with Ann Lee and a variety of other spirits. After his death, spirit messages virtually poured forth. Hundreds of messages and visions were recorded for the year 1841, more than for any other year, and the Harvard Ministry estimated that in the two months of December 1841 and January 1842, Believers at both communities recorded between seven hundred and a thousand pages of spirit messages.[15]

During this period the Shakers developed one of their most unique contributions to spiritualism—the incarnation of Holy Mother Wisdom, the female aspect of the Shaker's dual godhead, who made her first appearance in 1841. The Central Ministry planned Wisdom's visits well in advance and informed each Shaker village by letter of her impending arrival, giving them precise dates and instructions on how to prepare for her visit.[16]

On July 25, 1841, the spirit of Holy Mother Wisdom made her first visit to Harvard. One of her first acts was to appoint instruments—seven sisters and five brothers—to speak for her or "bear witness" to her presence. After choosing her instruments, Holy Mother Wisdom spent several days "marking" the Believers. Making her way through each family, Wisdom, through the agency of her instruments, placed a sign on all Believers, identifying them as her children. She also visited each building "to purge out the evil, wash away the stains and in lieu thereof to bestow her everlasting Peace, comfort, love and blessing, on every thing." On August 8, Wisdom went to Shirley, where she performed the same rituals, selecting five brothers and seven sisters as her instruments. She spent fourteen days at Shirley, and almost all the Believers "attended upon Holy Mother in meeting in some form, 50 hours in the time of her visit." [17]

Though Holy Mother Wisdom's first visit went smoothly, her second visit to Harvard created a small crisis. According to the Harvard Ministry, this visit occurred from December 27, 1841, to January 2, 1842. They claimed that this second visit "was as real to us all, as Her first visits," yet when they told the Central Ministry about it during a visit to New Lebanon in 1842, they were informed that the second visit to Harvard could not have occurred because Holy Mother Wisdom had been at New Lebanon and Watervliet during that same period. Apparently, Holy Mother Wisdom, though a spirit, could not be in two places at the same time. The Central Ministry explained away the incident to the Harvard Ministry by "intimat[ing] that it must have been [Holy Mother Wisdom's] Angels who were with us at that time" and not Holy Mother Wisdom herself. [18]

The Harvard Ministry returned home, dissatisfied with the answer they had received. A challenge to the Central Ministry's authority was rare, but in October the Harvard Ministry informed New Lebanon that they could not tell the people of Harvard that Mother Wisdom herself had not made the second visit. Not only would this admission embarrass the instruments who claimed to have seen Mother Wisdom, but it would also damage the people's belief in spirit manifestations in general. The Harvard Shakers maintained their position. The spirit messages in the collection of inspired writings from Mother Wisdom's second visit to Harvard have not been changed to reflect the Central Ministry's claim that Mother Wisdom was at New Lebanon and not at Harvard on the days in question. [19]

New Lebanon responded publicly to Harvard's challenge in November 1842. Seth Wells composed an open letter concerning the writing and editing of inspired messages to be sent to all villages. The content of spirit messages, claimed Wells, should always agree with previously recorded facts. He singled out Harvard and Shirley as two villages that had not followed this rule. Having dared to challenge New Lebanon, the communities were held up as public examples of disobedience. [20]

The Central Ministry also intervened in the course of the revival in 1842 by ordering all Shaker meetings closed to the world (Harvard closed their meetings on June 5), partly to preserve the sacred nature of the spirit visits and partly to ensure the safety of Believers. The Central Ministry feared that the ecstatic behavior of the Believers would lead to persecution by the world's people. This fear was not unfounded. In 1839 the Shakers at Harvard and Shirley received threats of persecution from the world, and several Shakers at the Harvard South family had visions of a mob attack which never came to pass. The Harvard Ministry knew the potential volatility of the situation and, after a "lively and free" public Sabbath meeting in January 1841, warned the Shakers not to say anything that would anger their worldly spectators.[21]

Having closed public meetings and removed themselves from worldly contact, the Believers began a period of intense introspection. Their search for renewal reached its apex in the spring of 1842, when each village, which by now had adopted a spiritual name (Harvard became Lovely Vineyard, and Shirley became Pleasant Garden), began celebrating a holy feast or passover ritual. Also called a "mountain meeting," the event was held twice a year on a specially prepared and named feast ground located on a hill outside the Shaker village; the focal point of each feast ground was a spiritual fountain. Before attending this feast, Believers underwent a period of preparation, sweeping away unbelief with spiritual brooms and donning special spiritual garments. On August 29, 1842, the Harvard Church family held its first passover, a six-hour affair, on the Holy Hill of Zion and recorded the event in a special journal. At 12:30 P.M. the Ministry elders, ten instruments (five of each sex), five scribes, and sixty-three brothers and sisters marched to the Holy Hill. When they reached the fountain, they "drank" from it, "washed" in it, and "sprinkled" each other with holy water. The climax of this event was the spiritual feast. Believers "dined" on honey, fruit, and cake covered with love, and "drank" wine from the spiritual winepress. Believers at Shirley celebrated similar feasts on the Holy Hill of Peace.[22]

In the autumn of 1842 New Lebanon initiated the gift of "taking in" native spirits. Spirits of "primitive" peoples, such as Native Americans or Hottentots, visited the Believers for the purpose of learning about and converting to Shakerism. One morning, for example, a native spirit came to the Shirley Church while the Believers were kneeling in prayer after breakfast and asked for instruction in saying grace before a meal. Such visits were very real to the Shakers. In January 1843 they reported that several tribes of Native American spirits were camping in wigwams at Harvard. The area got rather congested when several other groups of spirits moved in and soon a scuffle ensued between groups of native, Turkish, and French spirits. The Shakers "labored" with the spirits and finally wrangled a promise from the Indian chief to keep his men under control.[23]

Spirit activity continued through the spring of 1844, then slackened but picked up again in early fall with a unique visitation from Holy Father, the male aspect of the deity and the counterpart of Holy Mother Wisdom. The Shakers began preparations in August, appointing male and female instruments for his visit—three men and four women at Harvard, four women and five men at Shirley. Holy Father specified that his messages could be only be given to the sisters through a female instrument. He came to Harvard on September 1 and later that month went to Shirley. His visits deeply affected the young Believers, especially the boys. When Holy Father's instruments went into a meeting on September 20, eight young boys were "struck down" and rolled on the floor for an hour, groaning uncontrollably. The next day while the Shakers were eating, angels who were present in the dining room exclaimed, "Awake, clear the way." Some of the instruments responded and were caught up in the spirit, especially the male instrument known as "the mouth of the Lord Jehovah to his people," who began turning around the room. When the spirit of Holy Father finally left Harvard and Shirley, he had spent almost two months in the communities.[24]

By the time of Holy Father's visit in the mid-1840s, some Shakers had begun to question the validity of spirit activity, bothered by the excessive behavior of some of the instruments. When the Central Ministry realized that the power of the revival was waning, it sought to strengthen its position by codifying many of the regulations promulgated during the revival in a stringent set of rules known as the Millennial Laws of 1845. These laws were not new, having first been published in 1821, but many of the regulations included in the 1845 edition were excessive, even by Shaker standards, and represented the end of spiritual retrenchment and introspection for Believers during the Era of Manifestations. According to Theodore Johnson, a Shaker historian and theologian who resided at the Sabbathday Lake, Maine, Shaker community until his death in 1986, the 1845 Millennial Laws were "perhaps the final attempt of those most closely associated with the spirit manifestations to turn the tide of disinterest and distrust which was making itself so evident. Like most rear guard actions it seems to have proved to have been a highly unsuccessful attempt at redeeming a lost cause."[25]

Belief in spirit manifestations waned, but no one event marked the end of the revival at Harvard and Shirley. Spirit manifestations dwindled after Holy Father's visit but did not cease. The Shepherdess, a gentle female spirit who came to look after her "flock," appeared later in the year, and spirits still manifested themselves at the yearly meetings on the feast grounds. Two worship meeting journals kept from 1851 to 1854 indicate sporadic spirit activity. Much of the activity was familiar—native spirit visitations or sisters "turning like tops"—yet changes were also evident. By 1853 the sisters "pitched" most of the songs and did most of the singing; the period of ecstatic singing by all Believers was apparently over.[26]

The Shakers also became interested in the worldly spiritualist movement inaugurated by the 1848 "rappings" of the Fox sisters in Hydesville, New York. Claiming they could communicate with the dead, the Fox sisters struck a chord with the American people, and séances became popular events.[27] Even though this wider spiritualist movement was of worldly origins, the Shakers were favorably disposed toward it. The Harvard Ministry heard about the rappings from Shaker brothers who attended séances while in the cities on business. Eternally optimistic, the Harvard Ministry declared the rappings to be a sign that Mother Ann had begun her work in the world. Convinced that people would be converted by the rappings, the Ministry began preparing for the long-awaited influx of new Believers and took an active interest in spiritualism.[28] 1848, then, is a useful date to mark the end of the Era of Manifestations at Harvard and Shirley; after that time, Shaker spiritualism became increasingly entwined with worldly spiritualism.

In writing about the Era of Manifestations, it is easy to get caught up in the fantastic descriptions of Shaker behavior and overlook the deeper significance of this period in Shaker history. The revival was, in fact, a complex event infused with a variety of religious symbols manifested in visions, messages, and spiritual gifts. These symbols are important, telling us much about Shaker social organization during this period, because the symbols are not "merely a sign of . . . social structure," nor do they "simply prescribe or transcribe social status. Rather they transmute it, even while referring to it."[29] Thus, an analysis of the symbols used by the Shakers during the revival casts certain aspects of their social organization—spiritual kinship, androgyny, the biological family, and suffering—in a new light as they tested the bonds of community and searched for a useable past.

One of the important symbols employed by the Shakers during the revival was food imagery, the significance of which dates back to the stories of Ann Lee found in the 1816 *Testimonies.* Kathleen Deignan highlights the food symbolism in these early stories as reflections of Shaker theological conceptions of Ann Lee. Deignan, for example, parallels the miracle of Lee's feeding the hungry crowds with Jesus' miracle of the loaves and fishes. Both acts symbolized spiritual nourishment and were signs of the inauguration of a new age, the "messianic age" of Jesus and the "millennial age" of Ann Lee. In these stories the Believers, despite their rejection of any type of "sacramental system," maintained "a rich spiritual food tradition" which emphasized Ann Lee's Christlike role as healer and nurturer and resembled medieval Christian depictions of Christ as a "mothering" figure who "nursed" his children from the wound in his side.[30] The androgynous nature of Christ's character is reflected in Ann Lee, who also suffers for her flock and nurtures her children with spiritual food.

Food symbolism reappeared during the Era of Manifestations in the form of spiritual food gifts. This imagery was not accidental, for food reflects a culture's values and conceptions of itself. "Man knows," writes Jean Soler, "that the food he ingests in order to live will become assimilated into his being, will become himself. There must be, therefore, a relationship between the idea he has formed of specific items of food and the image he has of himself and his place in the universe. There is a link between a people's dietary habits and its perception of the world."[31]

If Soler is correct, then one should be able to determine, at least partially, the Shakers' view of themselves by analyzing their use of spiritual food. The type of spiritual food that Believers "ate," for example, indicates that they saw themselves as a "refined" people. Like most spiritual gifts, spiritual food was far different from what the Believers ate in real life. Shakers received dainty cakes covered with honey, or delectable and unblemished fruit, even white oranges and cherries, but rarely meat, except when given by native spirits. The food often carried biblical overtones, such as the twelve varieties of fruit, signifying the "twelve Christian virtues," which an instrument picked from the Tree of Life, or the spiritual fish and bread Believers received from Christ commemorating his own miracle of the loaves and fishes. The Shakers "consumed" food that was out of the ordinary, "the food of Angels," because they believed that such nourishment not only enabled them to live out their extraordinary calling but also connected them intimately to the spiritual world.[32]

This connection to the spirit world was important, because one of the Believers' goals during the Era of Manifestations was the conversion of "heathen" spirits. The sharing of spiritual food between the Shakers and the spirits facilitated these conversions by establishing feelings of intimacy and kinship among the various groups. African American spirits brought the Shakers what many probably considered typical "black" food—watermelon, muskmelon, boiled fish, and honey—while American Indian spirits shared with the Believers many feasts of wild turkeys, deer, barley bread, fruit, corn, and ground nuts. By partaking of food offered up by the "Other," the Believers yoked themselves and the spirits to the cause of Mother Ann's Work.[33]

The passover feasts, in which much of the spiritual food was "eaten," were especially important rites of bonding between the natural and the spirit world and the closest the Shakers ever came to employing a sacramental system. The feasts also reified the Shaker social order and the concept of androgyny as a paradisiacal ideal. As Karen Voci Zimmerman has observed, the passover feasts "elevated [Believers] to the level of the spirits" because the meetings were conducted on "the holy mountain which marked the intersection of heaven and earth. . . . The mountain top was neither earth nor heaven, but was ambiguously both," thus allowing the Shakers to "draw on the most profound symbols in their universe to assert that the basic contradictions of their cosmos were not that at all but the divinely ordained form of existence for all mankind." On the mountaintop, Shakers were neither male nor female but a union of both.[34]

The intermixing of male and female attributes is evident in an account of a feast that Eunice Bathrick attended with the spirit of Holy Mother Wisdom in August 1842. The feast, she wrote, was "beyond description," the tables laden with cakes, wine, honey, pies, fruit, and butter. The Shakers' "Holy and Eternal Parents" attended the feast, and eating the "food of Heaven" with them was an experience Bathrick deeply cherished. The crowning moment came when Christ, in a classic image from medieval Christianity, fed the Believers from his own hand, and Bathrick later kissed his feet in ecstatic joy. Christ, the male counterpart of Ann Lee, was identified with the feminine attributes of feeding and nurturing and "physically" acted out this part for the Believers' benefit.[35] Bathrick's interaction with a nurturing Christ is a powerful image, similar to the visions of medieval women mystics in which they were "fed" the eucharistic elements by Christ's own hand. For the Catholic sisters, such visions would be interpreted as an abrogation of clerical authority.[36] But for the Shakers, who had no sacerdotal system to subvert and who believed that the Christ spirit dwelled in each individual, Bathrick's experience on the Holy Hill affirmed, rather than denied, the Shaker belief system. At the moment when Christ fed Bathrick he became the androgynous ideal, and the blending of sacred space and sacred food embodied in the act gave Bathrick a personal and present connection with Christ's past sufferings.

The passover meals on the mountaintop also emphasized the importance of passivity in receiving spiritual gifts. Unlike medieval Christians, who "increasingly viewed the role of recipient, of pious lay person, as a female role,"[37] Shaker men and women both received food at the hands of the spirits. Both sexes were passive recipients of God's benevolence, and neither men nor women acted, like priests, as the sole conduit of grace between heaven and earth. Passivity, therefore, was associated with both sexes and contributed to the androgynous ideal of Shaker behavior.

One of the main goals of the revival, partly achieved by sharing spiritual food with the spirits, was strengthening the connection between themselves and the past. The Believers established relationships with the spirits both of deceased Shakers and of Biblical and historical figures, placing themselves within the larger context of human history. In 1843, for example, the Old Testament prophet Iddo "visited" Harvard and revealed that God had chosen that place as the site for the Square House before Ann Lee migrated to America. This house, continued Iddo, "has ever been a place of peculiar delight to the Ancient Patriarchs, because it is a place where blessed Mother performed so many of her labors. And we bow in reverence when we pass it, in commemoration of her sufferings, and the sufferings of those faithful witnesses who stood with her." Having revealed the sacred and historic roots of the Square House, and hence of Harvard, Iddo prompted the Shakers there to renew their loyalty both to the "gospel" and to their own village and its special heritage.[38]

Deceased first-born Shakers established links to the past when they sent messages to living Shakers. Some messages contained words of thanks for the families who took care of them while they were alive or words of encouragement to the young Believers. Other messages were more frank. Deliverance Whittemore told the Shakers that her heavenly reward far exceeded her expectations. She gave this message as a comfort to those Believers who, like herself when on earth, sometimes felt that their physical labor went unnoticed by their peers and elders.[39]

Believers also visited with a host of historical figures who had converted to Shakerism in the spirit world. American spirits such as George Washington and William Penn, the latter purported to be one of Shakerism's first converts in the spirit world, were important links to the Shakers' immediate past. George Washington, reflecting the Shakers' own feelings about living under a democratic form of government, told Believers that he fought the American Revolution at the Holy Spirit's command so that Believers would be free to practice their religion in the future.[40]

Earlier Christian and historical figures also regaled the Shakers with stories of their conversions. Spirits as diverse as Joseph of Arimathea, John Calvin, George III, and Queen Isabella recounted tales of their "sufferings" in the spirit world until they heeded the Shaker message in the afterlife. Isabella, being Catholic, was an important convert for the Shakers. The Shakers shared with many Protestant Americans a jaundiced view of Catholicism that included lurid stories associated with priests and nuns. These stereotypes appear in the Shakers' descriptions of the Catholic spirits. The Shakers noted, for example, that when Pope Clement VIII entered the spirit world he maintained a very "lofty" attitude until his housekeeper revealed his secret: during his lifetime he had satisfied his sexual needs with twelve girls that he kept hidden in the papal palace. Even worse, he had ordered that one of them be killed when she rejected him. Having suffered in hell for several centuries for these "abominations," Clement told the Believers that he would become a Shaker if it would end his torment.[41]

With the conversions of John Calvin, George III, William Penn, George Washington, Queen Isabella, and Pope Clement VIII, the Shakers established their supremacy over both secular and religious history. Royalty set aside their exalted positions as defenders of their faith to adopt the teachings of the humble and illiterate Ann Lee. John Calvin, one of the premier representatives of the Protestant Reformation, and the pope, the leader of the Catholic Church on earth, both renounced their religion for Shakerism. With a few well-placed conversions the Shakers subdued the two main branches of Christianity and established the primacy of Ann Lee as the pivotal religious figure in salvation history.

The Shakers, however, did not limit their concern with spirit conversion to historical figures or native spirits. The Believers were also concerned with their own biological families in the spirit world. Many spirit messages came from deceased family members of Shakers living at Harvard and Shirley. Often these people had died as unbelievers, but because of the virtuous life of their believing family members had converted in the spirit world. The role of Believers in the salvation of their dead relatives was established by Ann Lee with the practice of "bearing" for the dead and continued to be a part of Shaker practice.[42] A female apostate from the Harvard South family, who lived there during the Era of Manifestations but left sometime before 1850, commented on this practice: "Many persons suffering from acute pain in their shoulders, or diseased lungs, caused by colds, really suppose it to be the weight of their dead relations,—this they call bearing the state of the dead."[43] Joseph Parker of Harvard received a series of messages from his natural mother and sisters recounting their conversions in the spirit world. After Mrs. Parker's conversion, Ann Lee "took" her to Harvard to "see" Joseph. "I am his spiritual Mother," Lee told Mrs. Parker, "and he is a faithful child of mine. I marked him, and set on him my blessing when quite young, and it is through his faithfulness that you have been enabled to obtain this great privilege." As a Believer, Joseph Parker wielded power, and Ann Lee predicted that when he died he would "stand at the head of [his] natural kindred, and sound the everlasting trumpet of salvation to their poor lost souls."[44]

Visits by deceased family members also filled the lacunae in Believers' own personal histories. Sally Loomis's father, for example, abandoned his family when she was two years old; in 1842 his spirit finally explained to her why and told her of all he had suffered since then. As so often happened, he became a Shaker in the afterlife, and Sally was his agent of conversion. As he explained it, his "first understanding" of the gospel "came through" her "first understanding."[45]

An even more creative attempt by an instrument was made on behalf of Lucy Bodge of Shirley. For quite some time, claimed instrument Joanna Randall, she had sensed that the spirits possessed a message concerning the "mystery" of Bodge's birth and biological parents. (Bodge was the foster child of Nathaniel Bodge and Sally Kendall Bodge, a cousin of Hannah

Kendall. She was sent to the Shirley Shakers when she was nine because her foster father was a heavy drinker and the family was poor.) Randall told the Ministry and the elders about her feelings, and they agreed that she should write Bodge's genealogical message. Alone in her room, Randall prayed for help in this endeavor, and Holy Mother Wisdom responded by asking Lucy Bodge's biological mother, who lived in the spirit world, to write to Bodge. Through a series of messages given to Randall, the full story unfolded. Bodge's real mother was Mary Sylvester, a wealthy and educated young woman from Manchester, England, whose family had known and believed in Ann Lee. Bodge's father was Francis Duerwit, a Spanish aristocrat who seduced Sylvester twice but never married her. The second time, Sylvester's parents sent her to Boston to have the child; this child was Lucy Bodge. After Bodge was born she was given to a foster family, Sylvester being too ill to care for her. Sylvester returned to England soon after and died of consumption; two years later she became a Shaker. Other family members, including Bodge's father, her grandmother, and a great aunt, also became Shakers in the spirit world and sent messages to Bodge through Randall, creating a full-fledged genealogical tree. These revelations were important to Bodge. Apparently her concern over her biological roots was known within her family, prompting one of her Shaker sisters to provide the missing information through inspiration. More importantly, the Ministry sanctioned Bodge's quest and Randall's messages, acknowledging once again the power of the biological family within the Shaker community.[46]

Lucy Bodge's inner turmoil over her biological origins reflects one of the main themes of the revival—suffering. Suffering had always been an integral part of the Believers' experience. Ann Lee and her followers underwent mental, spiritual, and physical suffering as they planted the gospel in America. After the Shakers gathered into communities, they suffered persecution at the hands of nonbelievers and apostates. Believers at Harvard and Shirley had their own model of a "suffering servant" in Eleazer Rand. The spirit messages received during the Era of Manifestations reinforced the need for, indeed the inevitability of, suffering if the gospel was to be opened to a lost world. A message from Christ to the Harvard Believers reiterated that "Mother [Ann Lee] suffered in this place to lay a foundation, and it is done; and the work shall increase, it shall not go down, for here is a place that souls shall come to, and hear the word of God. Do be willing to suffer in the cause of virtue and innocence."[47] Instruments in particular were called to suffer. Before Holy Mother Wisdom made a visit to Harvard she sent an angel to inform her instruments that the suffering which was to come over the people there would first be experienced by the instruments; these instruments would then act as models for other Believers.[48] Many accounts of the sufferings of Christ and the ancient prophets and martyrs were also received through inspiration by both male and female instruments.[49]

Lest they forget the persecution of early Believers, the Shakers commemorated the sufferings of Christ and Ann Lee through eating rituals. Periodically they breakfasted on nothing but bread and water, a combination that symbolized hard times. On one occasion Ann Lee's spirit came to the kitchen where the Believers were eating and retold stories of her own suffering and persecution, reminding Believers of their present life and "comfortable surroundings." The fact that Harvard's prosperity was purchased at the expense of Lee's sufferings was left unspoken but understood.[50]

Visions also personalized suffering. Eunice Bathrick, during a morning meeting in March 1842, sensed the presence of a sword-wielding angel who had come to reveal the "secret intents of the heart" quite literally by slitting the Believers' breastbones. The operation itself seems to have been a test for the Believers. Bathrick felt that those who underwent the procedure would become strong Shakers, while those who resisted would eventually fall away. Bathrick, being a good Believer, acquiesced and watched while the angel performed the operation on her; the seven-inch incision, she recorded, was painful and bloody. At that moment, spiritual and physical suffering became one in Bathrick's visionary experience.[51]

For visionists such as Eunice Bathrick, the Era of Manifestations led to a deeper understanding of their Shaker faith. The effects of the period on the villages of Harvard and Shirley, however, were more mixed. The revival, for example, created divisions within the two villages. Antagonisms developed between the Church families and the out families when it became clear that the Church families were slower in obtaining spiritual gifts.[52] This lack of activity in the Church families was thoroughly discussed in the spirit world and attributed to a general disbelief in spirit manifestations. In 1840 Hannah Kendall's spirit told the Harvard Church that its members could receive "beautiful" spirit gifts if they would only open themselves to God. In 1841 the spirit of Eleazer Rand reiterated that the Harvard Church's dearth of gifts was a result of the people's "lack of faith." When members did come under the power of the spirit, they acted inappropriately, revealing information that was supposed to be secret and giving messages without first checking with their elders. Overall, the Harvard Church family's initial efforts to participate in the revival were less than enthusiastic, despite the Ministry's promptings, and Hannah Kendall chastised the Church family elders for the lukewarm participation of their members in worship meetings.[53]

The revival also disrupted intrafamilial relationships. In 1841 Ann Lee admonished Harvard Church family sisters to focus on the spirit messages rather than on trying to ascertain who the instruments were that had given the messages. This exhortation was reiterated in 1843 when the spirits warned that it was wrong for people, when given an admonitory message, to inquire after the instrument in order to discredit the message. Apparently, some Shakers were pointing out the foibles of the instruments as proof that these instruments were no more able to live up to the demands of their messages than other Believers and so had no authority to chastise others. In short, instruments were seen as uppity because they indicted other Believers for their failings. The spirits deplored these accusations, arguing that the messages applied to everyone, instruments and noninstruments alike. It is no wonder that the spirits warned the instruments that they would undergo mortification and suffering, cut off from their fellow members who accused them of a "holier than thou" attitude. One can understand the feelings of several young sisters who admitted that they resisted the power of inspiration, afraid that their peers would think them "bold and forward [in] desiring to teach more than to be taught."[54]

The Ministry's lack of control exacerbated the tensions. Initially, the Ministry had allowed the instruments to assess the validity of their own visions and messages so as not to staunch the flow of spirit activity. But the Ministry's members were admonished several times in 1841 to keep the "reins of government" in their own hands and control the instruments, especially the young Believers in the out families who were pointing out the hidden sins in the Church families. The hubris of the young Believers was fueled by a few elders in the gathering families who encouraged their members to believe that because they had more visions than the Church families they were more advanced spiritually.[55] Out family members, then, sometimes capitalized on the chance to embarrass the Church families when they had the opportunity.

Despite divisions that occurred in the villages, the revival was ultimately beneficial to the Shakers. Ideas that had become the basis for community formation at Harvard and Shirley were articulated and validated by the spirits. The androgynous ideal was reinforced during the Era of Manifestations when Christ appeared as a nurturing mother at the mountain meetings. Biological family bonds and spiritual kinship bonds were strengthened when the Shakers communed with their deceased relatives and native spirits, and the Believers' historical identity was validated by contact with historical spirits. The revival, as a liminal phase, also helped the Believers to maneuver successfully through the changes facing their society and helped them understand the suffering that their communities experienced.

The Era of Manifestations was the ultimate test of the Shakers' communal bonds, and despite the tensions generated within and between families, the Believers found these bonds to be strong and resilient. Emboldened by their convictions, the Shakers turned from their introspection and found new reserves of energy as the revival came to a close. Inspired by the outbreak of worldly spiritualism in the late 1840s, the Shakers of the 1850s launched a campaign to expand their community further into the world through active proselytizing and energetic reforming of their societies. Aligning themselves with current reformers on social and women's issues, the Shakers strengthened even further their connections with the world.

8

The Woman Question

THE GROUP AT HARVARD AND SHIRLEY that benefited the most from the Era of Manifestations was the Shaker sisters. Female imagery used during the revival and the public role of women as instruments increased the power of the sisters dramatically. This power was not transitory; after the revival ended, the heightened awareness of women's issues resulted in a concerted effort to deal with the problems of women, both within and without the Shaker community. Focusing on issues of marriage, the family, and women's health, the Believers sometimes led the way in nineteenth-century America's attempts to address the "woman question."

The status of women received a boost during the Era of Manifestations through messages and visions that glorified the role of the female nurturer. In a spirit message to the Shaker sisters, Mary Magdalene, writing for all of the "Apostolic Sisters" who lived during Jesus' lifetime, used the imagery of birthing, mothering, and feeding to emphasize the importance of the uniquely female contribution of Shaker women to their communities. She noted that when the long-promised opening of the gospel in the world occurred, the "children of this world" would "bring their wives to the city of freedom, and give them up to God." When these "spiritual children" came to the Shakers, hungry for the gospel, it would be the women's job to "feed" and care for them because the job of nurturing was "woman's work," both in the natural and the spiritual family.[1]

Female "fecundity" was also an important attribute of Shaker sisters. Holy Mother Wisdom spoke through the prophetess Elizabeth, the mother of John the Baptist, to her "daughters" at Harvard, exhorting them to prepare for their future role as spiritual mothers. The sisters were first admonished to "*wash* . . . [their] souls in Godly sorrow and repentance" as they awaited their bridegroom. They were then called to fulfill their maternal role in the society: "Sit not still, . . .for ye are called to be bearing Spirits, to bring forth children unto God. . . . And as Mothers in nature are called to bring forth children, so shall ye be called to bring forth spiritual children, for on you will I place the bearing Spirit even as I did on your blessed Mother before you." Finally, Holy Mother Wisdom warned the sisters that they would suffer in this process, "even as a Mother in nature [suffers] . . . when her time draweth nigh."[2]

Even more important than the spirits' acknowledgment of women's contributions to society was the legitimacy that the revival conferred upon the female "voice." Believers at Harvard and Shirley had been accustomed to women who spoke their minds freely, such as Hannah Kendall, or expressed their thoughts through vision-inspired hymn writing, such as Eunice Wyeth. During the revival, however, many more women took an active part in articulating their faith by acting as instruments for the spirits. The sheer number of female instruments indicates the increasing role of women in the public sphere of religion, a role legitimated by the very act of speaking for the spirits. "Spirit communication carried its own authority," writes Ann Braude. "If one accepted the message, one had little choice but to accept the medium."[3]

The female voice was important, not only because it provided a fresh perspective on Shaker society but also because it bestowed social power on women by allowing them to move within the male sphere as well the female. What Laurie Finke has written about medieval women mystics is also true for female Shaker instruments: "The basis of the power the female mystic enjoyed was both discursive and public, not private and extralinguistic. The mystic's possession of a 'public language' [gave] her the ability to act not just within a 'woman's culture,' but in a 'man's world' as well."[4]

Shaker women's use of public language is clearly illustrated in a spirit communication given by the Angel of Comfort and Blessing through the instrument Fidelia Grosvenor concerning the doctrine of predestination, a tenet the Shakers did not hold. Grosvenor's message explained both how the erroneous doctrine had come about in the first place and how the Shakers understood the Pauline passage on which the doctrine was based. She claimed that a lack of understanding, even by Paul himself, led to a misinterpretation of the concept of election. Uninformed people, argued

Grosvenor, thought that predestination meant that God chose some to be saved and others to be damned. What Paul really meant, she said, was that God called only some people "to work for the salvation of others." Election referred to this calling of working for others, not to a person's ultimate salvation or loss. Laying out her own theological musings, Grosvenor justified her position by pointing out that a truly just God could not and would not preordain people to an eternal and fiery punishment.[5]

Grosvenor, as many women before her, used revelation and her "spiritual voice" to legitimate her words and encroach on traditional male territory. Women did not generally expound on theological topics, but Grosvenor openly engaged in scriptural exegesis and presumed to approach her Shaker sisters and brothers on the grounds of rationality rather than emotion. Her writing reflects a knowledge of traditional and Shaker biblical interpretation and presumes the same on the part of her audience, both male and female.

The increasing prominence of Shaker women and their attention to women's social roles led some sisters at Harvard and Shirley to question women's place—or rather the invisibility of women's place—in history. Their interest was heightened by messages received from long-departed sisters. Elizabeth, the mother of John the Baptist, told the sisters about her "sufferings" after her husband was murdered. She said that Holy Mother Wisdom had encouraged her to record her story so that the sisters at Harvard could begin to understand women's experiences in Biblical times, given that women's lives rarely appeared in sacred texts.[6] The reason for this historic dearth of information about women, noted Elizabeth, was that most of them had lived before the dawn of the "female day" (inaugurated by Ann Lee) in a society that cared little about women's lives. Foretelling Lee's redemption of women, she concluded,

> I often felt the fallen and degraded state of the female, [and knew that in many cases she was held in contempt in the Sight of the male notwithstanding their strong attachment to her; and I often groaned, sighed and cried for deliverance.] And in one of my scenes of humiliation and heart felt grief, I received the consoling promise from an Angel of God, that a day should come, when the female would again stand in her lot, redeemed from under the curse, and promised that in that day I should be a ministering spirit to the people of God.[7]

The influx of messages from "ancient sisters" sparked an interest in women's history among the Harvard Shaker women. Other prophetesses repeated the claims that women had always been a part of sacred history, "laboring" and "prophesying" like men, but left out of the written records. Betty Babbitt, eldress of the Harvard Ministry, was particularly interested in learning more about the ancient sisters and received messages from a variety of women saints and martyrs, including Elizabeth, who was a cousin of John the Baptist, and Caroline Dunva, a medieval woman beheaded in England for "obeying Christ."[8] By reclaiming the stories of ancient sisters, Shaker women contextualized their own lives and gave meaning to their own actions and thoughts.[9]

As always, however, the Shakers retained some ambivalence about the nature of women, most vividly illustrated by contrasting views of Holy Mother Wisdom. While the Shaker belief in a dual godhead has been seen as a forward step for women, some scholars have observed that Holy Mother Wisdom still held a position subordinate to Holy Father.[10] Conflicting views of Wisdom at Harvard and Shirley suggest that the Believers themselves were not quite sure how to interpret this female personage. In some messages she appears as a strong, independent personality. She exercises both judgment and mercy, and, like Jehovah, she has the power to forgive sins. She also claims equal responsibility with Jehovah in the creation of the world. At other times, however, Holy Mother Wisdom is portrayed as powerful yet subordinate to the Lord Jehovah. She is represented as an emissary of God the Father, a merciful mother who begged an angry God to avert his wrath from the Harvard Shakers. She calls herself the Lord's helpmeet and downplays her role in creation, claiming that though she and God are one entity, he created heaven and earth while she stood by as a consultant. God is power and she is wisdom; they are equivalent, but they are not equal.[11]

Indeed, some messages strongly reinforced the concept of "separate spheres" for men and women. On one occasion the spirit of William Lee addressed the Harvard Church family office sisters. Lee exhorted the women to be the "strength & support" of the male deacons with whom they worked because the men, who dealt directly with worldly business and all its pitfalls, were "more exposed to the enemy" than the sisters, who worked behind the scenes in the office, presumably guarding morality in the domestic sphere.[12]

Nevertheless, the long-term effects of the revival were important for the Shaker sisters at Harvard and Shirley. Because of women's enhanced position during the Era of Manifestations, Shaker sisters in the postrevival era played an increasingly important role in their communities. Shaker women (and men) of this generation turned their interest toward the woman question so prevalent in the last half of the nineteenth century. In this debate, the Shakers were at the fore in acknowledging that patriarchal marriage and family structure could contribute to women's oppression. Indeed, many feminists in the nineteenth century argued that traditional ideas about marriage, divorce, child care, and housework oppressed women. Yet, the solution proffered by these reformers—restructuring the family—was not an easy task.[13] As Norma Basch writes, "The very absence of property rights and the very persistence of other gender-based inequities in marriage laws during the first third of the nineteenth century demonstrated the determination of the state, the all-male state, to preserve the legal aspects of patriarchy in its most fundamental unit of social organization—the family."[14]

Even before feminists and women's rights advocates began analyzing the potentially oppressive nature of marriage, the Shakers had done away with the institution and restructured the family along spiritual kinship lines, practicing for seventy years what activists had only begun discussing. The rise of reform movements in the 1840s and 1850s and the growth of spiritualism, with its links to women's rights,[15] however, turned the attention of an increasing number of Americans to the plight of women in the United States and prompted many to take notice of Shaker beliefs. For the Believers of Harvard and Shirley, this scrutiny was particularly intense because of their proximity to Boston, a major hub of reform and feminist activity.

Mary McDaniels, a Shaker sympathizer, informed Grove Blanchard that she thought the world was now more willing to seek out the Shakers because of "the influence of the Female spirit on society which . . . has its foundation and origian from the Spiritual world . . . which so fully acknowledges that in Christ there is neither Mail nor Female."[16]

Ironically, the Believers' views on sex and marriage—views which had often evoked scorn or even persecution from the world—sparked a new interest in Shakerism among nonbelievers as a concrete solution to social problems. The Shakers themselves, perhaps influenced by the increasing attention paid to them by the world, began to acknowledge the social as well as the spiritual benefits of celibacy, particularly for abused wives. In

1850 the Massachusetts state legislature enacted a law that allowed the spouse of a person who joined a religious sect that renounced marriage to obtain a divorce after three years if the latter did not "cohabit" with the former during that time. Some legislators worried that the act would simplify divorce to the point "that it would open a door for such females as were sick of their condition to go to the Shakers, and there seek refuge until the term of 3 years would deliver them from their bondage." A more sympathetic legislator told a Shaker brother that he was surprised that more women did not leave their husbands "to get clear of abuse and to save their lives." The brother asked the legislator why marital abuse was not considered murder as much as "the taking of life in any [other] way." The legislator answered that he did not see any difference between the two, and Believers felt that he and some of the other legislators "gave much credit to the Shakers' principal [sic] on this wise."[17]

The Shaker brother's equation of wife abuse with murder, the assertion that both actions destroyed life—whether physically, emotionally, or mentally—as well as the implication that Shakerism provided a safe haven for battered women, attest to the Shakers' contact with reform movements. By the middle of the century, the Shakers had developed close friendships with non-Shaker reformers, providing the Believers with access to the latest reform ideas. A prime example of this type of friendship was that established between the Shaker sisters of Harvard and Shirley and Harriot K. Hunt, "the celebrated Female Physician of Boston." Often credited with being America's first female medical doctor, Hunt was also an abolitionist, an avid health reformer, and an advocate of women's rights. Through her, Shaker women met many early feminists and reformers and were exposed to the current issues surrounding the woman question.[18]

Harriot Hunt first visited the Shirley Shakers in 1848, and the Believers readily befriended her when they discovered that she was a physician. The sisters were particularly drawn to Hunt, and she became close friends with several of them, including Eliza Babbitt, Olive Hatch, and Roxalana Grosvenor. Hatch sewed for Hunt, bought clothes for her, and distributed copies of Hunt's recently published autobiography to the Shaker sisters. Hunt visited Harvard and Shirley often, and when sisters were in Boston on business they lodged with her.[19]

It was in Hunt's home that the Shakers met a variety of reformers. They talked with Paulina Wright Davis, a suffragist, health reformer, and lecturer on female anatomy and physiology; Lydia Folger Fowler, the second woman in the United States to be granted a medical degree; Lydia's husband, Lorenzo Fowler, an avid phrenologist and part owner of a family business that published books and journals on phrenology, health, and diet reform; Charlotte Fowler Wells, Lorenzo's sister, who was active in the family business and lectured on phrenology and women's rights; Samuel Wells, Charlotte's husband and business partner in the Fowlers' company; and Dr. Josiah Foster Flagg, a homeopathic dentist and an advocate of women's rights.[20]

Hunt herself was an ardent believer in women's rights and attended the first and second national Woman's Rights Conventions held in Worcester, Massachusetts, in 1850 and 1851. Because so much of her life was devoted to the woman's movement, it is inconceivable that she did not discuss women's issues with the Shaker sisters. In fact, when Shakers from Enfield, Connecticut, visited Harvard in 1850, they met Hunt and learned all about her feminist leanings. They noted her acquaintance with many of the reform-minded "literary females" and her position as president of the planning committee for the 1850 Woman's Rights Convention.[21]

Both Harriot Hunt and her sister practiced holistic medicine, believing that disease was as much a spiritual problem caused by "heartbreak"—for instance, infidelity in marriage—as it was a physical problem. Her treatment included obtaining "heart histories" from her female patients in which they described the emotional trauma of their lives. She conducted many "heart histories" among the Shaker sisters and concluded that Believers were committed feminists who provided a necessary haven for women who had suffered from abusive relationships and intemperate husbands.[22]

In 1851 Marianne Finch, an Englishwoman who later published a book on her experiences in America, spent some time with Harriot Hunt, who took her to visit the Harvard and Shirley Shakers. She enjoyed her stay with the Shakers and found the sisters good-natured and affable. Like Hunt, Finch was impressed by the Believers' concern for the aged. Her description of the elderly sisters at the Square House, "chatting and knitting in a large, warm, comfortable sitting-room," epitomized the domestic tranquility of the Believers. Finch left Harvard and Shirley with a high opinion of Shaker communities, recognizing that within them women had "female legislators" to act on their behalf. She characterized this system as "parental" rather than as "paternal despotism" because both men and women (acting as "fathers" and "mothers") were in charge of its administration. Moreover, the female influence of "tenderness and right feeling" held "tyranny and injustice" in check.[23]

Hunt and Finch provided a social interpretation of Shaker celibacy that de-emphasized, indeed ignored, the Believers' theological reasoning behind the practice and highlighted the beneficent environment the Shaker system provided to abused and elderly women. Although the Shakers, too, began to emphasize the social benefits of celibacy in the 1850s, they never abandoned its theological justification. Instead, they incorporated theology and sociology into a broader critique of marriage, family, and society.

Lorenzo Grosvenor, a Harvard Shaker and author, was one of the more prolific defenders of celibacy during the 1840s and 1850s. In several works, Grosvenor critiqued the non-Shaker social order and proffered celibacy as the only solution to a corrupt society. In 1849 he published *Circular Letter in Defence of the United Society of Believers*, providing a Shaker interpretation of Luke 14:26, the passage in which Jesus says that no man can be a disciple who does not hate his wife. Grosvenor wrote that "hate" does not mean merely loving one's wife less than God, a common interpretation of this passage. For Grosvenor, hating one's wife translated into hating "carnal relations." "Our argument is this,—If any place be allowed for leaving, forsaking, hating the wife, (not the woman,) it must be in the very principle which originally MAKES HER A WIFE," that is, her legal and "wifely" duty to have intercourse with her husband. He went on to write that some people wondered whether it was possible to "love the wife and hate the woman." Grosvenor replied that many men did, and "sad work do they make of it. Many [women] by this means are driven to the brink of despair." Here Grosvenor succinctly presented the Shaker analysis of worldly society. Inverting the intended social order by placing the legal construction of marriage, and the concomitant notion of wifely "duties," above love of the actual woman (an indictment of the common law doctrine of marital unity), degraded individual human beings and corrupted society. Only celibacy could restore the proper balance to human relationships.[24]

Grosvenor addressed the issue of celibacy again in *Testimony of Jesus Concerning Marriage*, published sometime in the 1850s. In this tract, Grosvenor refuted the idea that sexual intercourse could ever be a pure or neutral act. He was arguing against two related ideas: that intercourse was only impure when one "abused" the sex act, and that if one engaged in intercourse only from pure motives "pure" children would be the result. Grosvenor turned to the Gospel of John, which he considered a treatise on the "true science of the heavenly generation," to show that the only way to produce "pure" children, that is to say, children of God, was by renouncing a life of the flesh through the power of Christ. Grosvenor represented the mainstream of mid-century Shaker theology that did not accept the procreative function of sexual intercourse as a justification for the sexual act, and he legitimized his approach to sexuality by giving it the cast of "science." For Grosvenor, spiritual birth was the "true and only process by which the sons and daughters of God are supplied."[25]

While Grosvenor commented on some of the social benefits of celibacy, these benefits were made even more clear in 1869 when the first (and perhaps only) pamphlet in the series "Shaker Tracts for the Times" was published at Shirley. Writing in *True Love: What it is, and what it is not*, the author, A. B. Davis (perhaps Shirley Shaker Alpheas Davis), attempted to explicate the Shaker theological view of love and celibacy. The main thrust of Davis's argument is that celibacy is a social good. "Our graveyards, could they speak," the author writes, "would send forth a sad and sickening wail from the young wives and mothers who have been placed there, the victims of matrimonial abuse of the sexual function. . . . [Cemeteries] are dotted with graves of young and middle-aged women, whose lives have been offered up as a sacrifice to the lustful passions of their husbands."[26] Such abusive relationships, even though legally sanctioned through marriage, were certainly not models of "perfect love." Indeed, argued Davis, there was an "intimate and inseparable" relationship "between body and soul," and true love, therefore, could not exist alongside lust.[27]

The theological and ideological shifts that occurred within Shaker society affected the lives of female Believers in practical ways. Although their humanity was preserved by the practice of celibacy, Shaker sisters also became more involved in active proselytizing and public speaking. Abigail Cook, for example, was a gifted speaker who often preached in worship meetings and was a popular speaker on missionary trips, whether giving her personal testimony or lecturing to factory girls in the Lowell textile mills.[28] Her life also reflected the increasing participation of Shaker women in financial and business affairs that previously had been reserved for men. In 1851 she wrote to Joseph Tillinghast, arranging for the distribution of Shaker brooms in New Bedford because Dennis Pratt, who normally made these arrangements, had been ill. She claimed to be "legally commissioned to do business in this Office." When Pratt found out what Cook had done, however, he immediately wrote to Tillinghast, indignant that a sister would meddle in his business.[29]

Despite Pratt's reaction, the male Shakers at Harvard and Shirley generally included the sisters in financial and business decisions that were once considered men's domain. Olive Hatch, who became elder sister in the Ministry in 1851, recorded several occasions in the Ministry's journal when she was included in important economic decisions. On August 11, 1852, the Ministry, including the women, went to the North family to discuss where to build the family's new house. In October Hatch attended a meeting in which they discussed fixing up the meetinghouse and moving a building on their property. On some occasions, women even initiated decisions about property. In 1864 Eliza Babbitt of the Ministry talked with Lucy Clark and Charlotte Priest about building an addition onto the Harvard Church family dwelling house. That evening they called all the elders together to discuss the project. Though Babbitt noted that the sisters "had quite a labor" making the elders understand just what they wanted in the way of remodeling, they were eventually successful.[30]

Shaker sisters also continued to play a prominent role in the medical field, although they were patients as much as practitioners. In the 1840s, hydropathy, or water cure, became popular at Harvard and Shirley. The premise of hydropathy, developed by Vincenz Priessnitz in Graefenberg, Austria, was that illness or disease could be healed by applying cold water to various parts of the body, either by wrapping the patient in wet sheets or giving the patient various kinds of baths. Hydropathy came to America in 1843 when two water-cure institutions opened in New York City. Harvard and Shirley adopted water cure soon after. In February 1845 the Ministry very excitedly wrote about the success and popularity of water cure at the two communities. They noted in particular the three cold baths installed in the basement of the Shirley Church dwelling house, one for men, one for women, and one for the boys, who enjoyed the water so much that their caretakers had to restrain their use of the bath.[31]

The Believers were in constant contact with water-cure physicians. Dr. E. A. Kittredge of Lynn, a regular physician who learned the methods of hydropathy and opened water-cure establishments first in Lynn and then in Boston, was a frequent visitor of and physician to the Harvard and Shirley

Shakers and was also visited by them when they were in Lynn. Dr. H. Foster, the physician at a water-cure establishment in Lowell, visited Believers and was plied with questions about hydropathy and requests for medical advice. The Believers practiced hydropathy themselves, particularly at the Shirley North family, but they also began to frequent Foster's newly opened establishment. In 1847 two Shaker sisters from Shirley boarded there for two weeks, and one of them returned later that year for three more weeks. The Shakers' belief in the validity of water cure must have been strong, for cures taken at an institution were not inexpensive. Aiming to attract a middle- and upper-class clientele, rates at Massachusetts water-cure institutions ranged from five to ten dollars a week; Foster's rates were six to ten dollars a week.[32]

As both Susan Cayleff and Jane Donegan have shown, women played an important role in the water-cure movement. Unable to obtain degrees in regular medicine, women turned to hydropathy, as they had earlier turned to Thomsonianism, as an outlet for their medical ambitions. Consequently, hydropathy practitioners, many of whom were women, tended to focus on issues relating to women's health. Seeing a connection between the body and spiritual and moral health, hydropathists were also concerned with issues of diet and dress reform and hoped to cure the ills of their society by curing the ills of its individual citizens.[33]

The precepts of hydropathy fit well with Shaker beliefs in perfection. The danger in the practice was that it could be too appealing to the Shaker sisters, many of whom seemed to enjoy their invalid status. In fact, the excessive sickness of the Shaker sisters worried the female leadership of Harvard and Shirley, who believed that the women in their bishopric were ill an inordinate amount of time. In the Shirley North family alone, the eldress had been sick for one hundred consecutive days. Frustrated by the situation, Eldress Sally Loomis vented her feelings and asked for advice in a lengthy letter to the female members of the Central Ministry in February 1851. Noting a recent scourge of sickness among the sisters at Harvard and Shirley, Loomis pointed out that most of the women suffered from "weakness," a vague ailment for which there was no cure. Loomis was also troubled by the apparent rise in the deaths of young women. She calculated that Elmira Adams's death on December 23, 1850, at the age of thirty-two, brought to twenty-four the number of young females who had died in the Harvard Church family since 1813. Of those twenty-four sisters, seventeen had been less than thirty years of age, and seven had been between thirty and forty-three years old.[34]

The sickness of the sisters, however, did not bother Loomis as much as the women's overreliance on the world's doctors, even though the Ministry prohibited the use of worldly physicians. Loomis's dilemma was that she wanted to keep Shaker order and appease the sisters at the same time, an almost impossible task given the situation. As an eldress she had final say over the use of the world's doctors, and while sisters could offer logical reasons for calling in a physician, Loomis was uncomfortable with breaking the rules, preferring that the sisters develop the gift of healing among themselves. When she told the women this, however, they often became angry and accused her of denying them the medical care that their conditions required. Caught in the middle, Loomis hoped that the Central Ministry would advise her on how to handle this delicate situation.[35]

Loomis herself tried to help the sisters by organizing a series of meetings for the women in which she read aloud to them feminist reformer Mary Gove Nichols's *Lectures to Ladies on Anatomy and Physiology*, a book written to enlighten women about their bodies and issues of female health. Loomis's efforts, however, yielded few results, and she perceived many problems within the communities rooted in the excessive illness of the women. She thought, for example, that some of the older women had become "spoiled" by being treated as true invalids when they were really only "half sick." Such women often took advantage of their situation, claiming that they were too tired to attend meeting, yet finding the energy to participate in activities they enjoyed. It was this spiritually dangerous side of illness that Loomis feared the most.[36]

In December, when Sally Loomis still had not received a return letter from the Central Ministry, she went over the leaders' heads and took her problem directly to the spirit world. She wrote a letter that Samuel Myrick, a gravely ill Believer expected to die any day, was to give to the spirits of Hannah Kendall and Eleazer Rand when he entered the spirit world himself. In this letter Loomis enumerated the social and economic problems that the continual sickness of the Shaker sisters caused their families. When Shaker women produced shoddy products that the public would not buy, the family's income fell; the sisters countered that they were too weak and sick to perform up to the standards set by the society. This led to many problems. First, the rest of the family, especially the young, had to work extra hard to make up for the lost income, leading many to believe that the Shakers were taking advantage of them. Second, the reduced income and the loss of able bodies caused the elderly Believers to feel that they were not being cared for adequately, even though many were capable of taking care of themselves. Third, and worst of all, those who were "weakly" resented having to go to worship meetings, so they sat glumly through the service, too tired to participate, and put a damper on the meeting for everyone else.[37]

Loomis believed that the sisters' obsession with sickness was destroying the spiritual, social, and economic health of their communities. Because spiritual healing did not seem to be working, and because the Central Ministry had not rescinded the general ban on world's doctors, Loomis pushed diet reform and hydropathy as ways to restore a healthy balance to the bishopric. She received backing from Seth Wells, who wrote a manuscript sometime around 1846 called "Temperance the best preserver of Health." Like many reformers of his day, Wells believed that physical illness was rooted in an "improper" diet: "high[ly] seasoned and heterogeneous mixtures in cookery tend to clog the system, vitiate the blood, obstruct the free circulation of the fluids, and produce a variety of diseases." He therefore advocated that the Believers practice temperance in their eating habits, as well as in other areas of their lives, by eliminating rich or spicy foods from their diet and by limiting the variety of foods eaten at one meal. It was imperative that the Shakers change their diet, he concluded, for sickly Believers made poor examples of the gospel when scrutinized by the world. Sally Loomis read Wells's manuscript and corresponded with him on the subject, hoping for greater success in changing the Believers' diet and in renewing the Shaker commitment to self-denial.[38]

The Shaker sisters' excessive sickness paralleled the phenomenon in nineteenth-century America of chronic female complaints and the belief that women were inherently weak and infirm.[39] The sisters' female frailty is also one case which highlights the impact of worldly ideas on supposedly nonworldly Shaker women; many of the sisters at Harvard and Shirley perceived themselves as weak and overworked and appropriated the status of invalids for themselves. By the same token, however, the Shaker leadership at Harvard and Shirley took vigorous pains to squelch this sickly behavior. Hannah Kendall had scolded the sisters under her care for excessive sickliness and challenged the women to "move lively." Sally Loomis wanted no less from the Shaker women she knew. Loomis intended to correct that situation, promoting what Frances Cogan has identified as the "Ideal of Real Womanhood." This ideal, uncovered by Cogan through an analysis of nineteenth-century advice and health manuals, novels, short stories, and periodicals, conveys an image of nineteenth-century women that is vastly different from that found in the better-known "Cult of True Womanhood." "Real Women" were healthy and robust, educated and knowledgeable, hardworking, and morally upright.[40] These were the qualities the Shaker leadership wanted in their female members and that they, too, most certainly gleaned from the medical and reform literature of the day. Indeed, with Boston as the central hub of health reform activity in antebellum America,[41] the Shakers at Harvard and Shirley were well aware of the problems of female health. Yet the leadership's constant discussion of such matters with the sisters in their charge indicates that they were not always successful in eradicating the idea of women as fragile and sickly beings, even within the Shaker community.

Of less concern to the Shakers than health reform was dress reform. Initially, Believers had no rigid rules about clothing but continued to wear the styles worn in New England in the late eighteenth century. Changes in Shaker clothing may have been made partly as a concession to fashion, as when men stopped wearing breeches in 1805, a change nearly contemporaneous with the movement in men's fashion from breeches to trousers, but comfort and practicality were also considerations. Shaker sisters stopped using stays around 1804 because they did not like them and because they adopted a modified version of the Empire gown, popular in America since the late eighteenth century. The gown's high waistline precluded the use of stays, and while this style was popular, many women gave up their corsets. When styles changed again around 1820 and waistlines dropped, corsets once again became fashionable and an integral part of a well-bred lady's wardrobe. Shaker sisters, however, retained the Empire waistline and did not reintroduce stays into the society. Because Shaker women did not change their wardrobes to follow the current fashions and because they did not use corsets, they lacked two major incentives for taking part in the concerns of mid-nineteenth-century dress reformers, who found women's fashions, particularly the corset, degrading, oppressive, and physically harmful.[42]

There is evidence, however, of a deeper strain of radical reform in the

Harvard community than was officially articulated. Eunice Bathrick, who expressed her opinions freely to Jeremiah Hacker, indicated in one of her letters that she had been reading *The Laws of Life*, a periodical edited by Harriet Austin and James C. Jackson. Austin, a hydropathist and well-known advocate of dress reform, is said to have designed the first "American costume," a knee-length dress with comfortable sleeves and a "natural" waistline worn over trousers; the outfit was similar to that popularized by Amelia Bloomer.[43] Bathrick was taken with the American costume and told Hacker that if she was "otherways situated" she "would adopt it, even at my advanced age" of seventy years. She considered women's clothing oppressive and "a figure of the bondage to which females have too long been consigned."[44] Bathrick's sentiments were not echoed in the official writings of Believers. While Shaker leaders were concerned about the inferior condition of women in society, they never advocated dress reform as a means of liberation for women. Believers were able to accept psychological androgyny, but they did not seem to want physical manifestations of this androgyny. Indeed, too much reform was not considered a good thing. In 1859 the Central Ministry warned Believers about the "inexperienced becoming contaminated with [the world's] spiritual theory and vain ideas of reform."[45]

Despite the Central Ministry's concern about worldly theory, the Shakers of Harvard and Shirley incorporated many elements of reform into their communities. Women were the primary beneficiaries of these changes. Beginning with the Era of Manifestations, women expanded their power within Shaker communities. More than in any previous time in Shaker history, women entered the men's sphere as proclaimers of God's word; they also revealed a growing concern with their social and historical roles. This concern became, in the postrevival era, an active attempt to address the woman question. Aligning themselves with worldly reformers, the Shakers addressed the social problems faced by women, offering their way of life as a viable solution to those problems. Union with the world, however, exacted a price from the Shakers. By opening themselves even more to the outside, they allowed for the introduction of potentially harmful ideas into their villages.

9

Embracing the World

SHAKER CONCERN OVER THE PLIGHT OF WOMEN and their increased use of sectarian medical practices were only two indications of greater Shaker openness to the world after 1848. When the Era of Manifestations ended, the Believers threw aside any reservations they may have had and openly embraced the world by actively proselytizing, adopting worldly ideas, establishing close friendships with some of the world's people, and developing stronger economic ties to the world. These trends were apparent in Shaker society as early as the 1820s, but the successful testing of boundaries that occurred during the Era of Manifestations convinced the Believers that they could risk even stronger ties to the world.

One of the primary reasons for the Shakers' increased traffic with the world after the Era of Manifestations was the outbreak of worldly spiritualism that had rekindled their belief in the promised ingathering.[1] Calvin Green wrote to Lorenzo Grosvenor in 1852 of his confidence that worldly spiritualism and the Shakers' spiritual practices were increasingly "merging" and that the prophecies concerning a large ingathering would be fulfilled. He predicted that places like Shirley, "those lovely & tried branches of Zion will yet become powerful & strong."[2]

The Shakers began a concerted effort at proselytizing even before the revival was over, taking advantage of the stir caused by William Miller and his followers, the Millerites or Adventists. Miller was a fervent millennialist minister who claimed that Christ's return was imminent. After several failed attempts to predict the time of his return, the Adventists set October 22, 1844, as the definitive date. When this day, too, passed without incident, disillusionment set in among the Millerites, and the Shakers moved in with their message that Christ had indeed already returned in the form of Ann Lee.[3]

Adventists began visiting the Harvard and Shirley Shakers in 1846, and in September Shaker brother Enoch Jacobs, a converted Adventist, spoke at Harvard, attracting large crowds of both nonbelievers and Millerites. The Shakers welcomed these meetings not only because they brought in prospective members but also because they were a change from the ordinary. One Shaker appreciated Jacobs's preaching as one of the highlights of 1846 "after being shut up from all access to the world for 3 years."[4]

By January 1847 seven Adventists had joined or were in the process of joining the Harvard and Shirley Shakers. Many of the Adventists lived in nearby towns and cities such as Boston, Lowell, Groton, Littleton, and Westminster. Much visiting occurred between the two groups, and the Believers recruited actively among the Adventists, even to the point of bringing wagonloads of them to Harvard on Saturday and housing them overnight so that they could attend public Sabbath meeting. In September a group of Harvard and Shirley Shakers attended a joint meeting of Adventists and Believers in Stowe, and two Shaker brothers went to an Adventist meeting in Groton.[5]

Some of the Believers' most extensive missionary work took place in the cities of New Bedford and Fairhaven, Massachusetts. Sometime around 1848 the Shakers at Harvard and Shirley became acquainted with Joseph Tillinghast, a prosperous and influential merchant and shipper in the Quaker town of New Bedford, and his cousin Pardon Tillinghast.[6] Joseph, himself a Quaker who sympathized greatly with Shaker ideas, introduced himself to the Believers and became a trusted ally and friend. He was a generous man and provided the Harvard and Shirley Shakers with the financial backing for their missionary efforts in the New Bedford area and for the publication and distribution of Shaker sermons and pamphlets. The Shakers' first mission to New Bedford took place in January 1849 at his request. His influence in the community opened the door to five Shaker missionaries, and thousands of people turned out to hear them. William Leonard, one of the main speakers, gave a discourse on celibacy as a requirement for salvation, while Abigail Cook offered a moving conversion narrative to her listeners. Cook played an especially important role on the trip because, as a former Methodist turned Adventist, she could relate her religious experiences to people of other Protestant denominations and sects. The Shakers were pleased with their first meeting and held more meetings in New Bedford in the spring and summer of 1850. But opposition to Shaker ideas was growing in New Bedford, and the Believers soon received a "civil invitation" not to proselytize there anymore.[7]

The Believers tried particularly hard to draw converts to Shirley because it was smaller than Harvard. Their hopes were raised by an outburst of interest in Shakerism spurred by missionary activity in Andover and the small town of Ballardvale. Both towns were close to the Lawrence textile mills, and the Shakers proselytized in the factory villages among English immigrants such as William Southdale, a Methodist carpet weaver. As a result of this activity, several English families moved to Shirley, including that of John Whiteley, future elder of the Harvard and Shirley bishopric. To house them Believers started a new gathering family, opening up the South family dwelling house, which had sat empty after the family was broken up in 1842 for financial reasons. This act, more than any other, symbolized the Believers' hope that the promised ingathering had begun at last.[8]

In their efforts to reach out to non-Shakers, Believers during this period began forming close friendships with a few of the world's people. The Believers had long cultivated working friendships with outsiders who could be useful to them, such as lawyers, judges, and doctors. Not until the late 1840s, however, did the Shakers at Harvard and Shirley take nonbelievers into their full confidence. Harriot Hunt is one example of this new type of friendship; Joseph Tillinghast, another. Even after their mission to New Bedford ended, the Shakers maintained contact with Tillinghast, and their relationship became increasingly close. Sisters made small gifts for him—a loaf of brown bread or a pair of gloves—and in return Tillinghast gave individual Believers money or sent them subscriptions to papers they would not ordinarily have received. He provided Believers with free property insurance, paid for the furnishing of Shaker rooms, and even covered the expenses for a group of Believers to take a "trip for their health."[9]

In addition to his role as a Shaker benefactor, Tillinghast served as a Shaker agent. He arranged children's indentures, conducted background checks on prospective members, and acted as the intermediary for the Shirley Shakers during the time that they owned a textile factory.[10] William Wetherbee described Tillinghast as "a sort of Elder on the outer wheel and a confidential friend."[11] The Harvard Ministry acknowledged Tillinghast's unique position by noting that he was "indulged . . . beyond the bounds commonly prescribed for enquirers." He was, for example, allowed to publish a pamphlet under his own name and distribute it among the Shakers.[12] Tillinghast expressed his closeness to Believers by referring to the Harvard community as his home.[13]

During the 1840s the Harvard and Shirley Shakers also developed an important friendship with Jeremiah Hacker of Portland, Maine, who was editor of *The Pleasure Boat*, a paper dedicated to his reformist views on religion and government. Hacker was a former Quaker and a friend of Joseph Tillinghast, from whom he probably heard of the Shakers. Tillinghast gave the Harvard and Shirley Believers a gift subscription to Hacker's paper, but both communities canceled the subscription after a few issues because they felt that some of the articles were not suitable reading material for some Believers.[14]

In 1847 Hacker visited New Lebanon to look over the community and to query the sisters about "their freedom or bondage." In 1848 he visited Harvard and began a long friendship with some of the Believers there, impressed by Shaker "temperance, honesty, industry, frugality and other virtues." Hacker also agreed with the Shakers' rejection of marriage, believing that the institution caused most couples more trouble than it was worth. Believers in the eastern communities reciprocated Hacker's feelings and visited him at his home in Maine as late as 1857. By June 1860, however, his opinions on marriage and the Shakers had changed. In a letter of that date, Hacker wrote to Joseph Tillinghast that he believed that the Shakers had erred in rejecting sexual intercourse rather than correcting its abuses. Hacker still believed that a majority of marriages were unhappy and that most children were products of "lust" rather than "true love." But he also believed that a few relationships based on "pure, divine love" did exist and that sexual intercourse within those relationships produced "pure" children. Hacker's changing opinions put him at odds with most Shakers, and his relations with Believers cooled considerably.[15]

Just as important as the effects of these friendships on the Shakers was the impact that the Shakers had on their worldly friends, especially their influence on the reformers and literati of the day. The Shakers' most notable contribution to nineteenth-century social theory was their reconstruction of the biological family, and many important thinkers of the day were acquainted with Shaker principles.[16] Harriot Hunt, Bronson Alcott, Charles Lane, and Ralph Waldo Emerson had visited the Harvard and Shirley Shakers and found, at least for a time, something intrinsically good in the Believers' altered social structure. Harriot Hunt valued the haven that Shakerism provided for abused and lonely women. The Transcendentalists, particularly Alcott and Lane, admired Shakerism's family structure. When outlining their plans for Fruitlands, their own communitarian experiment, Alcott and Lane wrote, "The Family in its highest, divinest sense is . . . our sacred earthly destiny." Holding up the Shaker spiritual family as a model of this "perfected" family, Alcott and Lane argued that the Shakers "are at least entitled to deeper consideration than they yet appear to have secured [on the topic of Family association]." [17] Alcott and Lane then noted,

> It is perhaps most striking that the only really successful extensive Community of interest, spiritual and secular, in modern times was established by A Woman. Again, we witness in this people the bringing together of the two sexes in a new relation, or rather with a new idea of the old relation. This has led to results more harmonic than anyone seriously believes attainable for the human race, either in isolation or association, so long as divided, conflicting family arrangements are permitted. [18]

Even Emerson, who at first viewed the Shakers with contempt, began by 1842 to appreciate their communal lifestyle "which so falls in with the temper of the times." His final acceptance came when he realized the security that the Believers offered his widowed cousin Rebecca Hamlin and her daughter Mary, both of whom lived with the Harvard Shakers. Though he would never choose to live with the Believers, he recognized the importance of the Shaker family for others. After one of the Hamlins' visits to Emerson in 1852, he wrote his brother, "They returned home today,—very tranquil well-behaved people, & to them & for them the plain fraternity at H. seems a sunny asylum." [19]

Once open to developing close friendships with the world, the Shakers widened their contacts even further by associating themselves with the spiritualist movement that swept the United States after 1848. Similarities existed between the Shakers and the spiritualists. Both groups believed that humans could communicate with the dead, and both groups also shared a fundamentally feminine bent. Although men could and did act as mediums, women were more likely to serve in that capacity, both in Shakerism and in spiritualism. [20]

The Believers at Harvard and Shirley adopted the trappings of worldly spiritualism, including séances. In 1851 William Leonard, after visiting La Roy Sunderland (a prominent spiritualist), Lewis Munroe, and several other mediums in Boston, invited them to Harvard. The mediums held several meetings there, but not all Shakers believed that the séances were real. Lewis Munroe then went to Shirley to conduct a séance but ran into difficulties. During the meeting, the spirits of Lucy Lion (a deceased Shaker sister), George Washington, and Ann Lee appeared. Munroe "tried to lead off in some things a number of times but finally had to give up & be led; he had to hear the word of Washington who exhorted him to faithfulness or he would be no more than any of the rest of the world." On this occasion Munroe's powers were overshadowed by the Shaker spiritualists. From his observations of the worldly mediums' performances, Leonard concluded that the Believers were much more spiritually advanced than the outside mediums. Yet he did not condemn the mediums and believed that they could communicate with the dead.[21]

Shaker interest in spiritualism continued into the 1850s, and the Believers frequently practiced rapping and levitation. The Shakers also continued to visit non-Shaker mediums. When Elijah Myrick was in New York City on business in 1858, he attended a lecture given by Cora Hatch, a celebrated medium of the period. That same year William Leonard cautioned Joseph Tillinghast "not to strike against [spiritualism] how ever imperfect it may seem. . . . All true Believers know it to be a work of preparation for the greater and higer [sic] work of God."[22]

Spiritualism and the many changes in and out of the Shaker communities in the 1850s compelled Believers to rethink some of their own theological positions as they awaited the long promised ingathering. From the beginning of the movement, one of the most asked questions of Believers was, "What would happen to the world if everyone became a Shaker?" According to the world's logic, universal adoption of celibacy would lead to the extinction of the human race. Thus, nonbelievers felt that the Shakers were hypocritical in their condemnation of procreation as "evil" when they relied on the "fruits" of sexual intercourse for new members.

For years, the Shakers' twofold response remained the same: universal celibacy would not lead to the total extinction of the human race so long as God continued to will the existence of the earth and its inhabitants, and sexual intercourse, no matter how beneficial the results, was always sinful.

By the 1840s, however, Believers felt so pressured by the world on this issue that during the Era of Manifestations the Central Ministry claimed that God had presented them with a solution to this dilemma. Through revelation, the Shakers learned that God planned to institute two orders on earth, the order of nature and the order of grace. The Shakers, as people who willingly adopted a celibate life to fulfill the commands of the new gospel, belonged to the superior order of grace. For those who were basically good and moral but who could not make the commitment to celibacy (almost everyone else), God would restore the order of nature as found in the Garden of Eden before the Fall. People living in this order would be judged according to natural law, which included the injunction that once every eighteen months couples could have intercourse for the sole purpose of conceiving a child. In October 1843 Seth Wells, the principal Shaker theologian of that time, wrote to Rufus Bishop, a member of the Central Ministry, concerning these revelations. He noted the resistance of some Shakers to this doctrine but promoted the idea as a way to eliminate obstacles between the Shakers and the world. In 1844 the doctrine made its appearance at Harvard in a spirit message delivered by Alfred Collier.[23]

The implications of this change in theology are enormous. Since the time of Ann Lee the Shakers had maintained certain religious beliefs and practices which set them apart from the world, even while they were drawing closer to the outside in other ways. Reiterating their beliefs in the face of attack, Believers developed a rhetoric of separatism that gave meaning to living apart from the world and endowed the Shakers with a feeling of moral superiority. Over time, however, Believers became more sensitive to attack and changed their long-held position on absolute renunciation of "carnal relations." By replacing their own Shaker standard for sexual behavior with a worldly, albeit modified, standard, the Believers threatened their own distinctive position as mediators between heaven and earth.

Outside influences, however, were not the only factors that affected Shaker theology and culture in the 1850s. Internally, villages polarized as Believers debated anew the future direction of Shakerism. Harvard and Shirley had dealt with this issue as early as 1828 when Grove Blanchard became elder of the bishopric, and the villages took a decided turn toward the world. The issue reached the level of the Central Ministry between 1849 and 1857 when the four men and women who had composed the Ministry for almost thirty years died, to be replaced by a new generation of leaders—Daniel Boler, Giles Avery, Betsey Bates, and Eliza Ann Taylor. This new Ministry, along with Hervey L. Eads of South Union, Alonzo G. Hollister of New Lebanon, and Henry C. Blinn of Canterbury, represented what Stephen J. Stein has identified as the "traditionalist faction" in Shakerism that "called for a return to a more sectarian perspective and to earlier religious patterns." Frederick Evans and Antoinette Doolittle led a second party, a "progressive faction" committed to change and ecumenism, centered at the New Lebanon North family.[24]

Though the two groups often disagreed about the future direction of Shakerism, both willingly accepted change in Shaker theology. Although this practice may seem inconsistent with the traditionalists' sectarian position, their acceptance of theological innovation was grounded in a basic tenet of Shakerism: "progressive revelation." The Shakers believed that God continued to speak to people through inspiration and revelation; the Bible was not the last word in God's design for the world. The Believers, then, were open to new ideas when revelation rendered previous ones obsolete. During the 1850s Frederick Evans, influenced by the ideas of Transcendentalism, Unitarianism, Universalism, and spiritualism, began promoting a "new theology" that challenged traditional Christian ideas such as the divinity of Jesus and the concept of hell as eternal punishment for sinners.[25] Not all Shakers were ready for change, and many were upset by these new ideas. But, ironically, the Central Ministry, despite its traditionalist bent, usually sided with Frederick Evans and other progressives in theological debates.

Harvard, as a community, generally disagreed with the "new theology," even though it was willing to embrace the world in other ways. Evans's essay denying the divinity of Jesus, for example, split the community. The Harvard leadership, including William Leonard, a respected elder and theologian, agreed with much of what Evans wrote, but many Harvard residents opposed Evans's work. Rather than stifle discussion, the Harvard Ministry encouraged the airing of opinions, and Leonard, though personally supportive of Evans, assumed the role of spokesman for the opposition, outlining their arguments in letters to Evans. Perhaps fearing Evans's reaction, Leonard confided to him, "We at Harvard have many imperfections, one of which is, we are too much of a talking people. And often in sentiments uttered by our advocates for free discussion, I have thot they had made themselves fully aware that they lived in a land of freedom of speech, and Republican liberty."[26]

The opposition gained strength when Elder John Lyon and other Believers from Enfield visited Harvard and spoke out against Evans. Lyon was outraged by Evans's ideas and cited Johann Lorenz von Mosheim's *Institutes of Ecclesiastical History* as proof that Evans was "reviving" an early heresy, the "Christian Gnosticism" of Cerinthus.[27] Cerinthus denied Jesus' divinity, claiming that Joseph was Jesus' biological, and only, father; Jesus' conception was in no way miraculous. This human Jesus was imbued with the "Christ spirit" only at his baptism and was later forsaken by the spirit prior to his Passion and crucifixion. Evans's beliefs also hinted at Arianism, the belief that Jesus Christ was neither divine nor coeternal with God (of the same substance as God) but created, like all other creatures, and later adopted by God as his only son.[28] Lyons's arguments and the circulation of Evans's writings among the Harvard Shakers drew even more people into the "opposition party." This opposition operated on two levels. Many Shakers rejected Evans's ideas, but even more were afraid of change in general and did not want to do what they thought the early church had done, that is, "[bring] in *new doctrines* after the Fathers fell asleep." The dissenters, fearing that the introduction of new ideas into Harvard would create a "sectarian spirit" in the village, wanted to maintain "the gospel *as delivered by Mother*," though Ann Lee had never made such complex Christological pronouncements during her lifetime.[29]

If many at Harvard and Shirley were afraid of change, William Leonard was not. A theologian in his own right, Leonard published *A Discourse on the Order and Propriety of Divine Inspiration and Revelation* in 1853. An ardent believer in the truth of Shakerism and an active proponent of proselytization, he wanted to make the simple truths of Shakerism available to the world. He believed that the only way people could understand these truths was through spiritual revelation and optimistically predicted that the Believers were on the verge of a period of growth and enlightenment: "Dreams, visions, prophecies, and revelations, the four chariot wheels that have carried forward God's work through all time, have begun to roll forward the great work of judgement."[30] To bring these new ideas to light, Leonard felt in his *"very bones"* that the Shakers would write many new and original works for the public after twenty years of stagnation, and he believed that his work had "set a precedent" for these new theological endeavors.[31]

Combined with Leonard's staunch faith in the supernatural, however, was a seemingly incongruous belief in the rational, even scientific, underpinnings of religion. When preaching to a Protestant congregation in Cohasset, Massachusetts, in 1867, Leonard laced his sermon with mechanistic imagery. "Man stands," he expounded, "as a monument of the highest mechanical skill of the Almighty on this earth; In that piece of living machinery he has placed a recording instrument, like a gasometer," upon which is recorded one's actions. On the final day of judgment, each person's "gasometer" readings would be measured against Christ's, a quantifiable indicator of Christianity in action. Salvation, then, could be studied scientifically, argued Leonard, and the best place to start was with the teachings of the Shakers.[32]

The Believers fully manifested their linkage of spiritual and scientific principles in their efforts at social reform, and William Leonard saw the Believers as pivotal to the spirit of reform that was sweeping the nation:

> The [Shaker] Church of the latter day is an accumulation of the best leading spirits of ages, in and out of the body. The power of this Church is felt thro this nation; tho unperceived by the internal or external workers. The reforms of the last century, have started with the American people; and these reforms are produced by the life germ, or spirit lights of the age, who have their highest existence in the Church.[33]

Leonard's statement reveals very clearly his belief that Shakers were not to remain isolated from the world. While acknowledging America's preeminent role in the reform movements of the nineteenth century, he makes clear that the Shakers led the American contingent, their influence subtle but strong. Through their many spiritual, intellectual, and cultural ties to the world, the Shakers were the "life germ" of reform. Bound to the world, they linked their own destiny with that of the United States.

The Shakers' intellectual and cultural ties to the world were firmly grounded in their successful integration into the American economy, seen in the frequent peddling trips that they conducted on established trade routes throughout New England and Canada. Though generally a profitable arrangement, financial dependence on the world meant that recessions and depressions in the American economy directly affected the Shaker economy. In the aftermath of the panic of 1837, Simon Atherton of the Harvard Church family returned from an eleven-day seed journey in October 1840 with only $120; the same trip twenty-five years earlier had yielded $600. "How we are to get our living," noted the Ministry, "we cannot say at present."[34]

The Harvard and Shirley Shakers weathered these periodic depressions and, except for a few families, entered a period of unprecedented prosperity in the mid-1840s and 1850s. Journals record a constant round of farm and family improvements. In 1846 the Harvard Church family added on to its milk house and renovated its dwelling house, and the South family built a new office. The next year the Church family built a windmill and began construction on a new Ministry shop. That same year, Shakers from New Lebanon visited the two communities. The visitors were impressed by Shirley's orchards, and Harvard they found "altogether pleasant, beautiful, & delightfully situated." They noted that Harvard's buildings were well maintained, some sporting slate roofs. The next year, Shakers from Watervliet described the Harvard Church family's new office "as neat as waxwork, and in the best of order." Seven years later visiting Believers from Ohio proclaimed that the Harvard North family was "done up in the best style," boasting "splendid" buildings and stone post-and-chain fences. One Shaker brother observed that "things about here bear the appearance of wealth."[35]

The key to Shaker economic prosperity after 1837 was the expansion of Shaker business enterprises, a decision that carried important ramifications for the Believers. Business expansion created the need for more labor and bigger markets, making withdrawal from the world increasingly difficult. As it was, the Shakers rarely had enough men to do hard physical labor and had to hire much of the work done. At the height of the Era of Manifestations, the Believers at Harvard and Shirley fired all hired hands in an attempt to cleanse the society, but they could not go for long without additional help; in 1846 the Harvard South family employed several outside carpenters and laborers while constructing a new dwelling house. In 1853 the family spent two thousand dollars on outside labor, illustrating the extent to which Believers relied on hired help.[36]

With labor costs rising, the Believers looked for new ways to tap into the American market. Like many Americans, the Harvard Church family joined in the brief fad of raising silkworms, which meant a side business in mulberry trees, but they eventually abandoned this venture for the more lucrative one of raising fruit trees, an enterprise begun in 1837. By the mid-1840s, the Harvard nursery business was thriving. The Believers sold fruit (pears, plums, peaches, quinces, and apples) to the world and raised saplings for local nurseries; William Leonard, head of the Shaker nursery, oversaw the planting of twenty-five thousand seedlings in the spring of 1846 alone. Harvard Church family members also experimented with new products. In 1846 they converted their sheep barn into a dovecote and began raising squabs for market, while a bumper crop of "extra large" pumpkins in 1847 prompted Believers to dry and grind the pumpkin and package the powder for sale.[37]

Access to outside markets was a major factor in the profitability of Shaker enterprises. Believers at Harvard and Shirley, therefore, were delighted when the Boston and Fitchburg Railroad commenced operation in 1845 with depots at Ayer and Littleton. (Because the railroad passed through Shaker property, the railroad company gave the Harvard Shakers $130 and gave all Believers at both villages passes for a free train ride.) Opportunities for reaching the world increased again the next year with the opening of the Worcester and Nashua Railroad.[38]

The Harvard Shakers immediately capitalized on the railroads. As early as 1845 the Shaker sisters used the railroad to facilitate their making of palm-leaf bonnets. Before this time, the women had to prepare the palm leaf themselves, splitting and bleaching it before it could be woven into hats. Now, however, the sisters could take the palm leaf into Fitchburg for this preparatory process, weave the bonnets at home, then return with them to town to be pressed. The railroad provided easy access to these services and eased the women's workload.[39]

The railroad also expanded Shaker markets. In 1845 the Harvard Church family, followed by the South family in 1846, began contracting with a dealer, usually from Boston, to sell their milk. Generally the agent supplied the milk cans, shipping boxes, and ice, while the Shakers provided the milk. Believers used the profits from their sales to purchase butter, cheese, and molasses from local farmers. The Harvard Shakers discussed this arrangement with several visitors from New Lebanon in 1846. The Harvard Believers argued that the enterprise was profitable—they had sold 1,054 gallons of milk the previous year—but the New Lebanon Shakers were not convinced that profits should take precedence over the Shaker tenets of hard work and renunciation of the world. One visitor claimed that he "love[d] butter & cheese made by clean hands, not defiled with sin—not only so but I think our Heavenly Parents will bless us if we strive to do our own work & not be idle." Undaunted, in 1850 the Harvard Shakers expanded their market even further by taking advantage of the California gold rush and shipping seeds, pickles, canned pumpkin, and horseradish to the West Coast.[40]

As the New Lebanon visitors feared, however, the quest for money did lead to "unshaker" behavior, seen when the Harvard deacons found themselves caught between trying to maintain union with fellow Believers and generating profits for their families. The deacons, who were responsible for selling Shaker products on peddling trips, were also in charge of buying provisions for their families. As good businessmen they tried to get the most for their money by buying the least expensive products they could find. This became a problem when the deacons had to choose between buying an item from the world at a lower price or from other Believers at a higher price. For many years they had simply purchased whatever they could from other Shakers, but more recently, in an attempt to save money, they had begun to buy from whomever charged the least. The deacons understood that Shakers charged more for their products than the world did because Shaker products were of a higher quality, and they considered this an equitable arrangement when they were dealing with outsiders. But when the Harvard deacons were trading with other Believers, they felt that they should be charged less than the world, and so they often found themselves in "a hard place to get over." Their dilemma, generated by the need for profit and the need for union, reflected the tension created when Shaker principles clashed with worldly realities.[41]

Despite the dangers inherent in trading with the world, the Shakers continued to expand their two most profitable industries, seeds and herbs. The impact of seed sales on the Shaker economy was significant. Between 1847 and 1857 garden seeds, on average, accounted for 8.6 percent of the total yearly gross income at Harvard, though the percentage for individual years ranged from 3.9 to 75.9.[42] But even more lucrative than the seed industry was Harvard's herb business. From its small beginnings in the 1820s, the industry grew quickly. By 1845 the Harvard Shakers were selling 197 kinds of "medicinal herbs," 8 varieties of "sweet herbs in canisters," and 13 "extracts." Three years later the Harvard Shakers erected a stone dry-house for drying the herbs, installed an herb press invented by Shaker brother George Whiting, and began construction on a large herb house which they finished in 1850. In 1853 the Harvard Shakers bought a machine that cut pressed herbs into one ounce blocks. They purchased a second herb press two years later and processed more than eighteen tons of herbs that year alone.[43]

The Shakers came to rely heavily on the income generated by the herb industry. A journal kept by Elisha Myrick, head of the Harvard herb indus-try, indicates that their herb business netted from $1,488.00 to $3,083.00 a year, depending on weather conditions, between the years 1847 and 1853.[44] In 1854 sales were down because of a drought. But in 1855, noted Myrick, the Harvard Shakers sold $11,682.40 worth of herbs, the most they had earned in one year since they began selling herbs.[45]

The success of the Shaker seed and herb industries and the building of the railroads sealed the Shakers' relationship with the world by making them almost entirely dependent on the outside for financial viability. At the same time, the Shakers reinforced this interdependence by strengthening their ideological and cultural connections to the world. While the short-term consequences of such open acceptance were financial prosperity and an infusion of new ideas, the long-term effects, as yet unforeseen by the Shakers, threatened the very bonds of Shaker community.

10

The Price of Worldliness

BY THE MIDDLE OF THE NINETEENTH CENTURY, the Believers of Harvard and Shirley had cause to question the price of worldliness for their communities. Economic disasters, dwindling membership figures, and doctrinal controversy, all of which stemmed largely from the Believers' accommodationist policies, combined with changes in Shaker social and economic structures to compel the Believers to reassess once again who they were and where they were going. How the Believers answered these questions was important, for the future of Harvard and Shirley hinged on decisions that the Shakers made in the 1860s and 1870s.

In some ways, the Shakers were, perhaps, not wary enough of the potential problems brought on by their interactions with the world. This was particularly true in regard to their economy, for though trade with the world brought about short-term prosperity for the Believers, the lure of profit also disrupted the order of Shaker life. Drawn increasingly into the world of market capitalism, the Harvard and Shirley Shakers found themselves walking a thin line between the demands of the Shaker world and those of the secular. At times, they made business decisions based on worldly economic principles rather than Shaker teachings. On these occasions the result was almost always disastrous, both financially and spiritually.

The most devastating example of what could happen when the Believers based their business decisions on the principles of market capitalism was the Shirley Shakers' decision to build the Phoenix textile mill on the Catacunemaug River. A three-story brick structure housing 130 looms, it was the largest cotton mill in Shirley. The Shakers finished the superstructure in 1850 and dedicated the mill in 1852.[1]

Building a factory was not, in itself, unusual for the Believers. Shaker vil-lages sometimes built textile factories to supply themselves with fabric, sell-ing leftover goods to the world.[2] There is no evidence, however, that the Shirley Shakers ever intended to use the Phoenix Mill to manufacture cloth for themselves. They built the factory solely as a money-making enterprise, intending to lease the factory and profit from the monthly rent. Although perhaps a solid business decision in worldly terms, building for "profit only" strayed far from fundamental Shaker ideas. Shaker industries had always been grounded in the needs of the community. Initially, Believers produced what they needed for themselves and sold only what was left to the world. Even when they began to produce for the world, the Shakers marketed items that were also used in their own communities. Financial success in the 1850s, however, convinced the Shirley Shakers to abandon traditional Shaker economic principles for the murky realm of speculation. The results were tragic.

In 1852 the Shakers leased the factory to the Steam Mill Company of New Bedford (later to become the Phoenix Manufacturing Company) for $1,652.35 a month and agreed to furnish enough water power to run a specified number of looms. What seemed a simple formula for profit quickly became a constant drain on the Believers' resources. The cost of construction was higher than the Shakers had anticipated, and contrary to Shaker rules, Believer Jonas Nutting, who oversaw the project, borrowed heavily from the world to finish the mill. As early as 1851 a bank loan of $3,000.00 came due, and the Believers appealed to Joseph Tillinghast to help them find a way to pay it back. A. G. Snell, the Phoenix Manufactur-ing Company's mechanic and overseer, was another problem for the Shak-ers. In March 1853 he charged the Shakers with breach of contract for not providing enough water to run the looms and sued the Believers for $6,000.00. In return for the Phoenix Company's dropping its lawsuit, the Believers agreed to fix the water problem at their own expense. To meet the costs, the Shirley Shakers borrowed money from the Watervliet Believers. The Harvard Ministry ruefully noted that the Shirley Shakers had expected to make a profit in a few years from the factory rent, but the enterprise had turned into a financial drain.[3]

Unfortunately, the Believers' troubles were not over. On July 2, 1856, a dam built as a joint venture between the Shirley Shaker trustees and nonbe-liever Samuel Hazen broke, releasing seven hundred acres of water over the countryside. The ensuing flood destroyed five bridges (including a railroad bridge), five dams, a sawmill, numerous buildings, and several fields of crops. Damage to the Believers' property amounted to $5,000.00, and total damages came to about $50,000.00, for which the Shakers were held largely responsible. The railroad sued the Shakers for $12,000.00, settling for a lesser amount; the Phoenix Manufacturing Company expected the trustees to cover the costs of all repairs and renovations necessary to keep the mill running; and the selectmen of the neighboring town of Lunenburg demanded that the Shakers replace one of the washed-out bridges and repair the roadbed damaged by the flooding, threatening to prosecute if the Shakers did not comply. The Shakers also reimbursed several landowners for flood damage. At the urging of the Central Ministry, the eastern Shaker villages donated $4,000.00 to Shirley so that the community would not have to borrow from the world to pay its debts.[4]

In 1861 the Central Ministry ordered an examination of the Phoenix Factory records and gave William Leonard the task of straightening out the accounts. He discovered that the factory debt totaled $50,000.00; $30,000.00 of that had been borrowed from the world. The sad fact was that the mill had never turned a profit for the Shirley Shakers. Leonard calculated that between 1856 and 1861 the net profit of the mill had been a mere $1,250.48. This had not even covered the Shakers' interest payments, and they had to rely on the income derived from two lumber mills and the sale of "domestic manufactures" at Shirley to pay their debts. Leonard summarized the feelings of many when he wrote, "It was a *bad, bad,* enterprize; a bad hour when they planned it; a bad foundation to build upon; they fell upon a bad man to manage the Mill; he has made it bad for us, and bad for the company." In October 1866 the Shirley Shakers sold the mill and sixty acres of land to Samuel Rodman, owner of the Phoenix Manufacturing Company, for $42,200.00. The Believers' final assessment was that the Phoenix Mill had been a failure, and even Rodman, who resold the mill in 1881, considered the venture only "moderately successful."[5]

Factory troubles threw a pall over the community. When the Central Ministry visited Shirley in October 1863 they tried "to encourage the people to keep the way of God, and to struggle on, and get out of debt. The great debt here, like an incubus, paralyzes the community, and, there is very little energy to move forward in temporal things. Of course the spiritual suffers also."[6] The Shirley Believers, however, were not alone in accruing large debts to the world. Several Shaker villages—including Enfield, New Hampshire, and both communities in Maine—had recently suffered similar "pecuniary embarrassments," and the Central Ministry issued a circular in 1864 admonishing the Believers not to borrow money from the world. Disregarding this command, they warned, could lead to "the annihilation of our Society." The circular closed with a short but powerful reminder, "Where there is no Order, there is no God."[7]

Order was an important concept to the Believers. Following the rules and obeying one's elders were considered good order, as was living peacefully within one's family. The proper running of a Shaker village, including the responsible use of its financial resources, was also a necessary part of maintaining order. Thus the abandonment of Shaker economic principles and the resulting financial crises of the 1850s and 1860s threatened the Believers by undermining the economic viability of their communities and challenging both their notion of order and their claims of superiority to the world.

Accompanying the financial problems of the mid-nineteenth century was a precipitous decline in membership. Until the middle of the century the two villages had maintained relatively steady populations. In 1833 the Shakers reported 169 people at Harvard and 97 at Shirley. In 1846 a Shaker diarist indicated that Shirley had 90 members and that Harvard had actually grown to 188.[8] These figures corroborate Priscilla Brewer's and William Bainbridge's figures, obtained from federal census records. Both Brewer and Bainbridge calculate the 1840 population of Harvard and Shirley as 167 and 70, respectively, and Brewer places the 1850 populations at 178 and 81.[9]

After many years of relative stability, however, membership figures began to plummet in the 1850s. According to Brewer, 107 people lived at Harvard and 67 at Shirley in 1860; ten years later, Harvard's population had dropped to 83, while only 48 residents remained at Shirley. Bainbridge's statistics for 1860 show Harvard with 110 residents and Shirley with 67. In 1869 the Shakers themselves reported that the population of Harvard totaled 80 people and Shirley about 70. The peak year for both villages, then, was around 1850. This growth pattern paralleled that of Harvard town, whose population reached its zenith in 1850 with 1,630 residents. After that, the town began to lose about 10 percent of its population every year. Nourse attributed this attrition to the town's geographic isolation and its inability to attract industry because of a lack of waterways.[10] The Believers, in their own way, suffered from these same factors. In short, their rustic and agricultural way of life appeared outmoded to a world increasingly enamored with industry and bustling cities.

Although any decline in population was alarming, what worried the Believers most was the loss of young people, especially boys and young men. Alfred Collier, who eventually left the Shakers himself, recorded their steady exodus in his journal. Between May 19 and 27, 1859, for example, twelve-year-old Edmund Mornder, thirteen-year-old Samuel Hollis, and fifteen-year-old Henry Cook left the Shakers after a three- to seven-year residence. Such departures took their toll. By 1859 only six girls remained in the Harvard Girls' Order and one boy in the Boys' Order. Given such grim figures, the Ministry disbanded the latter in June; for the first time in thirty years, Harvard had no family for young boys. The Harvard Church family also showed signs of decline. Only fourteen men (average age forty-seven) and forty-two women (average age fifty-two) resided there. With fewer men to work the farms and contribute to Shaker industries and fewer young adults to accede to leadership positions, the future of the family looked bleak.[11]

Financial and membership difficulties took their toll on the villages. In 1859 the Central Ministry observed the "gloomy state" of Harvard as the people there "wad[ed] thro scenes of tribulation and trial, especially the Church Family in consequence of apostasy." The situation did not improve over time. While visiting Harvard in 1870, the Central Ministry stopped at the South family, noting that this gathering family was "now the scattering family. . . . We have no visit here, with the Brethren & Sisters atall [sic]. A sorrowful feeling here indeed."[12]

Ironically, the sagging spirits of Harvard and Shirley were temporarily rejuvenated by the outbreak of the Civil War, which distracted the villages from their own problems. The Shakers were relatively insulated from events, and eastern Believers felt the impact of the war much less than the Shakers in Kentucky. The main problem that eastern Shakers faced was the general economic instability precipitated by the war. The Central Ministry noted in 1862 that Believers everywhere were having trouble selling their seeds because the war had disrupted their markets.[13]

The war threatened the tranquility of Harvard and Shirley most directly in the form of the 1863 Conscription Act. Because of the small male population of these villages, the government found few men eligible for the draft—four at Harvard and eight at Shirley—and most of these suffered physical disabilities. Three Shirley Shakers were eventually drafted. Two were released because of their poor physical condition, but twenty-six-year-old Horace Tabor was ordered to report for duty, even though he had lost the use of his left eye. Because of his Shaker principles, Tabor did not appear on the appointed day and was arrested on September 28, 1863, for desertion. His imprisonment was a harrowing experience. He was shocked by the conduct of the other soldiers, "such swearing I never heard," and when his captors told him that he could either "bear arms or be shot," he wrote home to Shirley that "I almost wish they would shoot me, and put an end to my sufferings." The Shakers appealed Tabor's arrest, claiming that he was too ill to serve as a soldier. In addition to his partial blindness, Tabor suffered from neuralgia and bronchitis. After a second physical examination, Tabor was released and returned to Shirley, thirty-three days after his ordeal had begun.[14]

Despite their pacifist principles, the Harvard and Shirley Shakers supported the war to end slavery, as long as others did the fighting. Although never active abolitionists, the Shakers believed that the "peculiar institution" was an evil that should be stopped. William Leonard's position was typical of many northerners. He advocated the emancipation of the slaves and proposed their colonization under "kind hearted agents" in the unsettled parts of the United States. Antislavery sentiments were no doubt heightened when the Ministry and the Harvard Church family read *Uncle Tom's Cabin* aloud in 1852. The Believers also took an interest in fugitive slaves, sometimes sending money and clothes to those who asked for help.[15]

When war finally did break out, the Shakers generally approved. At a Sabbath meeting on April 21, 1861, Alfred Collier noted that "the War God seemed to rule & inspired every feeling soul, in the cause of the Country." A few days earlier a Shaker sister had recorded in her journal, "Great stir and excitement about *war*." Soldiers were stationed at Camp Stephens in the nearby town of Groton, and they periodically visited the Shakers, sometimes practicing their military drills in the street that ran through the Harvard Shaker village. On these occasions the Shakers supplied the soldiers with apples and beverages. In 1862 a group of soldiers worshiped with the Harvard Shakers at a public Sabbath meeting. Olive Chandler remarked on their "commendable deportment" and commented, "God's spirit is moving upon the face of the great waters, and I trust this mighty struggle will accomplish some universal good." Like many Americans, the Shakers believed in the providential nature of the Civil War. William Leonard believed that God had chosen Abraham Lincoln to destroy slavery and punish the south, and Leonard supported Lincoln's efforts, even though his Shaker beliefs prohibited him from actually fighting.[16]

For all their disdain of fighting, however, the Shakers were not above using the war for their own financial gain, and they took advantage of opportunities to supply the military with food and drink. During the war the Shirley Shakers traveled throughout Virginia, to Baltimore, and to Washington, D.C., selling wine and quart cans of applesauce to the Union army. Such behavior compelled the Shakers to justify their actions and sometimes left them looking rather hypocritical. Augustus Burns, though moved by the tragic deaths of the soldiers, considered his pacifist position to be a "higher calling." "Those of us that are faithfull," he wrote, "are a thousand times greater than the Heroes of the present war."[17] Two decades later, William Leonard penned a defense of the Believers' actions during the Civil War. He knew that many Americans saw the Shakers' refusal to bear arms as cowardice and viewed the Believers as hypocrites for "reaping the rewards" of the war without forfeiting Shaker lives. Nevertheless, he wrote, the Shakers had felt that they could contribute more to the war effort through their spiritual presence than through physical fighting; while the country fought within itself on the "political plane," the Shakers waged their own battle on the "spiritual plane." "This patriotic and Christian struggle," concluded Leonard, "beautifully blended to uproot treason, and restore peace and prosperity to the land."[18]

This spiritual battle was not merely rhetorical. During the years of the Civil War, the Shakers of Harvard and Shirley grappled with their own internecine struggle as the heresy of "purified generation" swept through their villages. The controversy came to a head at Harvard in 1865 when two biological sisters, Roxalana and Fidelia Grosvenor, leaders of the movement there, left the village. The ramifications of the controversy, however, were felt long after. The "Grosvenor affair" was a critical event at Harvard and Shirley, capping a growing sense of crisis in the 1850s and 1860s, and an analysis of the case reveals long-standing tensions in the communities generated by issues of female sexuality, women's roles in society, and relations with the world.[19]

The Grosvenor sisters had been faithful Shakers for many years. In 1819, when Roxalana was six and Fidelia was eight, they moved to Harvard with their parents, Mary and Ebenezer, and their two brothers, Augustus and Lorenzo. In their twenties both Roxalana and Fidelia achieved positions of responsibility in the communities. Fidelia became deaconess in the Harvard Church family in 1840 at the age of twenty-nine. In 1853 she moved to the East family to "take first care among the Sisters" and returned to the Church in 1856 as elder sister. In 1859 she left the Elders' Order to become "second" in the Physicians' Order. She moved to the North family in 1861 as an office sister, returned to the Church in 1863, and left the society in 1865. Roxalana's administrative career began in 1837 when, at the age of twenty-four, she became elder sister in the Harvard Church family. In 1847 she moved into the Harvard Ministry as elder sister and went to Shirley in 1851 as elder sister in their Church family. Ten years later she returned to Harvard to resume her elder sistership in the Church. She was released from this position on January 1, 1865, and left the society in August.[20]

The two women were capable administrators and well liked in their communities, yet their changing theological views ultimately forced them to leave the society. Roxalana and Fidelia were heretics, and their heresy was two-pronged. They advocated the doctrine of purified generation, and they denied that Ann Lee was the second appearance of Christ.

Adherents of purified generation taught that sexual intercourse between two spiritually pure people who were united by true love produced pure offspring. This idea had its origins in the nineteenth-century free love movement, whose advocates believed that relationships between men and women should be equal partnerships based on mutual desire rather than social or legal conventions. Some spiritualists took up the theme of free love, applying their own interpretive twist. Andrew Jackson Davis, for example, believed that "elective affinities" superseded earthly marriage relations. In other words, every person had a soulmate, and a married person who found this soulmate was justified in leaving his or her spouse to start a new relationship. Davis also believed that the quality of a marriage affected its offspring. "Evil" children came from "bad" marriages; "peaceful" children came from spiritual and harmonious marriages.[21]

Free-love ideas were repugnant to most Americans, who viewed marriage as the building block of society.[22] Even the Shakers, who had come to recognize the validity of marriage for some people, deplored such an application of spiritual values. The Central Ministry lamented, "Spiritualism in these days is making sad havoc of purity & morality by discarding the marriage legal relations and advocating congeniality of temperment as the only proper bond of union between lovers."[23]

Although the doctrine of purified generation posed serious moral questions for society, it also challenged the Shaker concept of "original sin." According to the *Testimony of Christ's Second Appearing*, lust caused Adam and Eve's fall from grace. God had initially sanctioned sexual intercourse for the purpose of procreation and planned to usher Adam and Eve into the "knowledge of generation" at the proper time. But Eve, unable to wait, gave in to her passions and convinced Adam to do the same. From that point on, all of humankind's motives and actions were corrupt. To regain the purity of paradise, the Shakers abased their passions through celibacy and established spiritual families that superseded corrupt biological ties.[24]

The Shaker position on original sin could logically lead to the doctrine of purified generation. If people succeeded in mastering their base passions and were truly living on a higher spiritual plane, then sexual intercourse would be the product of pure love and not lust. Having reformed the motivation, theoretically one could redeem the act of intercourse. The possibility of extrapolating Shaker doctrine to this point, not lost on the Ministry, created a dangerous situation for Believers.[25] The eradication of celibacy would change the whole nature of Shakerism, and Believers would have to deny what they gave up their worldly lives to defend.

Despite its radical nature, the doctrine of purified generation appealed to some Shakers and caused havoc in several villages. The first overt reference to the issue in the Central Ministry's journal is found on May 15, 1864, "Purified generation, for Believers, is now advocated by some, and they want to mingle flesh and spirit. A time of intense trial for Believers." In September, after spending the day with the Harvard Ministry, the Central Ministry noted, "A spirit is considerably troubling Believers in these days striving to amalgamate the old and New Creation[,] Generation, and Regeneration. Flesh & Spirit."[26]

The leaders of the purified generation movement at Harvard and Shirley were the Grosvenor sisters. Roxalana, the more prominent of the two, probably learned about the doctrine sometime between 1851 and 1861 while serving as elder sister in the Shirley Church. She may have first heard of the doctrine through a worldly medium, as she seems to have visited mediums frequently, or she may have been influenced by Jeremiah Hacker with whom she was in frequent correspondence and who was an adherent of purified generation.

The idea of purified generation in itself was threatening to the structure of Shakerism, but the Grosvenor sisters turned it into an even greater challenge for the Harvard and Shirley Shakers. Capitalizing on the anxiety created by the loss of membership, the two women admitted to other Shaker sisters that they believed that "Shakerism was played out."[27] If the Society was ever to flourish, a new order or dispensation would have to be established and the act of regeneration introduced among the Shakers. Believing that "no organs were made to be useless," the Grosvenors envisioned a time "when believers had become pure enough . . . [to] have intercourse, and produce a pure offspring."[28] Even more disturbing to the Shakers was the Grosvenors' claim that they would lead this new order. In 1864 their followers at Harvard, labeled "disorderly progressionists" by the Ministry, announced that Ann Lee was not the much-touted manifestation of Christ's second appearing but merely a "good woman" who, like John the Baptist, had come "to prepare the way of the Lord." According to worldly mediums, Roxalana and Fidelia Grosvenor were the chosen receptacles for the Christ spirit, placing them in a "high station above much order or discipline; and this sacred manifestation is surely to take place this year [1864]." When Shaker leaders responded with some "very plain testimony," the "New Lights," as they were also called, claimed that they were being "persecuted" for their beliefs.[29]

This new order was to be established outside the Shaker community, and to lure recruits, the Grosvenors engaged in aggressive proselytizing. They encouraged women to abandon their Shaker faith as outmoded and viewed apostates as "chosen instruments for the building up of the new work." As leaders in the community, the Grosvenors had easy access to the Shaker sisters, but their success was limited. Their non-Shaker doctrines offended most sisters. But a few, particularly those who were going through a period of doubt concerning their faith or had obligations to family in the world, fell in with the Grosvenors' teachings. Sylvia Persons admitted that the Grosvenor sisters first approached her when she was experiencing a "depression of spirit." They sensed her discontent and used the opportunity to preach to her. She resisted their teachings, but other sisters did not. Some women who were thinking of leaving the Society made the final decision to do so after talking with the Grosvenors. In fact, it appears that Fidelia Grosvenor, while elder sister in the Harvard Church family from 1856 to 1859, was part of a clandestine network of apostates called the "Underground Railroad." Recent apostates kept in touch with people still living with the Shakers through letters, both parties using assumed names. The Shakers involved would sneak off to the post office to retrieve their mail. The contents of the letters are never disclosed, but recipients of the letters often left the Shakers within a short period of time.[30]

It is not clear just when the Harvard Ministry became aware of the activities of the Grosvenor sisters or when those activities started. After she returned to Harvard in 1861, Roxalana told Sylvia Persons "that her ideas had changed, from a virgin life, to a belief that she was to become the first Leader in the Bishopric." The Grosvenors' missionary work probably began at this time as well; records do not indicate any disturbances at Shirley when Roxalana was there. The first mention of the Harvard Ministry's involvement in the controversy appears in its journal for 1862. Two entries for December indicate that Roxalana met with the Harvard Ministry, once to read aloud some of her correspondence. On January 6, 1863, the Ministry had "quite a talk" with Fidelia. The Ministry continued to talk with the sisters, and by May the elders felt that they had "labored" with the Grosvenors as much as was reasonable "and far more than they [the Grosvenors] were pleased with." Indeed, the sisters seemed unable to acknowledge the heterodox nature of their views, and Roxalana insisted that fellow Believers, through ignorance or malice, were misrepresenting her ideas to the Ministry. She even claimed that she and Fidelia were being persecuted for their beliefs, "that the Grosvenors," in fact, "were always persecuted." Despite Roxalana's recalcitrance, the Ministry allowed her to remain in the Elders' Order until the end of 1864, "fearing that she might do more hurt [if she was] displeased [by being released]."[31]

By the summer of 1865 the situation had become intolerable. In July Fidelia left Harvard "in a fit of self will," making her way to Mount Lebanon[32] to lay her complaints before the Central Ministry brothers. The men refused to talk to her and sent two sisters to meet her at the train station; they reported that "she appears to be evil crazy." Fidelia did not return to Harvard, and Roxalana left in August, easing the strain under which Harvard had lived for several years. They moved to Boston where Roxalana took up writing and Fidelia became a "magnetic physician."[33]

Having received only fifty dollars apiece when they left Harvard, the sisters brought a lawsuit against the Shakers in 1871. They claimed that they had been wrongfully expelled from the Society and deprived of the temporal support guaranteed to them in the covenant that they signed when they joined the Church. They took the Shakers to court to recover damages and back wages for services rendered while in the Society.[34]

The Grosvenors had little chance of winning their case. Not only had the Shaker covenant prevailed in a court of law countless times in the past, but claims against other communal societies with similar covenants had also consistently been dismissed by the courts. The case was heard in 1871, and the Grosvenors lost. They appealed, and the case was heard a second time in 1874 before the full bench of the Massachusetts Supreme Court. The Grosvenors lost again. Having left the community, whether by their own choice or by expulsion, the court ruled that the sisters were no longer a party to the covenant and could make no demands against the Shakers.[35] As William Leonard observed, "The battle lay between them & the covenant. That Book defeated them and all broke down."[36]

The Grosvenor affair is interesting in its own right as a heresy case, but it is even more important as an indicator of the state in which Shaker society found itself by the 1860s. Faced with numeric decline and painfully aware of the financial, spiritual, and social problems that close relations with the world had wrought, the Harvard and Shirley Shakers had reached a critical point in their history. The Grosvenor affair resulted from a conjunction of these problems. Many issues that the Shakers had faced throughout their history—sexuality, women's roles, relations with the world, and the parameters of orthodoxy and heterodoxy—came together in the Grosvenor case. Decisions that the Believers made in light of this case were of paramount importance for the future of Harvard and Shirley.

At the center of the controversy were the related issues of sexuality and the role of women in Shaker society. Roxalana and Fidelia, like all Shaker women, benefited from a system which gave them positions of responsibility and encouraged them to develop their leadership skills and their intellect, while releasing them from the daily duties of marriage and motherhood. Both women were capable administrators, and Roxalana was also an intellectual of sorts. The Ministry allowed Roxalana to receive reading material from non-Shaker friends. In 1853 William Leonard touted her abilities as an "English scholar" and noted her high scores on the teaching qualification exams. She also exhibited an interest in Shaker history, collecting testimonies and stories from the first Believers who were still living. The Central Ministry approved of Roxalana's literary exertions, circulating her manuscripts among the Shakers.[37]

As leaders in the communities, Roxalana and Fidelia were also allowed to maintain friendships with the outside world. Roxalana in particular developed close relations with Joseph Tillinghast, Jeremiah Hacker (who referred to her as "darling Sr. Roxalana"), and Harriot Hunt. Hunt, describing Roxalana as "one of the loveliest, noblest women," was "attracted . . . irresistibly" by Roxalana's "deep interest in the sick, her subdued, chastened bearing, . . .her humility." The two were also intellectual equals; Roxalana discussed theology with Hunt, and in return Hunt presumably discussed her own feminist views. Marianne Finch was also impressed by Roxalana, "the beautiful ministress of Harvard," who she claimed was descended from English aristocracy; "and neither, in respect to personal beauty nor dignity of manners, does she disgrace her stock."[38]

Friendship with people of the world was probably the most important factor in the Grosvenors' falling away from Shakerism. Exposed to ideas of free love, spiritual affinities, and women's rights, Roxalana and Fidelia sought to create a new theological system that would solve the myriad of problems that their society faced. Ironically, in order to do this, the Grosvenors were required to attack the very system that had empowered them.

The Grosvenor sisters began by directly confronting Shaker ambivalence about women's roles and female status. Despite the Shakers' genuinely positive view of female nature and the many opportunities the Shaker sisters had before them, the Believers' view of women, by definition, retained a certain ambivalence. Women *had* to renounce biological motherhood to become Shakers. Furthermore, even female leaders, from Ann Lee to the spirit of Holy Mother Wisdom, sometimes qualified their view of women's role in society by falling back on the traditional doctrine of spheres.

The Grosvenor sisters turned the Shaker ideal of women on its head. Roxalana and Fidelia argued that God had created no "useless organs," and that included regenerative organs. Thus, the one function unique to women, giving birth, was no longer condemned as sinful when it occurred in a pure and proper context. The Shakers had often used the metaphor of spiritual motherhood to describe the ideal station of women, but the Grosvenor sisters accepted women as they were created and redeemed the function of biological motherhood. They believed that women could be "pure" and still embrace all of their biological functions.

The Grosvenors' vision of a new dispensation was largely a "female vision." In the new order predicted by Roxalana and Fidelia, men were present mainly as bearers of the "seed." Childbirth, on the other hand, was depicted as a sacred and important duty. Even women who were thought to be too old to bear children would "be aided by the Holy Ghost to conceive the male seed, for holy offspring." Even so, some women "would not be able to help bring in this holy brood; but, there would be no antagonism between the parties."[39]

Unfortunately there is no record of the Grosvenors' plans for their new society beyond the introduction of procreation, and no way to know how far the women would have gone with their reforms. One wonders, for example, if Roxalana and Fidelia wanted to incorporate elements of free love into their community or introduce other measures that equalized relations between men and women. Given Roxalana's close friendship with Harriot Hunt, it would not be surprising to find other aspects of the "woman question" addressed in the Grosvenors' community.

Although their full plans cannot be known, it is apparent that Roxalana and Fidelia aimed their theology at the Shaker sisters. They conducted most, if not all, of their proselytizing among the women; all the testimonies and depositions concerning the Grosvenor case, for example, came from women. The only exception to this generalization is that Roxalana and Fidelia tried to recruit their natural brother Lorenzo to their cause, perhaps hoping that he would be a missionary among the brethren. Lorenzo, however, repudiated their theology of "sexualism," maintaining his staunch adherence to the doctrine of celibacy.[40]

In addition to addressing the important issues of sexuality and women's status, the purified generation controversy spoke to a major concern of the Shaker movement, the dwindling membership of the group. For the Grosvenor sisters the answer to the population problem was simple. Shakerism in its present dispensation was no longer a viable movement; without the benefit of procreation the Shakers would die out. Rather than sit passively and watch this happen, Roxalana and Fidelia, with promptings from the spirit world, reasoned that the time had come to inaugurate yet another dispensation, with new rules and codes of conduct. Their reasoning was not far removed from the Shaker use of progressive revelation to justify

changes in Shaker rules and conduct. What the Grosvenor sisters proposed, however, was so radical that most Shakers rejected their teachings,
choosing to remain celibate and accepting the consequences.

Although very few Shakers actually adopted the tenets of purified generation, there was no consensus among the Shakers about how to address
the needs of their communities. The Grosvenor affair merely highlighted
the fragmentation of Shaker society at the end of the nineteenth century.
"By 1875," notes Stephen J. Stein, "Shakerism had become openly pluralis-
tic." Increased contact with the world had jeopardized the distinctive nature of Shaker society, and factions developed within Shakerism over the
future direction of the movement. The conservatives wanted to reclaim
their sectarian past, while the progressives opted for a more open and ecu-
menical relationship with the world and pushed a "new theology" which
challenged the orthodox Christian beliefs held by many Shakers.[41] The
conservatives resisted the introduction of these new ideas, but the amount
of theological discussion taking place among Believers in the 1860s and
1870s indicates that as far as the leaders were concerned, the future of
Shakerism was up for debate.

Given the state of flux of Shaker society, the heresy of the Grosvenor
sisters becomes more intelligible. Because leaders such as William Leonard
advocated theological debate, and because the Harvard Shakers had a
"democratic" tradition of free speech and discussion of ideas, the apparent
openness of Harvard may have encouraged the women to develop their
ideas. Furthermore, there does seem to have been a stratum of radical thinking at Harvard, evidenced by the letters of Eunice Bathrick (who had en-
dorsed the American costume), a friend of the Grosvenor sisters as well as
of Jeremiah Hacker. In Bathrick's correspondence with Hacker she hints at
ideas that were not generally circulated within Shaker society. Though she
never clearly identifies these views, she informs Hacker that they share
many ideas that surpass the understanding of most Shakers. Indeed, on one
unidentified point, perhaps purified generation, Bathrick noted that the
Shakers felt "delicate about having an idea so foreign from our own advanced among us. . . . There are many things which have been revealed to
some that are far in the future, & should they be made public in our society
in its present condition the knowledge would be productive of evil instead
of good."[42]

In another letter to Hacker, Bathrick wrote that she agreed with much of what he had written to her and Roxalana Grosvenor, but "it will be a long time before [these ideas] will be developed so as to be understood by the body at large; so I forbear many times to express my views on many points lest a misunderstanding should be given." If she felt the situation warranted it, however, she would give her opinion, even if it offended someone, "for I had rather be bound to the car of progression than to a body that has become stationary."[43]

The Grosvenor sisters seem to have tapped into this undercurrent of radical thought at Harvard and tried to use their position among the women to gain recognition of their own theology. Unfortunately for the Grosvenors, most people were not as radical as Eunice Bathrick. Even Bathrick ultimately rejected the Grosvenors' claims and felt betrayed when the sisters left and revealed their preference for "the beggarly elements of this world." Bathrick's response reflected a general trend among the Believers. Rather than experiment with new-fangled solutions to their many problems, the Shakers preferred the comfort of familiarity. Thus, they placed an increasing importance on Ann Lee as a symbol of Shakerism and reiterated the role of celibacy in their collective identity.[44]

The Believers' response to the Grosvenor crisis was critical for the future direction of Shakerism at Harvard and Shirley. Presented with a theological system that could, theoretically, justify a change in Shaker practice and enhance their chances of survival, the Believers rejected this option, choosing instead to be true to the gospel as they knew it. Their decision set the stage for the beginning of the end of Harvard and Shirley.

11

The Dissolution of Harvard and Shirley

THE HARVARD AND SHIRLEY SHAKERS never thoroughly recovered from the economic and emotional upheavals of the 1860s and 1870s, and they watched anxiously as their numbers continued to dwindle and their financial position became more precarious. Their problems were worsened by the concomitant breakdown of the Shaker family unit. The ties that had once bound the Shakers were now becoming frayed and thin, exposing disruptive relationships and discontent among the remaining Believers. Personality conflicts and bickering had always existed in the villages, but they had been hidden within the larger Shaker family and tempered by a shared sense of community. The disintegration of the Shaker family, however, exposed and magnified community imperfections and challenged the Believers' capacity for solving problems relating to communal life.

However beleaguered the Shakers may have felt, the internal buffeting of their communities was not, as yet, apparent to the world, and many outsiders continued to uphold the Shakers as a model of the family ideal. The most avid late-nineteenth-century promoter of the Shakers in this regard was William Dean Howells. In 1875, he and his wife rented a house from the Shirley Shakers for six weeks and visited with the Believers almost daily. The bonds of intimacy that he saw among the Believers particularly impressed him. Writing about his stay in an article for *The Atlantic Monthly,* Howells described a sister's funeral at which many of the Believers reminisced about her life. "Each one who spoke had some special tribute to pay to her faithfulness. . . . What was most observable in it all was the familiar character; it was as if these were brothers and sisters by the ties of nature, who spoke of the dead." [1]

Howells continued to explore the Shaker concept of family in his books. Because, as Joel Jones argues, Howells saw the family unit as a "social sub-system in which . . . self-abnegation takes precedence over self-aggrandizement or self-adoration," he used the Shaker family as a central theme in four novels that were essentially commentaries on marriage and family in America. Although many critics believe "that Howells rejected the Shakers for their failure to adjust pragmatically to the world around them," Jones contends that Howells was more ambivalent than hostile in his feelings toward the group. Moreover, disenchanted with the corruption and selfishness of his day, Howells ultimately developed a "renewed respect for the Shaker ideal." In his last Shaker novel, *The Vacation of the Kelwyns,* "Howells . . . realized that to espouse marriage simply for the sake of marriage, or marriage for the sake of creating families, would do little to further his familial ideal." Howells concluded that Shakerism, celibacy notwithstanding, was one solution to America's social problems.[2]

Although Howells admired the familial ideal that he found at Shirley, as an outsider he did not detect the changes in the Shaker social structure that were having a devastating effect on individual lives. The journal of Olive Chandler, a faithful Shaker who lived the last years of her life at Harvard under a cloud of sadness and anger caused by the treatment to which she was subjected, chronicles the changing nature of life in community. For reasons left unexplained, she did not get along with Eldress Elizabeth Grover of the Harvard Church or Eldresses Eliza Babbitt and Maria Foster of the Ministry. Her relationship with these women was acrimonious at best, and their interaction was fraught with tension. Chandler, for example, suffered from poor health and was partially deaf, yet the eldresses periodically turned down her requests to spend a few curative days at the seashore, even though such trips had been standard practice among the Shakers for years. Finally, in June 1883, her request was granted, and she left that month for a six-day trip to the beach.[3]

Chandler felt betrayed by her elders. In 1882 the Ministry asked Chandler and another sister to sign a deed, evoking bad feelings on all sides. Chandler noted in her journal, "Much censure was proffered for imaginary evils; also false judging through ignorance—But thank God I kept calm through the whole ordeal." The next day, Chandler was removed from her position of responsibility in the herb industry. "This . . . seemed tinched with the same element to push against the wounds and pricks. I felt the waves rear and rise to the highest summit but my barque was not shattered—I braved the current." Chandler was most incensed, however, when her attempts to help others were thwarted. On one occasion, she voluntarily offered to help Sister Lottie Tremper wash the milkpails after the daily milking. For some reason, the Ministry intervened and "wrenched [the pails] out of my hands; and I was deprived of my arrangement to do a little good. I would say it was the most rude treatment that I have experienced since I entered the stage of womanhood." The final insult to Chandler, however, was accorded her in death. It appears that John Whiteley, Ministry elder since 1871, did not attend her funeral on March 10, 1887, believing it more important to conduct his planned business trip to Worcester, Boston, and Providence.[4]

To her credit, Chandler controlled her anger, channeling her emotions into her journal. Others exhibited disruptive behavior openly, and public worship meetings increasingly became the forum for disgruntled Shakers to express their discontent. On May 29, 1881, Leander Persons and another brother interrupted Shirley's morning meeting with a litany of complaints. In January 1882 Lorenzo Prouty of Shirley broke "out in one of his strange & unreasonable freaks . . . which in a great measure spoils the good we have gained." On August 15, 1886, the Shirley Shakers experienced yet another outbreak from Prouty—"Lorenzo & Mary Ann get into a squabble which spoils the meeting."[5]

The dwindling population of Harvard and Shirley magnified such public displays of dissension. In 1880 the entire Harvard community only totaled fifty-four people: thirteen men, two boys, thirty-three women, and six girls under the age of eighteen. Six of the men were seventy years of age or older, and twenty-one of the women were over sixty; fourteen sisters were over seventy years of age. Only seven adults were under the age of forty. Conditions at Shirley were not much better. Only forty people lived there in 1880: eleven men, twenty-three women, and six girls under eighteen. Of the men, only two were young (aged eighteen and twenty-two); the others ranged in age from fifty-four to ninety-five. The women, however, were younger overall than those at Harvard. Ten sisters were between twenty and thirty-five, two were in their forties, and eleven were fifty-eight or older.[6]

In an effort to correct the overall imbalance in population, the Central Ministry supplied members from its own dwindling numbers at Mount

Lebanon. In 1880 Marcia Bullard, from the Lower Canaan family, and Ellen Green, from the Upper Canaan family, "remove[d] to Harvard to be a help there." Bullard became an office sister in the Church family, and Green moved into the Church family as a regular member. In the ensuing years, ten more men and women were sent to Harvard from "the Mount." Stephen Paterwic labels this exchange of members "the Canaan Connection" and notes that by 1898, half of Harvard's adult female population consisted of former Mount Lebanon Shakers.[7]

The importation of outside Shakers did little to resolve the problems of Harvard and Shirley. The imbalance in the sex and age ratios remained, making it difficult to maintain the semblance of a natural family so important in sustaining the Shakers' sense of community. The forced closing of the Harvard Shaker school in 1898 because of low attendance further disrupted the life of the Believers. For years the Shakers had maintained the practice of taking in orphans or indenturing children whose parents could not take care of them. The Harvard Shakers were still doing so in the late nineteenth century, though they had only a handful of children in their care. Town officials argued that these few pupils would be better served by attending the town school, but the Believers disagreed. The Shakers felt obligated to maintain a constant watch over their charges, something they could not do if the children were sent away to school. To resolve this impasse, the Harvard Believers simply sent all school-age children back to their parents or caretakers and only admitted children fourteen or older to their community. "[I]t will be rather unpleasant for us[,]" wrote Maria Foster, "but we shall have to come to it. This is only the beginning of the end."[8]

The influx of outside Shakers also created problems within the communities. Those who had lived at Harvard their entire Shaker lives resented the newcomers, particularly when the latter acceded to positions of power. Annie Walker, who was actually born in the Harvard Shaker village, was very upset by the gradual transfer of power to the "Canaanites." She had held consecutive positions of leadership since 1878, when she was appointed elder sister to work with Eldress Elizabeth Grover in the Harvard Church family. In 1883 a complete change in the eldership occurred. Walker became first in the elders' lot, as did Elijah Myrick, who was also from Harvard. Appointed to work with them, however, were Ellen Green and Andrew Barrett, both from Mount Lebanon. Seven years later, Walker left her eldership to serve as Harvard's trustee.[9]

When Eliza Babbitt, Ministry eldress and native Harvardite, died on February 21, 1900, the Mount Lebanon Ministry appointed Mary Elston of Shirley in her place. Elston also continued to serve as a Shirley trustee, a position she had held since 1889. Margaret Eggleston, a Canaanite transplant and resident of Shirley, became second in the Ministry Order. The appointments shocked some Harvardites. Annie Walker noted in her journal, "Elizabeth E Grover is cut *very much* indeed." Having served as eldress in the Harvard Church family and currently working in the office, Grover thought that she should have received one of the appointments, but whether her anger was directed at Elston or Eggleston is not clear. Elston herself sensed the resentment generated by her appointment and suggested that she serve only two months, most likely thinking that the Ministry could find someone to replace her in that time. John Whiteley concurred with Elston's assessment and felt that she would have trouble retaining her eldership as "[c]onditions in her family are against her." [10]

Mary Elston outlasted such dire predictions, serving as eldress until her death on August 5, 1904. Upon her demise, the Central Ministry tried to balance the situation. They made both Eggleston, who was still living at Shirley, and Annie Walker, who remained at Harvard, Ministry eldresses. Walker also continued to serve as a trustee, while Eggleston and Josephine Jilson became trustees at Shirley. Walker did "not feel as tho she could submite [*sic*] to the change[,] but it is the best they could do for the present as timber is very scarce." [11]

Generational rivalry also created conflict at Harvard and Shirley. The friction generated by the efforts of Elijah Myrick, Harvard Church family elder, to renovate the physically deteriorating village is a case in point. Ultimately, Myrick was able to modernize parts of the village, including the laundry room (which helped the sisters tremendously), but he encountered strong resistance to his plans from the older generation of Harvard Believers. Andrew Barrett, who was helping Myrick as elder brother, commented upon the provincial nature of Harvard society. The village, he noted, has "always been 25 years behind the age there while drift of feeling has been *to lay by money.* Any sensible person would know the truth of this if they should go thro their houses and see the miserable condition of their cellars and drainage. . . . I don't wish to throw blame on any party for this. I look upon it as ignorance in not knowing the physical wants of humanity." [12] Nevertheless, Barrett went on to point out that Myrick had "at times to knock out of the way an old conservative post. . . . [A]ll the bugbears that ignorance could throw in his way has been done. This spirit of jealousy & prejudice . . . is ripe and *flowered* out in the old who call themselves members of the Church." 13

These self-identified "members of the Church" were those people who had lived their entire Shaker lives at Harvard. The oldest ones would have remembered the Era of Manifestations and the exuberant optimism, characteristic of that period, that a large ingathering was imminent. Afraid to move into unfamiliar territory, these "conservative posts" fought the expenditure of money for what they probably deemed unnecessary luxuries. By 1909, however, almost all of these "original" Shakers had died. With the death of Elizabeth Grover from pneumonia on January 20, 1909, Annie Walker noted that she was the only member of the "old family" still alive; "all the rest are new commers." 14

Underlying the personality conflicts and the lack of physical growth at Harvard and Shirley was the ever-present problem of finances. Both villages remained agricultural communities, but they also relied heavily on the sale of particular items—garden seeds and applesauce at Shirley; milk and herbs at Harvard; and brooms, mops, sieves, and "sisters' work" at both villages—to supplement their income. Moreover, the Believers at Harvard and Shirley continued to experiment with economic diversification. They became absentee landlords, buying real estate as far away as Missouri, Tennessee, and Michigan, and also indulged in transcontinental investing. In 1881 the Harvard Shakers became acquainted with Charles M. Hawkes, a New England "mortgage broker with a fair-sized Kansas business," and at some point began purchasing Kansas real-estate mortgages. By 1898, however, John Whiteley had given up on the venture as unprofitable. "We have lost all patience with Kansas Investments," he wrote Hawkes. "Shall send no more money. Make the best you can for us out of it—in some way, but don't ask [for] any more funds." Hawkes was persistent, hounding the Shakers to continue their investments. Finally, in 1901 an exasperated Whiteley wrote Hawkes that the Shakers did not want to invest in any more mortgages. "Is that plain English? *We want to be understood.*" His letter convinced Hawkes, and Harvard and Shirley's venture in Kansas mortgages came to a close. 15

No matter how much the Shakers at Harvard and Shirley tried to maintain their economic viability, however, the lack of able-bodied members who could maintain the villages was a daily reminder of the precariousness of their position. More than ever before, the Shakers were forced to depend on hired help for their livelihood. Hired men became indispensable in running the farms, and even the task of boiling the cider for Shirley's famous applesauce eventually fell to a hired man. The labor crisis was most noticeable, however, when, for the first time, the Shakers hired women to help the sisters. Washerwomen were engaged to help with the laundry, and outside women were often brought in to "cut apples" for applesauce. The Believers went so far as to use an employment agency to find a woman to cook for the hired help, relieving the office sisters of that duty.[16]

The Shakers' increased dependence on hired labor created a dilemma for the Ministry: What should they do about housing the workers? Though reluctant to bring unregenerate members into their communities, the Shakers knew that their survival depended on the daily presence of outsiders. To insure that the hired men were always available, it made sense to house them on the premises. Furthermore, as Shaker families shrank and disbanded, the Believers were left with a large number of abandoned buildings they could not maintain. After much thought, the Ministry decided to offer on-site housing to its hired employees. A typical arrangement was that made between the Harvard Shakers and Michael Donevan, who contracted to work for the Shakers for eighteen dollars a month, free housing, and all the firewood that he could gather in his spare time. Other workers rented Shaker buildings outright, and even the Square House, Harvard's most historically and spiritually significant building, became living quarters for the hired help.[17]

As the Shakers feared, the hired hands created disturbances in the villages. The workers often fought among themselves and left the Shakers without notice when they became disgruntled. The Believers, therefore, were always short of hands, and Whiteley spent a good deal of his time hiring and firing workers and seeking tenants for their buildings. Drunkenness was also a problem. Inebriated workers upset the sisters, and Whiteley fired at least one drunken foreman for "lack of interest" in his duties.[18]

Although the Shakers generally saw hired help as an unavoidable intrusion of the world, on rare occasions they accepted a worker as part of their community. Bliss Goss was one such laborer. He lived with and worked for the Harvard Shakers for many years, appearing in Shaker account books as early as 1876 and as late as 1906. He was hardworking and honest, and in later years he became foreman of the hired men. Unlike most of the help, however, he established personal relationships with the Believers, including the aging sisters, whom he helped with everyday chores, including laundry. The Shakers, in turn, included him in their Christmas celebrations and other events. In 1904 Goss, his daughter Daisy, and Annie Walker took a trip to the Louisiana Purchase Exposition in St. Louis. The Shakers' revealed their high estimation of Goss most fully, however, in 1894 when Andrew Barrett left his position in the Harvard Ministry to return to Mount Lebanon. Rather than seek out another Shaker brother for help, the Believers entrusted Goss with their "temporal concerns," including the sale of Shaker property.[19]

Despite the increased use of hired help and the other financial innovations adopted by the Harvard and Shirley Shakers, both villages were facing the worst economic crisis they had ever known. The problem at Shirley was largely one of leaders who were too old to function effectively. Leander Persons, who had first been appointed a trustee of the Shirley Church in 1843 at the age of thirty, was still the chief trustee in 1881 when John Whiteley had a frank discussion with him about the financial state of Shirley. "Leander opens his financial conditions to me or rather I press him so close he cannot get by telling me. It is very serious—And I do not wonder he should hesitate to tell." When Whiteley examined Persons' account books, he found them "very defective."[20]

Persons remained in office, however, and when the Central Ministry visited Shirley in 1883 it noted the "bad conditions of Society here. Everything, temporal, nearly running down, except some new enterprises of a Stove & grist mill." The next day the Ministry met "the whole family of the Sisters together, and hear[d] their trials, they are heavy." Finally, the Shirley Shakers had had enough, and in 1884 they retired Persons and appointed John Whiteley as the new trustee; Whiteley also continued as Ministry elder. At the time of Leander's retirement, the Shirley Church family debt totaled nearly $8,700, "but," the Central Ministry predicted, "it will overgo this."[21]

Unfortunately, the change in leadership did not improve Shirley's economic situation. In 1886 Whiteley wrote the Central Ministry that "the financial affairs are getting into a serious condition." The Shakers were so low on cash that they did not have enough money in the bank to cover the checks they had written and "had to depend on the kind feelings of the

Bank Officers who have consented to honor [the] checks." Times were hard. "Applesauce has had very limited sale indeed—and we have a larger stock of Brooms unsold than for a long time." The situation was so bad, in fact, that Whiteley was forced to use money given to him as a present (money that should not have been in his possession in any case, according to the rules of joint interest) to purchase flour for the Shirley community.[22]

The combined pressures of dwindling population, financial worries, and the loss of social cohesiveness took their toll on everyone, but the sisters were especially affected by the profound changes in their daily lives. As new leadership positions opened up to the sisters, increasing their power in some spheres, they lost influence in other areas of their lives. Most troubling of all, they began to realize the disturbing consequences that resulted from the deterioration of the bonds of sisterhood.

The most striking change that benefited Shaker women of the late nineteenth century was the power and responsibility they gained by serving as trustees, a position previously reserved for men. Traditionally, the male trustee possessed more power than his female counterpart, the office sister, because he handled all the financial and real-estate transactions of the community while her main responsibility was running the office, a place where the world conducted its business, ate its meals, and sometimes spent the night. Her duties, then, consisted largely of housekeeping and cooking. As the number of capable male trustees dwindled, however, the sisters had to take over the financial affairs of their communities. At Harvard, the sisters' accession to the trusteeship appears to have occurred when Annie Walker became a trustee in 1890 (although Lucy McIntosh was referred to as a trustee as early as 1830). In 1904 Josephine Jilson and Margaret Eggleston became trustees at Shirley, the first time the position had not been filled by at least one man. It is likely, however, that sisters working in the Trustees' Orders at both villages had exercised financial authority even earlier.[23]

All women, however, and not just female trustees, became more involved in their communities. Decisions that at one time had been made only by the leadership were now the responsibility of all "covenant members," most of whom were women. Journals record meetings in which members discussed their family's financial problems, made decisions about selling property, and removed and replaced their leaders.[24] The degree to which women were involved in these decisions is highlighted by an incident concerning the Shirley Church family's use of property. In 1882, the Ministry sisters asked the Shirley Church sisters' opinion about "letting" the family farm "on shares" to a tenant. In lieu of rent, the tenant would return one-third of the farm's profits to the Shakers at the end of his term, keeping the other two-thirds for himself. "The Sisters," Whiteley noted, "have Meetings on the subject—and get some relief to some of their anxious Questions." They were worried that the arrangement would rob them of needed supplies, a problem they were already experiencing with their Shaker brothers. As one sister noted in her journal, "[W]e all think that we don't feel as tho we could come to it without we can have all that we need of everything from the office[,] as the Brethren are taking all means to get any thing away from us. [W]e can get no answer from Leander [Persons] how much nor how little we can have[,] and so it is proposed that we go to the office in the eve and talk with Hamer [the proposed tenant] and find out what we can have and tell what we want." The sisters continued to talk over the "farm affair" for the next several days and concluded that it would be best not to rent the farm on shares; Whiteley concurred with their decision.[25]

In addition to their expanded role as decision makers for their communities, the sisters also continued to play a vital role in the Shaker economy through the sale of "fancy goods." The sisters kept busy, particularly during the winter months, making cushions, baskets, needle books, bonnets, and other items that they sold in stores located in the Church family offices. Harvard's store, run by trustees Elizabeth Grover and Annie Walker, was well known among the local populace. Norbert Wiener, the founder of cybernetics, lived on a farm outside Harvard town as a boy and recalled visits to this store. He particularly enjoyed the "sugared orange peel and enormous disks of sugar flavored with peppermint and wintergreen. These were ridiculously inexpensive, and were the one sort of sweet which our parents allowed us to eat as far as our appetites might go."[26]

In some years the store generated a crucial part of the sisters' income, reflected in an account book kept by the Harvard Church family sisters from 1875 to 1905. Between 1881 and 1885, according to the records, the sisters' expenses were more than their income, sometimes greatly so. In 1881, for example, expenses totaled $90.76 while the sisters earned only $74.64 ($35.89 from store sales, $38.75 from interest). Eighteen eighty-three was the worst year, with expenses of $366.11 and an income of only $171.96. Beginning in 1886, however, the situation improved, and the sisters generally broke even or made a profit thereafter. Store income fluctuated over the years, but the following figures, which represent the percentage of the total income earned by the store for the given year, indicate that the sale of "women's work" often made a substantial contribution to the sisters' total income: 1886, 16 percent; 1887, 31 percent; 1889, 34 percent; 1892, 15 percent; 1894, 41 percent; 1896, 56 percent; 1897, 24 percent. The sisters augmented their store income by the sale of fruit and garden products, knitting, and even old furniture that they no longer wanted.[27]

Another source of income for the sisters was interest on their investments. With the help of John Whiteley, the sisters bought stocks and bonds in various enterprises, including two thousand shares in the North Western Car Company, and waited anxiously for their interest payments. In some years, the income from interest was not insignificant. In 1881, for example, interest of $38.75 accounted for more than half of the sisters' income of $74.64.[28]

Despite the increased power and greater financial freedom that the sisters enjoyed in these later years, their position also deteriorated in many ways. Relations between Shaker brothers and sisters and among the women themselves were fraught with tensions. Suspicions mounted among the sisters as they worried about getting their "fair share" from the brothers. Whiteley himself did not always get along with the women. Though outwardly tolerant, he often made cutting remarks about individual sisters in his journal. In 1882, for example, he recorded that Harvard sister Susan Kendall lay bedridden, completely paralyzed "except [for] her tongue which *still moves*."[29]

The network of sisterhood that had united several generations of Shaker women in common bonds of work and worship also changed as the Shaker family broke down and women lost much of what their predecessors had valued. Personality conflicts had always existed among the Shakers, but the spiritual family, with its emphasis on love and union, had served as a buffer to ease the tensions of life in community. With the collapse of this spiritual family, relationships between the sisters grew strained and divisive. Olive Chandler's experience was only one manifestation of this general breakdown in the quality of women's relationships. Shaker women also lost the support of religious structures, including mediumship, which had empowered earlier generations of sisters. Olive Chandler, for one, tried to keep these channels open. She continued to have visionary experiences and was intent on maintaining contacts with outside mediums. On one occasion, she recalled in her journal, a visiting medium informed Chandler that she (Chandler) was a "developing medium" with the "gift of prophecy." Chandler agreed with this assessment and gave a message to Lizzie Persons, another Shaker sister, concerning Persons's "mediumship for the feminine Deity." Intermittent visionary activity also occurred at Shirley. Joanna Randall, a prominent instrument during the Era of Manifestations, sometimes had visions, and Whiteley maintained his belief in the presence of spirits.[30] Nevertheless, such activity was sporadic, and the closing off of these avenues of communication meant that Shaker women lost not only their role as mediators between this world and the next but also the spiritual power that they derived from that position.

One exception to this general deterioration of personal relationships among women, an exception that illustrates the strength that spiritual ties could possess, was the friendship several Shaker sisters maintained with the Grosvenor sisters, despite the trouble that these two women had caused the Shakers. The women seem to have visited the Believers fairly frequently and were allowed to talk freely with the Shaker sisters. As Ann Elizabeth Persons, a Harvard sister, remembered: "On one of [Roxalana's] visits here, since leaving our society; she remarked that . . . she was a hypocrite, while here, as she did not . . . believe many things, which she felt obliged to assume to believe . . . in order to hold her office. . . . [S]he enjoyed her freedom; for as she expressed it, it was always hard for her to work in the harness, which was put upon her."[31]

In 1877 Fidelia even tried to reenter the community through the back door, so to speak, by applying for a room at the Rural House, the former North family dwelling house that had become a summer resort under the management of John Sprague. Sprague, by order of the Shakers, refused to rent a room to Fidelia, so she spent a few days at Harvard before returning to Boston. Five years later, Roxalana paid a remarkable visit to Harvard. During her stay of several days, she, two female mediums, and Olive Chandler visited the Holy Hill of Zion. Though long since abandoned by the Shakers as a place of worship, these women chose this spot for its association with the spirit world; while there, one of the mediums received a "wonderful message" from the spirits. Surprisingly, Roxalana's visit did not evoke any comment from the Believers and was mentioned only in Chandler's journal.[32]

A few Shaker sisters remained faithful friends of the Grosvenors to the end. Mary Hill attended Fidelia's funeral in Boston on November 7, 1888. She also spent five days in Boston in October 1893 attending to Roxalana, who was gravely ill. On January 9, 1895, Maria Foster recorded Roxalana's death in her journal (Roxalana had died the day before), though she does not say if any Shakers attended the funeral, which was held at Boston's First Spiritual Temple.[33]

These occasional displays of female solidarity were not enough, however, to counter the growing instability of Harvard and Shirley, and while Whiteley tried to remain optimistic about the future, the financial burdens of the two communities were becoming too heavy to bear. Thus, the Shirley Shakers made a momentous decision in November 1899: "For the first time within the memory of the oldest member of the Shaker society, they have decided not to make any of the celebrated Shaker apple sauce this year." A sign that the end was fast approaching, the Shirley Shakers began to dismantle their village, beginning with the sale of two South family buildings in 1900. As Whiteley remarked in November of that year, "Finances look rather Blue—But it is not the first time."[34]

John Whiteley did not live to see the final dissolution of his community. He retired from the Ministry in August 1904 because of ill health; Joseph Holden came from Mount Lebanon to take his place. One year later, on August 12, 1905, Whiteley died, and the spirit of Shirley died with him. In 1908 the state of Massachusetts bought the village, now reduced to four Believers, as the site for the Shirley Industrial School for Boys. The sale netted $43,000, which was "held by Elder Holden in trust, the interest to be used as most needed by any place requiring help." Henry Hollister, the only surviving brother, joined the Hancock, Massachusetts, community. The three remaining sisters—Josephine Jilson, Laura Beale, and Annie Belle Tuttle—moved all their worldly goods to Harvard in January 1909. The change was traumatic. "[T]he poor Sisters feel terribly bad as [Shirley] has been their home so long." Annie Walker noted that they "were almost heart broken[.] Josephine was nearly prostrate[,] has been sick three weeks[.] [T]hey all had a terrible hard time picking up and streighting [*sic*] out things[.] I hope," she concluded, "they will get at home here."[35]

The breakup of Shirley created problems for more than these three sisters. In October 1908, when the Central Ministry came to Shirley to oversee the completion of the sale, they also visited Harvard and, according to Annie Walker, made "quite a disturbance[.] [T]ake Margaret Eggles[t]on to

Lebanon and Mary Ashby goes with her." Eggleston and Ashby later returned briefly to Harvard and then moved permanently to Mount Lebanon
in December 1908. This sequence of events caused a stir among the Harvard sisters because Eggleston took with her $100 of the money raised by
the sale of Shirley, $45 from Harvard's till, and numerous pieces of furniture
and household items. "[T]his is *abominable*," wrote Walker, "when she came
here without a cent to Harvard." Walker, as a trustee, was even more irked
that the deed was done behind her back. Eggleston, she concluded, was "a
perfect robber."[36]

The interpersonal problems of the Harvard residents were exacerbated
by Harvard's own economic plight. In 1894 the village suffered at least
$10,000 worth of damage from a fire that destroyed two barns, the tan
house, the ice house, and the provisions stored within; another fire in 1896
claimed their cart shed and cider mill. They were also plagued over the
years by repeated burglaries, which so exasperated Maria Foster that she
confided to her journal in 1896: "H H Holmns [*sic*] is hung. The burglars
broke into our barn last night, which has become quite a frequent occur-
rence. I wish they were hung too."[37]

The Harvard Shakers responded to their troubles, as Shirley had, by
gradually selling off their land. In 1890 they sold the East family—two
houses, a large barn, and more than one hundred acres of land—to George
Felch for $1,200. In 1912 they sold a parcel of land to the Harvard Medical
Company, and the next year Levi Phelps and his son bought a 150-acre
woodlot from the Shakers for $6,000.[38]

The Harvard Shakers also had to contend with a rapidly dwindling population. Eldress Annie Walker's death in 1912 left only ten women and
three men, most of them old and sickly, in residence at Harvard. The deaths
of Maria Wood, Stephen McKnight, and Louisa Green in 1914 and of Ellen
Green in 1915 further diminished their numbers. Unable to manage their
own affairs, the Harvard Shakers acquiesced as the Central Ministry began
searching for a buyer for the Harvard property and appointed Elder Arthur
Bruce of Canterbury, New Hampshire, to negotiate the sale. Fiske Warren,
a wealthy "social experimenter" with utopian plans of his own, seized the
opportunity to purchase the Shaker village and made an offer. The Central
Ministry accepted, and in 1918, 137 years after Ann Lee first gathered Believers at Harvard, they sold the property to Warren for $60,000 while the
Harvard Shakers stood silently by and watched their world collapse.[39]

If they had no say about the sale of their property, the remaining Shakers did have a choice about their future. They could either move to Mount Lebanon or begin a new life "in the world." Nathaniel Nilant, the sole remaining male Shaker, moved to a local residence, and the Shakers arranged to pay his bills each month. Three sisters also left Harvard for the world. Hattie M. Whitney settled with the Shakers for $1,850.00 and moved to Reading, Massachusetts, to live with friends. She took with her a bed, a bureau, a mirror and chest, a sewing machine, various other pieces of furniture, dishes, and clothing. Mary Jane Maxwell, "a semi-invalid," moved to the Home for Aged People in Brockton, Massachusetts, where the Shakers paid her monthly rent of $20.00. Myra McLean settled for the annual sum of $150.00, paid to her in monthly installments of $12.50, and an assortment of furniture, dishes, and clothing. The Shakers even settled with Bessie Bailey, who was not a member of the society. She took $100.00 and a good bit of furniture, household items, and clothing with her when she left.[40]

The remaining five sisters—Josephine Jilson, Annie Belle Tuttle, Laura Beale, Sadie Maynard, and Lottie Tremper—chose to remain with the Shakers. On July 29, 1918, these women, followed by "five Truck-loads of furniture and personal belongings," arrived at Mount Lebanon, New York, their new home. Jilson, Tuttle, Beale, and Maynard moved to the North family, and Tremper moved to the Church family. The change was traumatic for the sisters, but they coped admirably. Less than a month after their arrival, M. Catherine Allen noted that "the sisters from Harvard are getting nicely settled and have expressed themselves as finding things 'better' than anticipated. It will of course require some time to get the home feeling which permeated the very wall & pavements of places so long inhabited."[41]

The following spring found the sisters still adjusting to their new life. As Josephine Jilson put it, "We are all as well as usual but not quite at home yet." That summer the five sisters returned to Harvard, spending three weeks visiting their friends in the area, but it was clear that the era of the Harvard and Shirley Shakers was past. What remained were memories and, as a result of Jilson's efforts, artifacts that she had begun to collect from the two villages before they disbanded. She and M. Catherine Allen gave many items to Clara Endicott Sears, founder of the Fruitlands Museums. Jilson also started her own museum at the Mount Lebanon North family.[42]

Despite everyone's efforts, not all of the sisters could find a home at Mount Lebanon. The first to leave was Lottie Tremper. According to M.

Catherine Allen's account, Tremper had barely settled into her home at Mount Lebanon when she began corresponding with a male cousin, a widower twice over from Providence, Rhode Island. The two had been out of touch for forty years and reacquainted themselves through letters. When Tremper asked her cousin to visit her at Mount Lebanon, he did, and only a few hours after his arrival they decided to wed. They married in September 1919; Tremper was sixty-two. "Lottie said," wrote Allen, "she knew that she had a much nicer home here than she ever before lived in . . . but that she was used to going somewhere from home nearly every day when at Harvard . . . and that she wanted a freer life." Allen, who thought that Tremper should be satisfied with "her frequent calls at the *three* other families here and occasional auto rides to Pittsfield, with good Sabbath services, phonographs and much time on her hands for walks," considered Tremper ungrateful.[43]

Tremper's own assessment of her situation was somewhat different. After her marriage, she wrote to a friend that she would have remained at Mount Lebanon "if I could feel the freedom [there that] I did in H[arvard], to go where and when I liked, only by asking." The strict control of a fully functioning Shaker community was more than Tremper, used to the laxity of a community in decline, could bear. Her dismay, however, was deeper than that. In the same letter, she wrote that when her future husband visited her at Mount Lebanon she "told him that every thing was dead, and existing only for a short time." Too traumatized by the move to find meaning in her existence, she married and began life over again. In 1926, Lottie Tremper Gillette and her husband moved to Ayer, Massachusetts. Three years later she died of pneumonia and was interred in the Harvard Shaker cemetery, the last to be buried there.[44]

The remaining four sisters—Josephine Jilson, Annie Belle Tuttle, Laura Beale, and Sadie Maynard—banded together as the "Harvard Club," seeking to retain a separate identity within the Mount Lebanon community. Beale left the Shakers in 1924, returned, and left again. She died at Ayer, Massachusetts, in 1945. The other sisters remained committed Believers. In 1925 Jilson was the first "club member" to die and the last Shaker to be buried in the Shirley Shaker cemetery. Tuttle died in 1945 and was interred at Mount Lebanon. It was left to Maynard to experience, for a second time, the closing of a village and the upheaval of moving. In 1947 Mount Lebanon disbanded, and its members, Maynard among them, moved to Hancock, Massachusetts. Six years later she, too, died and was laid to rest there.[45]

Conclusion

SADIE MAYNARD'S DEATH brings the story of Harvard and Shirley to a seemingly abrupt end. What is particularly noticeable as the narrative progresses to its close is the story's "loss of poetry," so to speak, as it becomes difficult, and then impossible, to find the sisters' own words to describe their situation. By the time of her death in 1953, Maynard had been reduced to a statistic. How she felt about her life, her moves, first to Mount Lebanon, then to Hancock, her position as the last of the "Harvard Club," will never be known.

Yet Maynard's death was not really the end of the story of Harvard and Shirley, for the legacy of their inhabitants is embodied in the texts they left behind as well as in the physical presence of their buildings, many of which are still functional. Ironically, the Shirley village is now a prison. After the Shirley Industrial School for Boys was closed by the Department of Youth Services in 1970, one of the vacant buildings was used by a drug rehabilitation program until the Massachusetts Correctional Institute, a "pre-release center for adult felons," opened on the former Shaker site in 1972. Most of the buildings currently in use were built after the Believers left, but eleven Shaker structures (twelve if one counts the Shirley meetinghouse, which has been relocated to the restored Hancock Shaker village) remain; a few, including the Church family office, are still in use. Prisoners today provide the upkeep for the Shirley Shaker cemetery, but the Holy Hill of Peace has been obliterated. A red-and-white-checked water tower now stands where the Shakers once danced and prayed.[1]

The Harvard community met a somewhat different fate, although many of Harvard's buildings, like Shirley's, no longer exist. The North family dwelling/Rural Home, which served at various times as a resort, a sanitarium, and a home for Fiske Warren, was demolished in 1939. The remains of the Harvard East family site fell victim to modernization and to the construction of Route 2, which opened in 1950.[2]

Fortunately, many of Harvard's other buildings and important sites have been preserved. In 1972 the people of Harvard created the Shaker Village Historic District, which now encompasses the cemetery (with its unique "lollipop" grave markers) and what remains of the Church and South family sites. Residents have turned the old Shaker buildings into private homes, except for the Square House, which recently opened as a bed-and-breakfast, while the Harvard Conservation Commission saved Harvard's Holy Hill of Zion from destruction. The commission purchased the Holy Hill and surrounding lands, placed historic markers on the Hill, reconstructed part of the worship site, and preserved the lane, lined by maple trees, connecting the Church family to the feast ground. When the site was dedicated on May 21, 1976, Eldresses Bertha Lindsey and Gertrude Soule of Canterbury, New Hampshire, attended the ceremonies.[3]

Although preserving the physical remains of the Believers' past is important, the legacy of the Harvard and Shirley Shakers transcends the buildings and artifacts they left behind. Indeed, the lasting significance of their story lies in the themes that have wended their way through the pages of this book—the interconnectedness of family, community, and gender in the Shaker, and ultimately, the human, enterprise. As so many reformers knew, changing American society must necessarily begin with changing the family. What those reforms should be, even what constitutes a family, is open to debate. For many nineteenth-century Americans communitarian solutions seemed the answer. Certainly Ann Lee, though not a literate intellectual, promoted a form of communal living as the best way to secure the needs of her people. Later Shakers would refine the Shaker belief that spiritual ties were the only legitimate ties in a family. In 1875, Daniel Fraser and John Whiteley published *The Divine Afflatus*, in which they so eloquently stated that "Jesus Christ laid the axe at the root of the whole genealogical tree, introductory to founding a kingdom organically distinct from the procreative order." Elijah Myrick wrote *The Celibate Shaker Life* in 1889, noting that "the 'new commandment to love one another,' is an elimination from the exclusive family tie, broadening and transferring all the senses, loves, affections and sympathies, to higher and diviner uses." To "live the divine angelic life without distinction of family tie" was a Shaker's ultimate goal.[4]

Within the spiritual families that formed the basis of Shaker community, brothers and sisters worked and worshiped on an equal footing. The Believers' reconceptualization of gender relations, perhaps more than any other aspect of their belief system, reflects the transformative power of living in community. Basing the most fundamental aspect of community—human relations—on the theological principle that God is both female and male, the Shakers worked hard to build a system that valued equally the labor, the religious experiences, and the ideas of the men and women who committed their lives to Shakerism.

Many nineteenth-century intellectuals and reformers, some famous and some not so famous, acknowledged the Shaker experiment with spiritual families and gender equality, and many of them took particular notice of Harvard and Shirley. Their names have appeared throughout these pages: Ralph Waldo Emerson, Bronson Alcott, Charles Lane, Harriot Hunt, Jeremiah Hacker, William Dean Howells. The contributions of most of these people to nineteenth-century American thought are well known. Each critiqued, and often proffered a solution to, the ills of society. What has been less apparent, and perhaps cannot be measured, is the influence of the Shakers on these intellectuals. During the time that these reformers were in contact with the Shakers at Harvard and Shirley, they were engaged with the Shaker practice of spiritual families. This idea of the spiritual family, very apparent in Bronson Alcott's and Charles Lane's writings, most certainly affected the thoughts of those nineteenth-century intellectuals who chose to listen to the Shakers with an open mind. Thus, as odd as the Shakers' contemporaries liked to portray them, it is clear that the Believers were not altogether on the fringes of society. Intellectually, as well as culturally and economically, the Shakers were often at the center of the newest and latest developments in American society. While maintaining their distance from "mainstream" America, the Believers used and strengthened their ties to the larger world when by doing so they could strengthen their own communities. In this way, the Shakers helped to shape American ideas on family and reform as much as they themselves were shaped by outside forces.

Ironically, the one feature of Shaker life that drew them inexorably to the world was the family, or more precisely, the biological family. Despite their protestations to the contrary, biological families were very important to the maintenance of community at Harvard and Shirley. This conclusion was never more dramatically revealed than in the painful decline and eventual closure of the two villages. Not only did the presence of biological families dwindle, then disappear, from these shrinking communities, but even the semblance of a balanced family disappeared. When the structure of the family was compromised, entire communities fell apart. Without the grounding of the family, human relationships and gender interactions broke down, leaving frustration and discontent in their wake.

On the other hand, over the course of their 120-plus years of history, the Shakers of Harvard and Shirley created villages in which life within spiritual families was often better than life in the outside world. This was especially true for women. Attacking the patriarchal basis for most of American family life, the Shakers cleared the way for a new society where relationships were built on love and choice, not duty and obligation, and where traditional female characteristics were upheld as normative for society. Although the Shakers were not successful in obliterating sexism entirely from their communities, their efforts went a long way toward restructuring common perceptions about women's roles in society and about the value of women's lives. Women took on positions of responsibility, made choices about their bodies and their lifestyles, and were empowered by Shaker religious practices. In short, I believe that the majority of Shaker sisters were, indeed, happy. And of all the people who lived in community with the Believers, women benefited the most from life in Shaker spiritual families.

Through the medium of this book I have given these women, and their male counterparts, the space to reflect upon their lives in community. But ultimately, what I have presented in these pages is not merely a story about two villages but a deeper probing into the American consciousness. Just as understanding the Shakers requires examining them in light of the larger American culture, so, too, grasping the full picture of American history and culture necessitates rereading history through the eyes of its many participants. This is easy to do in the case of the Believers because they were an articulate people who left behind an extraordinary amount of material full of their observations on American life and culture. Central to the Shakers' analysis of society was their interpretation of history. They saw history, as did many nineteenth-century Americans, as a cosmic struggle between good and evil. And, like many Americans, they believed that the "good," personified by the United States, was winning. The Shakers, however, conflated American and Shaker history so that the Believers, over all other Americans, appeared as the leaders of the struggle; history, then, became the story of Shakerism's ongoing triumph over misguided secular and religious forces. The Believers also understood history as the reformulation of human relationships resulting from the Shakers' conquest of evil— that is, lust. It is this last component, in particular, that sheds new light on American history.

Relationships are central to understanding the past, whether one is analyzing an individual's relationship to a deity, to the state, to the political hierarchy, or to the localized community. The Shakers understood the relational nature of history, and so they focused their attention on the family. Unintentionally, perhaps, they created a model of enquiry useful to those who seek to understand America's past. As historians of the family know, focusing on the complex network of relationships that binds people to each other unveils an explanation for human behavior that goes beyond impersonal political or economic forces and recovers the "humanity" of history. The Shaker system of spiritual families allows scholars an opportunity to examine such issues in American history on a large scale and within a controlled environment. As the Shakers and their reformer counterparts debated the merits of life in community and life in the biological family, as they analyzed and discussed what constituted the "best" and most "normal" kind of relationship, they touched on issues that have vexed human society for centuries. The Shakers came down squarely on the side of community, and for a time, their way of life appealed to a segment of the American population. Historical circumstances have since changed, and the Shaker system of spiritual families no longer attracts followers as it did a century and a half ago; only a handful of people still live in community as Believers. Yet the Shaker legacy lives on, offering modern-day Americans a glimpse into what many nineteenth-century Americans already understood—the transformative power of communal life.

Appendixes

Notes

Bibliography

Index

APPENDIX A

Membership Statistics

THE FOLLOWING TWO TABLES are a compilation of the original members of the Harvard and Shirley Shaker villages.[1] Because the Believers did not keep comprehensive membership records, I have consulted the available membership rosters and other lists, many of which are incomplete, as well as local town histories and genealogies, to piece together as accurate a picture as possible of the earliest Shaker converts. Where I have not been able to verify a particular relationship but have probable cause to believe that it existed, I have bracketed the information. All members of a nuclear family are listed together under the surname, father first, mother second, and children below and indented. The birthplace, where known, is listed in parentheses next to the surname and refers to all family members unless otherwise indicated. I have also indicated whether each individual was an adult or child at the time he or she entered the community. I have counted the members of the Ministry as Harvard residents since that was their primary place of residence.

Key to Symbols and Abbreviations

*	original members who covenanted together to build the Harvard meetinghouse in 1791
#	heads of families who united at Shirley in 1792
?	fate unknown
ad.	admitted
Chh	Church family
d.	died
f.	family
H	Harvard
l.	left

m.   married
n.d.   no date
r.   removed to
rt.   returned
Sh   Shirley
Sq H Square House

Original Members of the Harvard Shaker Community, January 1791-January 1793

Adams (Chelmsford)
    *Oliver, adult, d. Chh 1804; m.
    Rachel, adult, d. South f. 1796
Adams (Chelmsford)
    Olive, child, l. Chh 1794
Ames [Eames] (Leominster)
    Phineas, adult, l. Chh 1800
    (His mother, Hannah, and his sister, Hannah Ames Knight, lived at Shirley.)
Avery (Hoosack, N.Y.)
    Park, adult, l. Chh 1792
Babbitt (Norton; Tabitha and Sarah born in Hardwick)
    Seth, adult, d. Chh 1826; m.
    Betty [Elizabeth], adult, d. Chh 1825
    —Sarah, child, d. Chh 1853
    —Tabitha [Betty], child, d. Chh 1865
Babbitt (Norton)
    Hannah, adult, d. Chh 1852
    (She was Seth Babbitt's sister.)
Bardeen
    *Thomas, adult, ?
Barrett (Lancaster)
    Sarah, adult, d. Chh 1832
Bean (Canterbury, N.H.)
    Elizabeth, age ?, ad. H Chh 1791, r. Sh Chh 1794, l. Sh Chh 1796
Blanchard (Harvard)
    Jemima, adult, d. Chh 1847
Bridges (Belchertown)
    Jonathan, adult, d. Chh 1833; m.
    Rachel, adult, d. Chh 1820
    —Persis, child, d. Chh 1803
    —Hannah, child, d. Chh 1875

Brocklebank (Rowley)

　　*Asa, adult, ad. Chh 1791, r. Sh Chh 1793, d. Sh Chh 1831

Brown (Weare, N.H.)

　　Mercy, age ?, ad. Chh 1791, r. Canterbury, N.H. Shakers 1793

　　(She came to Harvard from the Enfield, N.H., Shakers. Her brother, Elijah

　　Brown, lived with the Canterbury, N.H., Shakers.)

Burt (Harvard)

　　*Daniel, adult, l. Chh 1795

　　(His mother, Beulah; his brother, Oliver; and James, who was probably his

　　son, lived at Shirley.)

Burt (Mason, N.H.)

　　Oliver, Jr., child, l. Chh 1801

　　(His parents, Oliver and Sarah, and sister, Sarah, lived at Shirley. Daniel Burt

　　was his uncle.)

Clark (Harvard)

　　*Jonathan, adult, d. as Shaker n.d.; m.

　　Mercy, adult, d. East f. 1815

　　—*Jonathan, Jr., adult, l. Chh 1799; rt., d. East f. 1850

Clark (Lancaster)

　　William, child, l. Chh 1797

Cody

　　Abiathar, age and fate ?

Cooper (Cambridge)

　　Sarah Prentice, widow, adult, d. Sq H 1807

　　—*Simon, adult, l. in or prior to 1797

　　—Jonathan, child, l. Chh 1797 to live with his father

　　—*Solomon, adult, d. Chh 1819; m.

　　　　Frances, adult, d. East f. 1806

Cooper

　　Rebecca, age and fate ?

Cooper (Grafton)

　　Abigail, widow, adult, d. Chh 1816

　　—Deliverance, adult, d. Chh 1840

　　—Beulah, adult, d. Chh 1837

Cooper (Harvard)

　　*Samuel, adult, l. n.d.; m.

　　Sarah Willard, adult, l. Chh 1801

　　[—Isaac, child, l. Chh 1800]

　　[—Samuel, Jr., child, l. Chh 1800]

Cox (Cambridge)

　　Lydia, adult, d. Chh 1825

Crouch (Harvard; Mary Brown Crouch born in Rowley; Sarah Stearns Crouch
    born in Littleton)
    *David, adult, d. East f. 1793; m.
    Mary Brown, adult, d. Sq H 1814
    —Elizabeth, adult, d. Sq H 1813
    —*David, Jr., adult, r. Sh Chh 1806, d. Sh Chh 1849; m.
        Sarah Stearns, adult, d. Sq H 1833
    —Daniel, child, ?
    —Levi, child, ?
    —*Jonathan, adult, d. Chh 1837
    —Mary, adult, d. Chh 1826
    —*Caleb, adult, d. Chh 1841
    —Moses, adult, d. Chh 1857
    (David and Mary's daughter, Patience, and David Jr. and Sarah's son, Ephraim,
    lived at Shirley.)
Crouch (Stow)
    Mehitabel, child, l. Chh 1801; rt., d. North f. 1821
Daby (Harvard)
    Susanna, widow, adult, d. Sq H 1815
Dodge (Cambridge)
    Deliteth, adult, d. Sq H 1826
Dodge (Harvard)
    Elizabeth, adult, l. Chh 1800
    Reuben, adult, l. Chh 1799
    John, adult, l. Chh 1795
    [The three were probably siblings.]
Dow (Hamstead, N.H.)
    Daniel, adult, l. Chh 1795
Dwinnel (Sutton)
    *David, adult, d. Chh 1812
    —Elijah, adult, l. Chh 1795
    —Mehitabel, child, l. Chh 1795
    —Humanity, child, l. Chh 1795
    —David, Jr., child, l. Chh 1796
Eddy (Taunton)
    Abiathar, adult, d. Chh 1816; [m.]
    Hannah, adult, d. Chh 1823
Edson (Bridgewater; children born in Enfield, N.H.)
    Hosea, adult, l. Chh 1802; rt., d. North f. 1829
    —Susanna, child, l. Chh 1795

—Bezaleel, child, l. Chh 1801
—Sarah, child, l. Chh 1801
Farnham (Sansonbush, N.J.)
Asa, adult, d. Chh 1796
—Gilbert, child, l. Chh 1799
Farr (Groton)
William, child, l. Chh 1792
Farrar (Chelmsford)
Patty, adult, d. Chh 1844
Finney (Attleborough)
Elizabeth, adult, d. Chh 1813
Fletcher (Mendon)
Elizabeth, adult, d. Chh 1839
(She left her husband and children to join the Shakers.)
Frizzel (Petersham)
*Solomon, adult, d. Chh 1814
*Earl, adult, l. Chh 1799
(Solomon and Earl were brothers.)
Frost (Cambridge)
Joseph, adult, d. Chh 1827
Mary, adult, d. Chh 1801
(Joseph and Mary were siblings.)
Godding (Lexington)
*Henry, adult, d. North f. 1830
Godding (Rindge, N.H.)
Sarah, adult, d. Chh 1835
Grace (Lexington)
David, child, l. Chh 1795
Hammond (Petersham)
Mary, adult, d. North f. 1824
—Thomas, adult, l. 1793
[—Polly, child, l. Chh 1797]
Hawkins [Hankins]
Abigail, adult, r. New Lebanon, N.Y., d. South f. New Lebanon,
N.Y., 1813
Hayward (Sheffield born in Mendon; Lavina born in Upton)
Sheffield, adult, l. Chh 1792
Lavina, adult, l. Chh 1800
(Sheffield and Lavina were siblings. Their parents, Moses and Lois, lived at
Shirley.)

Heath
Isaac, age and fate ?
Heath (Hastow, N.H.)
Jacob, child, ad Chh 1791, r. Enfield, N.H., 1795
Jewett (Littleton; Mary born in Rowley; Mary [wife of Aaron] born in Grafton;
Elizabeth born in Peperell)
*Abel, adult, d. Sq H 1806; m.
Mary, adult, d. Chh 1791
—*Aaron, adult, d. Sq H 1816; [m.]
Mary, adult, d. Sq H 1814
—Abel, child, d. Chh 1859
—Aaron, Jr., child, l. Chh 1800
—Daniel, child, d. Chh 1813
—Sarah, adult, d. Chh 1822
—Elizabeth [Betty], adult, d. Chh 1838
Keep (Harvard; Phebe born in Westford)
Phebe, adult, d. Sq H 1826
—Sarah, adult, d. Chh 1809
—Elizabeth, adult, d. Chh 1796
—Mehitabel, adult, d. Sq H 1822
—Rebecca, child, l. Chh 1800
Keep (Connecticut)
Ruth, adult, d. Chh 1794
Kendall (Woburn)
"Mother" Hannah, adult, d. Chh 1816
(She converted with her family in 1781 or 1782. Most of her family moved to
New Lebanon.)
Lathe
*Ezra, adult, d. North f. 1807; [m.]
Anna, adult, d. North f. 1832
[—Phebe, child, ?]
Lathe
Eunice, adult, d. South f. 1794
Locke
*Benjamin, adult, ?
Longley (Shirley)
Lydia, adult, l. Chh 1796
(Lydia's mother, Lydia, and her sisters, Abigail and Sarah, lived at Shirley.)
Lyon (Worcester; Luther born in Grafton; John and Aaron born in Alstead,
N.H.)

Mary, adult, d. Sq H 1843

—Luther, adult, l. Chh 1801

—John, child, l. Chh 1796

—Aaron, child, l. Chh 1797

(Mary's husband, Aaron, and their daughter, Mary, lived at Shirley.)

Mixer (Westborough; Olive born in Hardwick; Betty born in Phillipston)

Joseph, adult, l. Chh 1801; m.

Olive, adult, l. Chh 1801

—Betty [Elizabeth], child, l. Chh 1801

Perham (Concord)

Dorothy, adult, d. Chh 1838

(Her father, Peter, and her brothers, William and David, lived at Shirley.)

Perry

Darias, age ?, l. Chh 1796

Pierce (Westmoreland, N.H.)

John, child, l. Chh 1795

(His father, Joshua, lived at Shirley.)

Powers

Miriam, adult, d. Chh 1796

Pratt

*Phineas, adult, r. Sh, d. Sh North f. 1828

Prentice (Cambridge)

Deborah Wyeth, widow, adult, d. Chh 1811

—*Daniel, adult, l. Chh 1796

(Deborah's nephew was Joseph Wyeth, and her sister-in-law was Sarah Prentice Cooper.)

Prescott (Westford)

Bethiah, adult, d. Sq H 1813

—Bethiah, see Willard, Bethiah Prescott

—Lucy, adult, ad. Chh 1791, r. Alfred, Maine 1793

—Martha, adult, l. Chh 1795

—Elizabeth, age ?, l. n.d.

—Phebe, age ?, l. n.d.

—Hannah, see Wait, Hannah Prescott

Procter (Chelmsford)

Rebecca, adult, d. Sq H 1833

Proctor

*Isaac, adult, l. Chh 1796

Proctor (Jeffrey, N.H.)

John, child, l. Chh 1801

Rand (Charlestown)
"Father" Eleazer, adult, d. Chh 1808
Robbins (Lexington)
*John, Jr., adult, ?
Sarah, adult, d. Chh 1835
Anna, adult, d. Chh 1852
Ruth, child, d. North f. 1853
Hannah, child, l. Chh 1799
(The five were siblings.)
Robbins (Lexington)
Exene [Xene], adult, d. North f. 1826
Deborah, see Williams, Deborah Robbins
(Exene and Deborah were sisters and cousins of the above Robbins.)
Robbins (Harvard)
Jonathan, adult, l. Chh 1795
Roberson [Robinson] (Petersham)
Oliver, adult, d. Chh 1838
John, adult, ad. Chh 1791, r. Sh 1810, d. Sh Chh 1845
Nathan, age and fate ?
[The three were probably brothers.]
Safford (Harvard)
Sarah, adult, ad. Chh 1791, r. Sh 1793, d. Sh Chh 1838
(Her daughter, Lucy, lived at Shirley.)
Stanhope
Abigail, adult, d. Sq H 1814
Stearns (Littleton)
Ruth, adult, d. Chh 1822
Stevens (Harvard)
John, adult, d. Sq H 1807
Tiffany (Enfield, Conn.)
Daniel, adult, d. Chh 1793
(Tiffany was sent to Harvard from the Hancock, Mass., community in January 1792 to help Eleazer Rand in the Ministry.)
Turner (Petersham)
Mary, adult, l. Chh 1800
Nathaniel, adult, l. Chh 1794
Robert, child, l. Chh 1796
[These four Turners were probably siblings. Sarah Turner at Shirley was probably their sister.]

Turner

John, age ?, l. South house, 1799

Turner

Eben, age and fate ?

Wait (Westford)

Hannah Prescott, adult, ad. Chh 1791, r. Sh Chh 1794, l. Sh 1796

(Hannah's mother was Bethiah Prescott.)

Warner (Lancaster)

John, adult, d. Chh 1834

Levi, adult, d. Chh 1825; m.

Phebe Wilds, adult, l. n.d.

—Elijah, child, d. Chh 1814

(John and Levi were brothers. Their mother, Prudence, and five siblings lived at Shirley.)

Whittemore (New Ipswich, N.H.)

Samuel, adult, l. n.d.

—Deliverance, adult, r. Sh Chh 1793; rt. H 1793, d. H Chh 1827

—Lucy, adult, r. Sh Chh; rt. H 1795, l. Chh 1801

(Samuel's wife, Olive, and three children, Ruth, Nathan, and Rebecca, lived at Shirley. Their daughter Sarah, a Believer, died in 1786 at New Ipswich, N.H.)

Wilds (Shirley)

Eunice, adult, d. Chh 1855

Abigail, child, ad. Chh 1791, r. to Sh Chh 1794, l. 1816

Olive, child, r. Sh 1793; rt. H 1793, l. H Chh 1800

(The three were sisters. Their father and mother, Elijah and Eunice, lived at Shirley.)

Willard (Harvard)

*Isaac, adult, d. with Shakers, n.d.; m.

Hannah, adult, d. South f. 1816

—*Jeremiah, adult, l. Chh 1796; m.

   Bethiah Prescott, adult, d. Chh 1832

—Susanna, child, l. Chh 1800

Willard (Harvard)

Susanna, adult, d. South f. 1792

(Susanna was the sister of Isaac Willard.)

Williams (Lexington; Aaron, Sr., born in West Cambridge)

*Aaron, adult, ?; m.

Deborah Robbins, adult, d. Sq H 1815

—Aaron, Jr., adult, l. Chh 1794

—Deborah, Jr., child, l. Chh 1794

[—Sarah, child, ?]

Williams (New Ipswich, N.H.)

*Nathaniel, adult, l. 1795

Williams

Hannah, adult, d. South f. 1791

Wood (Upton)

Rachel, adult, d. Sq H 1810

Worster (Harvard)

Abijah, adult, d. Chh 1841

(His sister, Molly, lived at Shirley.)

Wyeth (Cambridge)

Joseph, adult, l. Shakers; rt. and d. Sq H 1837; m.

Eunice, adult, rt. home; rt. to H and d. Sq H 1830

[—Jonathan, child, l. Chh 1796]

(Eunice returned home with Joseph to take care of a crippled daughter. She continued to live as a Shaker during the many years in which she lived at home.)

Original Members of the Shirley Shaker Community, 1792–1793

Ames (Leominster)

Hannah, widow, adult, d. Chh 1812

—Hannah, see Knight, Hannah Ames

(Her son, Phineas, lived at Harvard.)

Barrett (Lancaster)

Samuel, adult, d. Chh 1835

Susannah, see Warner, Susannah Barrett

Salome, adult, d. with Shakers 1832

(The three were siblings.)

Barrett (Lancaster)

#Reuben, adult, d. North f. 1833

[Reuben was probably a brother of the above Barretts.]

Beckwith (Lancaster)

#Abel, adult, d. Chh 1812; [m.]

Martha, adult, ?

Bigelow

Elisabeth, adult, l. Chh 1795

Blanchard

William, adult, l. Chh 1796

Blood (Lancaster)

#Ebenezer, adult, ? [m.]

Sarah, adult, d. Chh 1801

[—Lucy, child, l. Chh 1796]

[—Rebecca, child, l. Chh 1796]

Brocklebank

Asa, adult, came from H in 1793, d. Sh Chh 1831

Burt (Shirley)

Beulah, adult, d. Chh 1820

—#Oliver, adult, d. Chh 1834; m.

Sarah, adult, d. Chh 1843

—Sarah, Jr., child, l. 1800

(Oliver and Sarah's son, Oliver, Jr., lived at Harvard. Oliver's brother, Daniel, also lived at Harvard.)

Burt

James, child, l. Chh 1799

[James was probably the son of Daniel Burt, who lived at Harvard.]

Buttrick

Amos, adult, r. H 1813, rt. Sh Chh, d. Sh Chh 1844

Mercy, adult, d. Chh 1813

(Amos and Mercy were siblings.)

Clark (Shirley)

#Daniel, adult, d. Chh 1809; m.

Lydia, adult, d. North f. 1810

—William, child, l. Chh 1832, rt. Sh, d. North f. 1849

—Annis, child, d. Chh 1850

Cook

Jonathan, adult, d. South f. 1809

Cooke

Lyman, age and fate ?

Coolledge

John, adult, l. Chh 1800

—Flavel, child, l. 1801

Coolledge

Elisha, Jr., age and fate ?

Coolledge

Relief, age and fate ?

Crouch
> Patience, adult, ad. Chh 1793, r. H Chh 1795, d. H Chh 1843
> (Patience's parents, David and Mary, and her six siblings lived at Harvard.)

Crouch
> Ephraim, child, l. Chh 1800
> (Ephaim's parents, David, Jr., and Sarah, and his siblings lived at Harvard.)

Dodge
> Sarah, widow, adult, d. South f. 1792
> [—Sarah, child, l. Chh 1796]

Draper (Lyme, Conn.)
> Martha, adult, ad. Sh Chh 1793, r. H Chh 1805, d. H Chh 1838

Druce
> Betty, adult, d. South f. 1809

Hayward [Howard] (Lancaster)
> Moses, adult, d. South f. 1829; m.
> Lois [Louisa], adult, d. South f. 1822
> (Their children, Sheffield and Lavina, lived at Harvard.)

Holt
> Susannah, adult, d. Chh 1848

Houghton
> Ruth Kilbourn, adult, d. Chh 1824
> (Ruth was a sister of Samuel Kilbourn and Lydia Kilbourn.)

Kilbourn (Shirley)
> #Samuel, adult, d. South f. 1807
> —Samuel, Jr., child, l. Chh 1796
> Lydia, adult, d. South f. 1835
> Ruth, see Houghton, Ruth Kilbourn
> (The three were siblings.)

Kinney [Kenney] (Shirley)
> #Jonathan, adult, d. North f. 1825; m.
> Susannah, adult, d. Chh 1830
> —Joshua, child, l. Chh 1801

Kinney
> Lydia, widow, adult, d. South f. 1794

Knight
> Hannah Ames, adult, d. Chh 1826
> (Her brother, Phineas Ames, lived at Harvard.)

Longley (Shirley)
> Lydia, adult, ?

—Abigail, adult, d. Chh 1817

—Sarah, adult, d. Chh 1818

(Lydia's daughter, Lydia, lived at Harvard.)

Lyon

Deborah, adult, d. South f. 1794

—#Aaron, adult, l. n.d.

—Mary, adult, l. Chh 1798

—Ebenezer, adult, r. H Chh 1794, l. H Chh 1801; m.

Matilda, adult, d. South f. 1834

—Hannah, child, d. Chh 1858

(Aaron's wife, Mary, and his sons, Luther, John, and Aaron, lived at Harvard.)

McIntosh

William, child, l. Chh 1797

Melvin [Melven] (Lancaster)

#John, adult, l. Chh 1796

—John, Jr., age and fate ?

Melvin

David, adult, d. Chh 1834

[John and David were probably brothers.]

Melvin

Daniel, child, l. Chh 1797

[Daniel was probably the son of either John or David.]

Merrill

Dorothy, adult, d. Chh 1825

Osgood (Lancaster; Abigail born in Petersham)

#Ebenezer, adult, d. South f. 1831

[—Sarah, adult, d. Chh 1847]

[—Relief, child, d. Chh 1866]

[—Abigail, child, r. H Chh 1814, d. H Chh 1866]

Perham

Peter, adult, l. Chh 1801

—David, child, l. Chh 1801

—William, child, d. Chh 1795

(Peter's daughter, Dorothy, lived at Harvard.)

Phillips (Lancaster)

#Ethan, adult, d. with Shakers 1792

Priscilla, adult, d. Chh 1813

Elizabeth, adult, d. Chh 1816

Grace, adult, d. Chh 1817

(The four were siblings.)

Pierce (Harvard)

#Joshua, adult, d. Chh 1810

(His son, John, lived at Harvard.)

Proctor

Anna, adult, d. South f. 1798

Randall (Shirley)

#Samuel, adult, ?

Reed

Elizabeth [Betty], child, d. Chh 1850

Robbins (Lancaster)

#Eleazer, adult, l. Chh 1796; m.

Martha, adult, d. with Shakers in or before 1796

Robbins (Lexington)

Ruth, adult, d. Chh 1811

(Ruth's sisters, Exene Robbins and Deborah Robbins Williams, lived at Harvard.)

Safford

Sarah, adult, ad. to Chh from H 1793, d. Chh 1838

—Lucy, child, l. Chh 1799

Temple

John, adult, l. Chh 1800; [m.]

Judith, adult, d. North f. 1834

Turner

Joshua, adult, l. Chh 1796

[—Joseph, child, l. Chh 1796]

Turner (Petersham)

Sarah, adult, ad. Chh 1793, r. H Chh 1793, l. H Chh 1794

[Mary, Nathaniel, and Robert Turner of Harvard were probably her siblings.]

Warner (Lancaster)

Prudence Wheelock, widow, adult, d. South f. 1792

—Abigail, adult, d. Chh 1844

—Elizabeth, adult, d. Chh 1818

—Frances, adult, d. Chh 1850

—Lucy, adult, d. Chh 1822

—Prudence, child, d. Chh 1829

(Prudence's sons, John and Levi; her daughter-in-law, Phebe; and her grandson, Elijah, lived at Harvard.)

Warner (Lancaster)

Susannah Barrett, adult, d. Chh 1847

Wheelock (Shirley)

Anna Wilds, widow, adult, d. Chh 1838

—Olive, adult, d. Chh 1841

(Anna's parents were Elijah and Anna Wilds.)

Whitney (Lancaster)

#Samuel, adult, d. South f. 1842; m.

Lucy, adult, d. Chh 1852

—Phebe, age ?, l. South f. 1815

Whittemore (Lancaster; at least some of the children were born in New Ipswich, N.H.)

Olive, adult, d. with Shakers 1812

—Ruth, adult, d. Chh 1843

—Lucy, adult, ad. Chh 1793, r. H 1795, l. H Chh 1801

—Deliverance, adult, ad. Chh 1793, r. H 1793, d. Chh 1827

—Nathan, child, l. Chh 1796

—Rebecca, age ?, l. Chh 1800

(Olive's husband, Samuel, lived at Harvard.)

Whittemore (Lancaster)

Susannah, adult, d. Chh 1854

[Susannah was probably Samuel Whittemore's sister.]

Wilds (Shirley)

Elijah, adult, d. with Shakers 1791; m.

Anna Hovey, adult, d. with Shakers 1804 or 1805

—#Elijah, adult, d. Chh 1829; m.

Eunice Safford, adult, d. Chh 1819

—Anna, child, l. Chh 1800

—Martha, child, d. Chh 1827

—Olive, child, ad. Chh 1793, r. H 1793, l H Chh 1800

—Anna, see Wheelock, Anna Wilds

—Olive, see Wheelock, Olive

—#Ivory, adult, d. Chh 1817; m.

Hannah Estabrook, adult, d. Chh 1826

—Nathan, child, l. Chh 1795

—Levi, child, l. Chh 1801

—Phebe, see Warner, Phebe Wilds

—Susanna, adult, d. Chh 1817

(Elijah and Eunice's daughters, Eunice and Abigail, lived at Harvard.)

Willard (Lancaster)

    #Nathan, adult, d. Chh 1832

Woodward

    Hannah, widow, adult, d. South f. 1798

    —Elizabeth, adult, d. Chh 1845

    —Hannah, Jr., adult, d. South f. 1809

Worster (Harvard)

    Molly, adult, d. South f. 1835

    (Her brother, Abijah, lived at Harvard.)

APPENDIX B

Population Statistics for Harvard and Shirley

TABLE 1

Population Statistics for Harvard, January 1791-January 1793

Females

	Total	Adults	Under 18 in 1791	Age unknown
Came with family and remained	46	41	5	
Came with family and left	23ª	9	12	2
Came alone and remained	18ᵇ	17	1	
Came alone and left	2ª		1	1
Moved to another village (came with family)	5ᶜ	3	1	1
Moved to another village (came alone)	2ᵈ	1		1

ª These figures include those whose ultimate ends are not recorded but who most likely left the community because they disappear from the records.

ᵇ This figure includes those who left the community but later returned and died with the Shakers.

ᶜ Three moved to Shirley, two of whom eventually left, one of whom died there. One moved to Canterbury, N.H., and one moved to Alfred, Maine. Their ultimate fates are unknown.

ᵈ One moved to Shirley and left. One moved to New Lebanon and died there.

TABLE 2

Population Statistics for Harvard, January 1791-January 1793

Males

	Total	Adults	Under 18 in 1791	Age unknown
Came with family and remained	28[a]	25	3	
Came with family and left	36[b]	19	16	1
Came alone and remained	4	4		
Came alone and left	16[b]	7	4	5
Moved to another village (came with family)	2[c]	2		
Moved to another village (came alone)	3[d]	2	1	

[a] These figures include those who left the community but later returned and died with the Shakers.

[b] These figures include those whose ultimate ends are not recorded but who most likely left the community because they disappear from the records.

[c] Both moved to Shirley and died there.

[d] Two moved to Shirley and died there. One moved to Enfield, N.H., and his ultimate fate is unknown.

TABLE 3

Population Statistics for Shirley, 1792–1793

Females

	Total	Adults	Under 18 in 1792	Age Unknown
Came with family and remained	50	45	5	
Came with family and left	11[a]	3	6	2
Came alone and remained	6	5	1	
Came alone and left	2[a]	1		1
Moved to another village (came with family)	6[b]	4	2	
Moved to another village (came alone)	1[c]	1		

[a] These figures include those whose ultimate ends are not recorded but who most likely left the community, because they disappear from the records.

[b] All moved to Harvard. Three of them left; three of them died there.

[c] This woman moved to Harvard and died there.

TABLE 4

Population Statistics for Shirley, 1792–1793

Males

	Total	Adults	Under 18 in 1792	Age Unknown
Came with family and remained	19[b]	17	2	
Came with family and left	21[a]	9	11	1
Came alone and remained	3	3		
Came alone and left	4[a]	1	1	2
Moved to another village (came with family)	1[c]	1		

[a] These figures include those whose ultimate ends are not recorded but who most likely left the community, because they disappear from the records.

[b] This figure includes those who left the community but later returned and died with the Shakers.

[c] This man moved to Harvard and left that village in 1801.

Notes

Shaker Manuscript Collections and Abbreviations

AAS   American Antiquarian Society, Worcester, Mass.

ASC   Andrews Shaker Collection, Henry Francis du Pont Winterthur Museum, Winterthur, Del.

CAN   Canterbury Shaker Village, Canterbury, N.H.

FM   Fruitlands Museums, Harvard, Mass.

HSV   Hancock Shaker Village, Inc., Hancock, Mass.

LC   Library of Congress, Washington, D.C.

NYPL   Shaker Manuscript Collection, Manuscript and Archives Division, New York Public Library, Astor, Lenox, and Tilden Foundations.

NYSL   Manuscripts and Special Collections, New York State Library, Albany, N.Y.

OC   Emma B. King Library, Shaker Museum, Old Chatham, N.Y.

SL   Shaker Library, United Society of Shakers, Sabbathday Lake, Maine.

WC   Shaker Collection, Williams College Archives and Special Collections, Williams College Library, Williams College, Williamstown, Mass.

WRHS   Western Reserve Historical Society, Cleveland, Ohio.

Introduction

1. For a thorough discussion of Ann Lee's life in England and the early years of Shakerism in America, see Clarke Garrett, *Spirit Possession and Popular Religion: From the Camisards to the Shakers* (Baltimore: Johns Hopkins Univ. Press, 1987).

2. Edward Deming Andrews, *The People Called Shakers: A Search for the Perfect Society*, enl. ed. (New York: Dover, 1963); Stephen J. Stein, *The Shaker Experience in America: A History of the United Society of Believers* (New Haven, Conn.: Yale Univ. Press, 1992). Priscilla Brewer's *Shaker Communities, Shaker Lives* (Hanover, N.H.: Univ. Press of New England, 1986) focuses on villages in the eastern states through 1904.

3. John Brenton Wolford, "The South Union, Kentucky, Shakers and Tradition: A Study of Business, Work, and Commerce" (Ph.D. diss., Indiana Univ., 1992); Julia Neal, *By Their Fruits: The Story of Shakerism in South Union, Kentucky* (Chapel Hill: Univ. of North Carolina Press, 1947); Deborah E. Burns, *Shaker Cities of Peace, Love, and Union: A History of the Hancock Bishopric* (Hanover, N.H.: Univ. Press of New England, 1993); Edward R. Horgan, *The Shaker Holy Land: A Community Portrait* (Harvard, Mass.: Harvard Common Press, 1982).

4. Clara Endicott Sears, "The Shakers of Harvard, Massachusetts," (Paper read at the Bay State Historical League, Harvard, Mass., 22 July 1939), SL.

5. The literature on nineteenth-century Boston's significance as a major American city and influential center of culture and reform includes William H. Pease and Jane H. Pease, *The Web of Progress: Private Values and Public Styles in Boston and Charleston, 1828–1843* (New York: Oxford Univ. Press, 1985); Michael Broyles, *"Music of the Highest Class": Elitism and Populism in Antebellum Boston* (New Haven, Conn.: Yale Univ. Press, 1992); Martha H. Verbrugge, *Able-Bodied Womanhood: Personal Health and Social Change in Nineteenth-Century Boston* (New York: Oxford Univ. Press, 1988); Betty G. Farrell, *Elite Families: Class and Power in Nineteenth-Century Boston*, SUNY Series in the Sociology of Work (Albany: State Univ. Press of New York, 1993).

6. I agree with William L. Smith that "scholars have inadequately conceptualized [the incompatibility of family and community] because there is still confusion over the nature of communes and the role of the family within communes" (*Families and Communes: An Examination of Nontraditional Lifestyles* [Thousand Oaks, Calif.: Sage Pub., 1999], 6). It is certainly true that Shakers valued the concept of family even as they rejected biological ties.

7. On the importance of restructuring child care in the empowerment of women, see Muriel Nazzari, "The 'Woman Question' in Cuba: An Analysis of Material Constraints on Its Solution," *Signs* 9, no. 2 (1983): 246–63.

8. Carl N. Degler, *At Odds: Women and the Family in America from the Revolution to the Present* (New York: Oxford Univ. Press, 1980), vii, 74, 144–68, 175. On the patriarchal family, see Lawrence Stone, "The Rise of the Nuclear Family in Early Modern England: The Patriarchal Stage," in *The Family in History*, ed. Charles E. Rosenberg (Philadelphia: Univ. of Pennsylvania Press, 1975), 13–57; and Gerda Lerner, *The Creation of Patriarchy*, Women in History, vol. 1 (New York: Oxford Univ. Press, 1986). Women faced many problems when they challenged the patriarchal family. Norma Basch argues that the major obstacle to nineteenth-century women's attempts to enact married women's property laws in New York was "the determination of the . . . all-male state to preserve the legal aspects of patriarchy in its most fundamental unit of social organization—the family" (*In the Eyes of the Law: Women, Marriage, and Property in Nineteenth-Century New York* [Ithaca, N.Y.: Cornell Univ. Press, 1982], 41, 198). Nancy F. Cott analyzes the same problem in the 1920s, when wives and mothers who worked outside the home were considered "enemies of society" and a threat to patriarchal family authority (*The Grounding of Modern Feminism* [New Haven, Conn.: Yale Univ. Press, 1987], 190–91, 272–73).

9. See Carolyn Johnston, *Sexual Power: Feminism and the Family in America* (Tuscaloosa: Univ. of Alabama Press, 1992); Stephanie Coontz, *The Social Origins of Private Life: A History of American Families, 1600–1900*, Haymarket Series (London: Verso, 1988); Steven Mintz and Susan Kellogg, *Domestic Revolutions: A Social History of American Family Life* (New York: Free Press,

1988); Michael Grossberg, *Governing the Hearth: Law and the Family in Nineteenth-Century America*, Studies in Legal History (Chapel Hill: Univ. of North Carolina Press, 1985).

10. See Linda K. Kerber, *Women of the Republic: Intellect and Ideology in Revolutionary America* (Chapel Hill: Univ. of North Carolina Press for the Institute of Early American History and Culture, Williamsburg, Virginia, 1980); Mary Beth Norton, *Liberty's Daughters: The Revolutionary Experience of American Women, 1750–1800* (1980; reprint, Ithaca, N.Y.: Cornell Univ. Press, 1996); Louis Kern, *An Ordered Love: Sex Roles and Sexuality in Victorian Utopias—The Shakers, the Mormons, and the Oneida Community* (Chapel Hill: Univ. of North Carolina Press, 1981), 30–32; Grossberg, 17–30.

11. Barbara Welter and Nancy Cott were two of the first historians to explicate fully Victorian domestic ideology. See Barbara Welter, "The Cult of True Womanhood, 1820–1860," *American Quarterly* 18 (1966): 151–74; Nancy F. Cott, *The Bonds of Womanhood: "Woman's Sphere" in New England, 1778–1835* (New Haven, Conn.: Yale Univ. Press, 1977).

12. Marilyn Dell Brady, "The New Model Middle-Class Family (1815–1930)," in *American Families: A Research Guide and Historical Handbook*, ed. Joseph M. Hawes and Elizabeth I. Nybakken (Westport, Conn.: Greenwood Press, 1991), 83.

13. Farrell has argued that the separation of Boston's upper-class women into a separate sphere merely "masked" the power of their role as the keepers of kinship networks, strengthening the power and economic functions of the elite family(18–19).

14. "Introduction," in *A Shared Experience: Men, Women, and the History of Gender*, ed. Laura McCall and Donald Yacovone (New York: New York Univ. Press, 1998): 1.

15. Suzanne Thurman, " 'Dearly Loved Mother Eunice': Gender, Motherhood, and Shaker Spirituality," *Church History* 66 (Dec. 1997): 750–61.

16. An important study of the fluidity of public and private spheres is Karen V. Hansen's *A Very Social Time: Crafting Community in Antebellum New England* (Berkeley and Los Angeles: Univ. of California Press, 1994).

17. Donald Yacovone, " 'Surpassing the Love of Women': Victorian Manhood and the Language of Fraternal Love," in *A Shared Experience: Men, Women, and the History of Gender*, ed. Laura McCall and Donald Yacovone (New York: New York Univ. Press, 1998): 195–221.

18. Barry Levy, *Quakers and the American Family: British Settlement in the Delaware Valley* (New York: Oxford Univ. Press, 1988), 6–11, 17–21.

19. Rodney Hessinger, "Problems and Promises: Colonial American Child Rearing and Modernization Theory," *Journal of Family History* 21 (April 1996): 125–43; David Hackett Fischer, *Albion's Seed: Four British Folkways in America* (New York: Oxford Univ. Press, 1989) passim.

20. See Lawrence Foster, *Religion and Sexuality: Three American Communal Experiments of the Nineteenth Century* (New York: Oxford Univ. Press, 1981); Kern.

21. Grossberg, 25, 27.

22. Jean M. Humez, " 'A Woman Mighty to Pull You Down': Married Women's Rights and Female Anger in the Anti-Shaker Narratives of Eunice Chapman and Mary Marshall Dyer," *Journal of Women's History* 6 (Summer 1994): 91.

23. Kathleen Deignan, *Christ Spirit: The Eschatology of Shaker Christianity*, ATLA Monograph Series, no. 29 (Methuen, N.J.: Scarecrow Press, 1992), 56.

24. On the functions of the family, see Michael Mitterauer and Reinhard Sieder, *The European Family: Patriarchy to Partnership from the Middle Ages to the Present*, trans. Karla Oosterveen and Manfred Hörzinger (Chicago: Univ. of Chicago Press, 1982), 73–84.

25. James Whittaker to his relations, 9 Oct. 1785, in [Joseph Meacham], *A Concise Statement of the Principles of the Only True Church, according to the Gospel, of the Present Appearance of Christ. As Held to and Practiced upon by the True Followers of the Living Saviour, at New-Lebanon, &c. Together with a Letter from James Whittaker, Minister of the Gospel in this Day of Christ's Second Appearance, to his Natural Relations in England* (Bennington, Vt.: Haswell and Russell, 1790), 17–24; Edward Deming Andrews, *The Gift to Be Simple: Songs, Dances and Rituals of the American Shakers* (1940; reprint, New York: Dover, 1962), 20.

26. Wolford noted that at South Union, Kentucky, certain families formed "dynasties"(213–21).

27. Rufus Bishop and Seth Y. Wells, eds., *Testimonies of the Life, Character, Revelations and Doctrines of Our Blessed Mother Ann Lee, and the Elders with Her; Through Whom the Word of Eternal Life was Opened in this Day of Christ's Second Appearing: Collected from Living Witnesses, By Order of the Ministry in Union with the Church* (Hancock, Mass.: Tallcott and Deming, 1816), 125; Richard Lovejoy, "Shun Thy Father and All That: The Enthusiasts' Threat to the Family," *New England Quarterly* (March 1987): 71–85.

28. See Gordon S. Wood, *The Creation of the American Republic, 1776–1787* (1969; reprint, New York: W. W. Norton, 1972), 91–124; Alice Felt Tyler, *Freedom's Ferment: Phases of American Social History to 1860* (Minneapolis: Univ. of Minnesota Press, 1944, passim); Ernest Lee Tuveson, *Redeemer Nation: The Idea of America's Millennial Role* (Chicago: Univ. of Chicago Press, 1968), 1–73.

29. R. Laurence Moore, *Religious Outsiders and the Making of Americans* (New York: Oxford Univ. Press, 1986), 208–9.

30. Andrews, *Gift to Be Simple*, 111–12.

31. Eunice Bathrick to Eldress Ann [Taylor] and Eldress Polly [Reed], 1881, OC.

1. Planting the "Gospel"

1. Bishop and Wells, 82–83.

2. Ibid.; Octavo vol., Harvard, Mass., Shaker Church Records,91, courtesy of AAS; "Testimonies And Wise Sayings, Counsel & Instruction of Mother Ann & the Elders, With Some of the Sayings of their Immediate Successors. Gathered from different Witnesses and Records. Collected & transcribed by Eunice Bathrick. Commencing 1869. Nov. 14.," 22, 32, 35, 185–87, WRHS, VI B 10; Stephen A. Marini, *Radical Sects of Revolutionary New England* (Cambridge, Mass.: Harvard Univ. Press, 1982), 90, 93.

3. Bishop and Wells, 85.

4. C. C. Goen, *Revivalism and Separatism in New England, 1740–1800: Strict Congregationalists and Separate Baptists in the Great Awakening* (New Haven, Conn.: Yale Univ. Press, 1962), 210, 314; Isaac Backus, *A History of New-England, with Particular Reference to the Denomination of Christians called Baptists. Containing The first principles and settlement of the country; the rise and increase of the Baptist Churches therein; The intrusion of Arbitrary Power under the cloak of Religion; The Christian Testimonies of*

the Baptists and others against the same, with their Sufferings under it, from the Begining [sic] *to the present Time. Collected from most authentic Records and Writings, both Ancient and Modern.* 3 vols. (Boston: Edward Draper, 1777; Providence, R.I.: John Carter, 1784; Boston: Manning and Loring, 1796), 2: 462; Octavo vol., Harvard, Mass., Shaker Church Records, 252, courtesy of AAS; Henry S. Nourse, *History of the Town of Harvard, Massachusetts, 1732–1893* (Harvard, Mass.: Warren Hapgood, 1894), 255.

5. Backus, 2: 209; Abijah P. Marvin, *History of the Town of Lancaster, Massachusetts: From the First Settlement to the Present Time, 1643–1879* (Lancaster, Mass.: pub. by the town, 1879), 781.

6. Nourse, *History of the Town of Harvard*, 253–54.

7. Thomas Hammond, "Sketches of Ireland, The Square House, Mother Ann, Father William & Father James," 5–7, WRHS, VII B 27; Nourse, *History of the Town of Harvard*, 256–57.

8. Octavo vol., Harvard, Mass., Shaker Church Records, 257–58, courtesy of AAS. On Ann Lee's cooptation of the Irelandites, see Marini, *Radical Sects*, 91.

9. Hammond, "Sketches of Ireland," 8–9, WRHS, VII B 27; Nourse, *History of the Town of Harvard*, 256–58; "A Collection of Harvard Shaker Manuscripts," copies of deeds, 115, FM Reel 1; Folio vol., "Sums [paid] . . . for the square house farm in Harvard," Harvard, Mass., Shaker Church Records, courtesy of AAS; "Circumstances respecting the Square House as related by Br. Abel Jewett, Jonathan Clark Jr & Others," collected and written by Roxalana L. Grosvenor, Sept. 1, 1846, SL.

10. Bishop and Wells, 223–24.

11. Ibid., 224.

12. Ibid., 224–25.

13. Quoted in Backus, 3: 181. On the dispute between the Baptists and the Shakers, see William G. McLoughlin, *New England Dissent, 1630–1833: The Baptists and the Separation of Church and State*, 2 vols. (Cambridge, Mass.: Harvard Univ. Press, 1971), 2: 712–17.

14. On the development of "radical sects" in New England during and after the American revolution, see Marini, *Radical Sects*. He includes a discussion of Jemima Wilkinson, another prophetic female leader, who founded a short-lived group known as the Universal Friends.

15. Amos Taylor, *A Narrative of the Strange Principles, Conduct and Character of the People known by the Name of Shakers* (Worcester, Mass.: printed for the author, 1792), 3, 11–12; Horgan, 24.

16. William Plumer, "The Original Shaker Communities in New England," ed. F. B. Sanborn, *The New England Magazine*, n.s., 22 (May 1900): 304–6.

17. Backus, 3: 180.

18. Thomas Brown, *An Account of the People Called Shakers: Their Faith, Doctrines, and Practice, Exemplified in the Life, Conversations, and Experience of the Author during the Time He Belonged to the Society. To Which is Affixed a History of their Rise and Progress to the Present Day* (1812; reprint, New York: AMS Press, 1972), 325–26; George Faber Clark, *A History of the Town of Norton, Bristol County, Massachusetts, From 1669 to 1859* (Boston: Crosby, Nichols, and Co., 1859), 533–34.

19. Roxalana Grosvenor, "Incidents Related by Jemima Blanchard of her experience and Intercourse with Mother Ann and our first Parents," 26, SL (hereafter cited as Grosvenor, "Incidents #1"); Roxalana Grosvenor, "Incidents related by Jemima Blanchard. Of her expe-

rience and intercourse with Mother and the Elders," 172–73, SL (hereafter cited as Grosvenor, "Incidents #2").

20. Frederic Kidder, *The History of New Ipswich, From Its First Grant in MDCCXXXVI, to the Present Time: With Genealogical Notes of the Principal Families, and Also the Proceedings of the Centennial Celebration, September 11, 1850* (Boston: Gould and Lincoln, 1852), 190–91; Grosvenor, "Incidents #1," 35, SL.

21. Bishop and Wells, 106.

22. Nourse, *History of the Town of Harvard*, 259–62; Bishop and Wells, 114–27.

23. Nourse, *History of the Town of Harvard*, 262–63; Bishop and Wells, 145–54.

24. Hammond, "Sketches of Ireland," 9–11, WRHS, VII B 27; Nourse, *History of the Town of Harvard*, 267; Stephen J. Stein, 24.

25. For a map of Ann Lee's missionary journey in New England, see Stephen J. Stein, 20–21.

26. Marvin, 368–71.

27. Kidder, 189–90, 441–42.

28. "Testimonies And Wise Sayings . . . transcribed by Eunice Bathrick," 160–63, WRHS, VI B 10; Church Family Register, typescript, 62–63, 65, FM Reel 1; Charles Hudson, *History of the Town of Lexington, Middlesex County, Massachusetts, From Its First Settlement to 1868*, 2 vols., rev. and cont. to 1912 by the Lexington Historical Society (Boston: Houghton, Mifflin Co., 1913), 2: 578.

29. Bishop and Wells, 290–91; "Sayings of Mother Ann and the First Elders, taken from Abijah Worster by Thomas Hammond, 1839–1850," 104–6, WRHS, VII B 22.

30. Grosvenor, "Incidents #1," 8–9, 22, SL; Bishop and Wells, 90–91.

31. Ethel Stanwood Bolton, *Shirley Uplands and Intervales: Annals of a Border Town of Old Middlesex County, with Some Genealogical Sketches* (Boston: George Emery Littlefield, 1914), 314.

32. Copy of a letter from James Whittaker to Elijah Wilds, 13 July 1786, WRHS, IV A 19.

33. William Bentley, *The Diary of William Bentley, D.D.*, 4 vols. (Salem, Mass.: Essex Institute, 1905–1914), 2: 149.

34. "Record of the Church of the United Society in Shirley. Commencing—1792," 54, WRHS, I B 62; "Testimonies And Wise Sayings . . . transcribed by Eunice Bathrick," 166, WRHS, VI B 10.

35. U.S. Bureau of the Census, *Heads of Families at the First Census of the United States Taken in the Year 1790, Massachusetts* (Washington, D.C.: U.S. Government Printing Office, 1908), 153, 222–25. The census did not differentiate the ages of females.

36. Marvin, 368; "A Collection of Harvard Shaker Manuscripts," copies of deeds, 115, 144, FM Reel 1; Harvard Church Register, typescript, 62–63, FM Reel 1; Eunice Bathrick, "A Biographical Sketch of Eunice Wyeth," WRHS, VI A 5.

37. Nourse, *History of the Town of Harvard*, 369.

2. Gathering the Believers

1. By this time Niskeyuna, the location's Indian name, was becoming more frequently known by its Dutch name, Watervliet.

2. Stephen J. Stein, 41–49; Andrews, *People Called Shakers*, 54–69; Henri Desroche, *The American Shakers: From Neo-Christianity to Presocialism*, trans. and ed. John K. Savacool (Amherst: Univ. of Massachusetts Press, 1971), 186–92.

3. "A Short Account of the Birth, Character, and Ministration of Father Eleazer and Mother Hannah, by John Warner, Harvard, Mass., 1824," WRHS, VI A 5.

4. Ibid.; Bishop and Wells, 119–21, 158.

5. "A Short Account . . . by John Warner," WRHS, VI A 5; "Incidents Related by some of the Ancient Believers of Their experience & intercourse with Mother and the Elders together with some other Interesting Statements, Collected and recorded by Roxalana Grosvenor," c. 1842–1847, Jemima Blanchard's testimony, WRHS, VI B 9.

6. "A Short Account . . . by John Warner," WRHS, VI A 5; Bishop and Wells, 155–56, 189, 201–2.

7. "Manifest Journal 1791–1806," 19–20, FM Reel 1; Harvard Church Register, FM Reel 1; "United Society of Believers, Shirley, Record of Deaths Previous to the Gathering of the Church, Record of the Gathering of the Church With the Individuals Admitted—Removals—Deaths—Etc." (hereafter cited as Shirley Church Register), CAN.

8. "Items of a Journey to Harvard, Shirley, Lynn, New York etc.," 16 Aug. 1846, WRHS, V B 140.

9. "Manifest Journal 1791–1806," 1–11, FM Reel 1.

10. Ibid.

11. I have left out of the calculations the eleven people at Harvard and the six people at Shirley whose ages are unknown.

12. These figures do not include those Shakers who left Harvard and Shirley and moved to another Shaker village.

13. In my calculations I have included those who had at least one other family member living among the Believers and those whose family relationships were highly probable, but not those whose ages were unknown. Had I included the latter the results would still have been statistically insignificant.

14. Charles Nordhoff, *The Communistic Societies of the United States: From Personal Visit and Observation* (1875; reprint, New York: Dover, 1966), 179–214. See also Stephen J. Stein, 242–53; Foster, *Religion and Sexuality*, 54–58. On the feminization of American religion generally see Ann Douglas, *The Feminization of American Culture* (New York: Alfred A. Knopf, 1977).

15. On the problem of retaining children, especially in the years after 1865, see Andrews, *People Called Shakers*, 191–94; Foster, *Religion and Sexuality*, 237–38.

16. Rosabeth Moss Kanter, *Commitment and Community: Communes and Utopias in Sociological Perspective* (Cambridge, Mass.: Harvard Univ. Press, 1972), 146.

17. Bishop and Wells, 93–98, 114–27, 145–54; "Testimony of Elisabeth Jewett," 4–5, WRHS, VI A 8; "Testimony of Deliverance Cooper," 12–13, WRHS, VI A 8; "Testimony of Nathan Willard," 18–19, WRHS, VI A 8; Kanter, 102–3.

18. Marini, *Radical Sects*, 4–6.

19. Nourse, *History of the Town of Harvard*, 253–55; "Testimony of Abijah Worster," WRHS, VI A 5; "Incidents Related by some of the Ancient Believers . . . recorded by Rox-

alana Grosvenor," testimony of Beulah Cooper, WRHS, VI B 9; Octavo vol., Harvard, Mass., Shaker Church Records, 252, courtesy of AAS.

20. Nourse, *History of the Town of Harvard*, 221; Bathrick, "Biographical Sketch of Eunice Wyeth," WRHS, VI A 5; Wilson Waters, *History of Chelmsford, Massachusetts*, (Lowell, Mass.: Courier-Citizen, 1917), 700; "Testimony of Sarah Burt," 17, WRHS, VI A 8; "Testimony of Elizabeth Woodward," WRHS, VI A 8; "Testimony of Nathan Willard," 18, WRHS, VI A 8; "Testimony of John Robinson," 20, WRHS, VI A 8.

21. Seth Y. Wells, "Testimonies concerning the character and ministry of Mother Ann Lee and the first witnesses of the gospel of Christ's second appearing; given by some of the aged Brethren & Sisters of the United Society, including a few sketches of their own religious experience; approved by the Church," 1827, 63–70, WRHS, VI B 52; Henry S. Nourse, ed., *The Birth, Marriage and Death Register, Church Records and Epitaphs of Lancaster, Massachusetts. 1643–1850* (Lancaster, Mass.: n.p., 1890), 84, 159, 300–303, 305, 307–309, 311, 320, 331.

22. Emil Oberholzer, Jr., *Delinquent Saints: Disciplinary Action in the Early Congregational Churches of Massachusetts*, Columbia Studies in the Social Sciences, no. 590 (New York: Columbia Univ. Press, 1956), 22–24; Rhys Isaac, *The Transformation of Virginia, 1740–1790* (Chapel Hill: Univ. of North Carolina Press for the Institute of Early American History and Culture, Williamsburg, Virgina, 1982), 164–65.

23. Marini, *Radical Sects*, 56.

24. Bishop and Wells, 90; Plumer, 304; Bentley, 2: 149.

25. Marini, *Radical Sects*, 96.

26. Nourse, *History of the Town of Harvard*, 209–10; Jackson Turner Main, *The Social Structure of Revolutionary America* (Princeton, N.J.: Princeton Univ. Press, 1965), 22–23; Robert A. Gross, "Culture and Cultivation: Agriculture and Society in Thoreau's Concord," *Journal of American History* 69 (June 1982): 56–58; Bolton, chaps. 2 and 3.

27. The approximate landholdings of Seth Babbitt and Jonathan Bridges are based on an analysis of copies of "A Collection of Harvard Shaker Manuscripts," copies of deeds, 129–30, 137, FM Reel 1. Evidence that the Willard and Jewett families were large landowners comes from Nourse, *History of the Town of Harvard*, 268; Octavo vol., Harvard, Mass., Shaker Church Records, 255, AAS; Marini, *Radical Sects*, 96; "A Collection of Harvard Shaker Manuscripts," copies of deeds, 116, FM Reel 1; Main, 214–15.

28. Deed from Jonathan and Hannah Searle to Reuben Barrett, 8 Dec. 1772, WRHS, I A 14; "Testimony of Nathan Willard," 19, WRHS, VI A 8; Seth Chandler, *History of the Town of Shirley, Massachusetts, From Its Early Settlement to A.D. 1882* (Shirley, Mass.: pub. by the author, 1883), 675, 680. Evidence concerning the Wilds family comes from Bolton, 185–87, 193, 312–13; Chandler, 268, 523, 675–79; Nourse, *History of the Town of Harvard*, 145, 267.

29. "A Collection of Harvard Shaker Manuscripts," copies of deeds, 116–17, 122, 130–31, FM Reel 1; Marini, *Radical Sects*, 96; Deed from William and Lydia Longley to Samuel Kilborn, 28 Jan. 1794, WRHS, I A 14; Deed from John Wheelock to Ethan Phillips, 24 Jan. 1755, WRHS, I A 7; Asa Brocklebank's Day Book, No. 9, 23 June 1829, WRHS, V B 188; Chandler, 523–26; Main, 82–83.

30. "Record of the Church . . . in Shirley," 55–56, WRHS, I B 62.

31. Sarah F. McMahon, "A Comfortable Subsistence: The Changing Composition of

Diet in Rural New England, 1620–1840," 3d ser. *William and Mary Quarterly*, 42 (January 1985): 54, 56.

32. "Testimony of Abijah Worster," WRHS, VI A 5; Nourse, *History of the Town of Harvard*, 301, 317, 322.

33. Christopher Clark, *The Roots of Rural Capitalism: Western Massachusetts, 1780–1860* (Ithaca, N.Y.: Cornell Univ. Press, 1990), 23–27, 30–38; Bettye Hobbs Pruitt, "Self-Sufficiency and the Agricultural Economy of Eighteenth-Century Massachusetts," 3rd ser. *William and Mary Quarterly*, 41 (July 1984): 337–38; Gross, "Culture and Cultivation," 45.

34. Stephen J. Stein, 45–46; "Covenant of the Church of Christ in New Lebanon, relating to the possession and use of a Joint Interest 1796," WRHS, I B 28.

35. "A Collection of Harvard Shaker Manuscripts," copies of deeds, 116, 127, FM Reel 1.

36. "A Collection of Harvard Shaker Manuscripts," copies of deeds, 119, 131, 140, 144, FM Reel 1; Harvard Church Register, typescript, 63, FM Reel 1.

37. "Record of the Church . . . in Shirley," 29–30, WRHS, I B 62.

38. Kenneth A. Lockridge, "Land, Population, and the Evolution of New England Society 1630–1800," *Past and Present* 39 (1968): 62–80; Robert A. Gross, *The Minutemen and Their World*, American Century Series (New York: Hill and Wang, 1976) 12–13, 79–83, 169.

39. Main, 20–22, 212–15.

40. Christopher Clark, 36.

41. "Aaron Jewett and Seth Babbitt's Book of Accounts in Dollars & Cents, 1799," 3, 31–32, 37–38, FM Reel 4; Lucius R. Paige, *History of Cambridge, Massachusetts, 1630–1877. With a Genealogical Register* (Boston: Houghton and Co., 1877), 516–17.

42. Harvard Church Register, typescript, 11, FM Reel 1; Paige, 516–17.

43. Bentley, 2: 149.

44. Ibid., 2: 150–55.

3. Constructing Community

1. Both Ann Lee and her brother, William Lee, experienced deep emotional and physical anguish, called "bearing," which the Shakers interpreted as vicarious atonement for Believers' sins (Bishop and Wells, 337, 341, 347–48).

2. "A Short Account . . . by John Warner," WRHS, VI A 5; Eunice Bathrick, "An Epic on Our Parents," 1856, WRHS, VII B 26; "Items of a Journey to Harvard," 14 Aug. 1846, WRHS, V B 140. In speaking about his special rock, Rand once told John Robinson that there were times when "if it had been the will of God, he should have been willing to breathe his last there." Robinson recalled that Rand would "go to that rock in the night, when he could not sleep for tribulation, and weep on that rock" ("Sayings of Mother Ann and the First Elders, taken from Abijah Worster," 97, WRHS, VII B 22).

3. "A Short Account . . . by John Warner," WRHS, VI A 5.

4. "Testimonies or the Wise Sayings, Counsel & Instruction of Mother Ann & the Elders With Some of those of their Immediate successors. Gathered from different Witnesses and Records and Written by Eunice Bathrick," 1869, 229–32, WRHS, VI B 11.

5. Calvin Green, "Number of Believers, 1803," WRHS, III A 17.

6. Seth Wells, "Record of a journey from Alfred to Harvard," 29 Aug., 4 Sept. 1822, WRHS, V B 1; "Number of Believers, 1803," WRHS, III A 17; Brewer, *Shaker Communities*, 215; Harvard Ministry to New Lebanon Ministry, 23 Dec. 1833, WRHS, IV A 23.

7. Octavo vol., Harvard, Mass., Shaker Church Records, 127–28, 130–31, 133, 139, 141, 145–46, 150–51, 154, 157–58, 160–66, 168, courtesy of AAS; "Record of a journey from Alfred to Harvard," 8 Sept. 1822, WRHS, V B 1; Harvard Ministry to New Lebanon Ministry, 23 Dec. 1833, WRHS, IV A 23; Brewer, *Shaker Communities*, 215; Joseph Hammond, "Account of the Shakers," in *A Gazetteer of Massachusetts Containing a General View of the State, With an Historical Sketch of the Principal Events from Its Settlement to the Present Time, and Notices of the Several Towns Alphabetically Arranged*, comp. Jeremiah Spofford (Newburyport, Mass.: Charles Whipple, 1828), 211–12; Harvard Ministry to New Lebanon Ministry, 23 Dec. 1833, WRHS, IV A 23.

8. "A *Journal Record* of the South and East Family of Young Believers at *Harvard*; County of Worcester, State of Massachusetts. Containing an account of all the important transactions of said families from the year 1813 of the former, and 1837 of the latter, up to the present time," see "Note" at beginning, WRHS, V B 35; Asa Brocklebank's Day Book, No. 4, 22 Oct. 1810, WRHS, V B 182.

9. Winifred B. Rothenberg, "The Market and Massachusetts Farmers, 1750–1855," *Journal of Economic History* 41 (June 1981): 289, 291.

10. "Oliver Burt's Garden Seed Book, 1805–1807," FM Reel 7; Asa Brocklebank's Day Book, No. 3, 20 Jan., 7 Feb. 1809, WRHS, V B 181; Asa Brocklebank's Day Book, No. 4, 24 Jan. 1811, WRHS, V B 182.

11. Asa Brocklebank's Day Book, No. 3, 25 Oct. 1808, 7 Feb. 1809, WRHS, V B 181; Asa Brocklebank's Day Book, No. 4, 5 Nov., 8 Nov. 1810, 28 Sept. 1811, WRHS, V B 182; Asa Brocklebank's Day Book, No. 5, 23 Feb., 3 Oct. 1815, WRHS, V B 183; Asa Brocklebank's Day Book, No. 10, 10 Oct. 1828, WRHS, V B 188.

12. Henry C. Binford, *The First Suburbs: Residential Communities on the Boston Periphery, 1815–1860* (Chicago: Univ. of Chicago Press, 1985), 30–44.

13. Asa Brocklebank's Day Book, No. 3, 10 May 1808, WRHS, V B 181; "Aaron Jewett and Seth Babbitt's Book of Accounts," 65–66, 90–91, FM Reel 4. It is possible that Benjamin Cooper was an "out family" Shaker rather than a nonbeliever, though I can find no direct evidence of this. Shaker payment of property taxes, however, was a practice maintained for Believers who still lived on their own farms near the Shaker village or lived with the Shakers but maintained private property.

14. Hammond, "Account of the Shakers," 211; Nourse, *History of the Town of Harvard*, 455; "The Shakers in Harvard are building a barn," *The Portsmouth Journal and Rockingham Gazette*, 27 Aug. 1831.

15. "Record of the Church . . . in Shirley," 74–75, WRHS, I B 62; Shirley Church Register, 2, 6, CAN.

16. "Sayings of Mother Ann and the First Elders, taken from Abijah Worster," 87–88, WRHS, VII B 22.

17. Amanda Porterfield, *Mary Lyon and the Mount Holyoke Missionaries* (New York: Oxford Univ. Press, 1997), 32–39.

18. Asa Brocklebank's Day Book, No. 3, entry at beginning of 1808, WRHS, V B 181; Asa Brocklebank's Day Book, No. 4, 22 Oct. 1810, WRHS, V B 182.

19. "Testimonies or the Wise Sayings . . . Written by Eunice Bathrick," 261, WRHS, VI B 11.

20. Asa Brocklebank's Day Book, No. 3, 10 May, 26 May 1808, WRHS, V B 181; Octavo vol., Harvard, Mass., Shaker Church Records, 115, 121, 140, courtesy of AAS; "A *Journal Record* of the South and East Family of Young Believers at *Harvard*," undated entries for 1813 and 1814, 11 June 1815, 5 May 1822, WRHS, V B 35.

21. "A Short Account . . . by John Warner," WRHS, VI A 5.

22. Whittaker to his relations, 9 Oct. 1785, in [Meacham], 23; Grove Blanchard's Journal 1815–1818, 1 Oct. 1815, WRHS, V B 196.

23. Kanter, 70–74, 80, 82, 92, 104–5, 112, 124–25.

24. Joseph Hammond's Day Book, No. 8, 18 Dec. 1826, WRHS, V B 200; Joseph Hammond's Day Book, No. 9, 4 April, 4 May, 12 Sept., 20 Oct., 1 Dec., 8 Dec. 1827, WRHS, V B 201; Joseph Hammond's Day Book, No. 11, 3 Jan., 17 April, 27 May, 30 May, 7 June, 10 June, 17 June, 8 July, 13 July, 15 July, 3 Aug., 14 Aug., 19 Aug., 26 Sept., 30 Sept., 16 Oct., 17 Oct., 18 Oct., 26 Oct., 5 Nov., 24 Dec. 1829, WRHS, V B 203; Harvard Ministry's Journal 1834–1836, 19 Oct., 25 Oct., 27 Oct., 29 Oct. 1835, WRHS, V B 214.

25. Shirley North Family Journal 1809–1836, 17 Sept. 1822, 2 July 1823, 15 Sept. 1825, 10 Aug., 11 Nov. 1826, 12 Oct., 7 Nov., 20 Nov. 1827, 26 May, 30 Aug., 15 Nov. 1828, 14 Jan., 7 Feb. 1829, 3 April, 5 June, 7 June, 20 Nov., 22 Nov. 1830, 24 Oct., 27 Oct. 1831, 19 May, 22 May, 24 May, 27 May, 1 June, 3 June, 28 June, 29 June, 7 July, 8 July, 3 Aug., 26 Nov., 30 Nov., 11 Dec., 12 Dec. 1832, 12 Jan., 24 March, 29 March 1834, WRHS, V B 190; Harvard Ministry to New Lebanon Ministry, 1 May 1831, WRHS, IV A 23; Henry M. Tower, *Historical Sketches Relating to Spencer, Mass.* 4 vols. (Spencer, Mass.: W.J. Heffernan-Spencer Leader Print, 1901–1909) 2: 56–62; Stephen Paterwic, "Necrology for the Shaker Society at Shirley, Massachusetts," *Shaker Quarterly* 20 (Fall 1992): 104–6.

26. Harvard Ministry's Journal 1834–1836, 14 April 1835, WRHS, V B 214; Harvard Ministry to New Lebanon Ministry, 31 Dec. 1827, WRHS, IV A 22.

27. "Testimonies And Wise Sayings . . . transcribed by Eunice Bathrick," 67–69, WRHS, VI B 10; "A Collection of Harvard Shaker Manuscripts," succession of elders, 235, FM Reel 1; "A Collection of Harvard Shaker Manuscripts," succession of trustees, 249, FM Reel 1; Bishop and Wells, 396.

28. Chandler, 675–79; Harvard Church Register, typescript, 3, 62, FM Reel 1; Shirley Church Register, 4, 5, 6, CAN; Asa Brocklebank's Day Book, No. 5, 13 June, 7 July 1816, WRHS, V B 183.

29. "Manifest Journal 1791–1806," 29 Oct. 1794, 2 June 1795, FM Reel 1; "Testimonies or the Wise Sayings . . . Written by Eunice Bathrick," 444, WRHS, VI B 11.

30. "Record of the Church . . . in Shirley," 53–54, WRHS, I B 62; "Items of a Journey to Harvard," 9 Aug. 1846, WRHS, V B 140.

31. "A Short Account . . . John Warner," WRHS, VI A 5.

32. Harvard Ministry to New Lebanon Ministry, 1 Jan. 1825, WRHS, IV A 22.

33. Suzanne Youngerman, " 'Shaking is No Foolish Play': An Anthropological Perspective on the American Shakers—Person, Time, Space, and Dance–Ritual" (Ph.D. diss.: Columbia Univ., 1983), 410–11; Jean M. Humez, " 'Weary of Petticoat Government': The Specter of Female Rule in Early Nineteenth-Century Shaker Politics," *Communal Societies* 11 (1991): 1–17.

34. Octavo vol., Harvard, Mass., Shaker Church Records, 90, courtesy of AAS.

35. Ibid., 72; Harvard [Ministry] to Mother [Lucy Wright], 22 Dec. 1807, WRHS, IV A 21; Harvard Ministry to Mother [Lucy Wright], 2 Feb. 1808, WRHS, IV A 21.

36. Harvard [Ministry] to Mother [Lucy Wright], 22 Dec. 1807, WRHS, IV A 21; Octavo vol., Harvard, Mass., Shaker Church Records, 72–73, 89–90, courtesy of AAS; Harvard Ministry to Mother [Lucy Wright], 2 Feb. 1808, WRHS, IV A 21.

37. Bathrick, "An Epic on Our Parents," WRHS, VII B 26; "A Short Account . . . by John Warner," WRHS, VI A 5; Octavo vol., Harvard, Mass., Shaker Church Records, 77–78, courtesy of AAS.

4. The Boundaries of Gender

1. Karen Armstrong, *The Gospel According to Woman: Christianity's Creation of the Sex War in the West* (1986; reprint, New York: Doubleday, 1987), passim.

2. Bishop and Wells, 310.

3. "A Short Account . . . by John Warner," WRHS, VI A 5.

4. "Testimonies or the Wise Sayings . . . Written by Eunice Bathrick," 283–85, WRHS, VI B 11.

5. Ibid., 279–80.

6. Judith Hoch-Smith and Anita Spring, "Introduction," in *Women in Ritual and Symbolic Roles*, ed. Judith Hoch-Smith and Anita Spring (New York: Plenum Press, 1978), 2.

7. Sally L. Kitch, " 'As a Sign That All May Understand': Shaker Gift Drawings and Female Spiritual Power," *Winterthur Portfolio* 24 (Spring 1989): 5; Sally L. Kitch, *Chaste Liberation: Celibacy and Female Cultural Status* (Urbana: Univ. of Illinois Press, 1989), 40–43, 87–91, 125–41, 174–76.

8. Kern, 133–34.

9. See Janice G. Raymond, *The Transsexual Empire: The Making of the She-Male* (Boston: Beacon Press, 1979), 156–60; Carolyn Heilbrun, *Toward a Recognition of Androgyny* (New York: Alfred A. Knopf, 1973), 3–45; Louis Ginzberg, *The Legends of the Jews*, 7 vols. (Philadelphia: Jewish Publication Society of America, 1925), 1: 66, 5: 88–89; Wendy Doniger O'Flaherty, *Women, Androgynes, and Other Mythical Beasts* (Chicago: Univ. of Chicago Press, 1980).

10. See Mary Daly, *Gyn/Ecology: The Metaethics of Radical Feminism* (Boston: Beacon Press, 1978), 388; Barbara Charlesworth Gelpi, "The Politics of Androgyny," *Women's Studies* 2 (1974): 151–60; Daniel A. Harris, "Androgyny: The Sexist Myth in Disguise," *Women's Studies* 2 (1974): 171–84.

11. Heilbrun, ix-x; Sandra Bem, "The Measurement of Psychological Androgyny," *Jour-

nal of Consulting and Clinical Psychology 42 (April 1974): 162. See also Ellen Piel Cook, *Psychological Androgyny*, Pergamon General Psychology Series, 133 (New York: Pergamon, 1985), 18–33; Mary Anne Warren, "Is Androgyny the Answer to Sexual Stereotyping?" in *"Femininity," "Masculinity," and "Androgyny": A Modern Philosophical Discussion*, ed. Mary Vetterling-Braggin (Totowa, N.J.: Littlefield, Adams and Co., 1982), 170.

12. See Caroline Walker Bynum, *Holy Feast and Holy Fast: The Religious Significance of Food to Medieval Women*, The New Historicism: Studies in Cultural Poetics, 1 (Berkeley and Los Angeles: Univ. of California Press, 1987); Caroline Walker Bynum, *Jesus as Mother: Studies in the Spirituality of the High Middle Ages* (Berkeley and Los Angeles: Univ. of California Press, 1984); Teresa M. Shaw, *The Burden of the Flesh: Fasting and Sexuality in Early Christianity* (Minneapolis: Fortress Press, 1998), 234–53.

13. B. J. Gibbons, *Gender in Mystical and Occult Thought: Behmenism and its Development In England* (Cambridge: Cambridge Univ. Press, 1996); Patricia Crawford, "Divine Androgyny and Female Activism: Gender and Religion in Early Modern History," *Gender and History* 10 (Aug. 1998): 303–6.

14. Richard Godbeer, " 'Love Raptures': Marital, Romantic, and Erotic Images of Jesus Christ in Puritan New England, 1670–1730," in *A Shared Experience: Men, Women, and the History of Gender*, ed. Laura McCall and Donald Yacovone (New York: New York Univ. Press, 1998), 51–77; Mark E. Kann, *A Republic of Men: The American Founders, Gendered Language, and Patriarchal Politics* (New York: New York Univ. Press, 1998), 16–22, 175–77; Yacovone, 195–221.

15. For observations on Shaker androgyny, see Virginia Weis, "Women in Shaker Life," paper delivered at the Bicentennial Conference, Sabbathday Lake, Maine, 1974, quoted in Flo Morse, *The Shakers and the World's People* (1980: reprint, Hanover, N.H.: Univ. Press of New England, 1987), 101; Rosemary Radford Reuther, *Sexism and God-Talk: Toward a Feminist Theology* (Boston: Beacon Press, 1983), 35–36, 60–61, 100–102, 110–11, 127–30, 133; Marjorie Procter-Smith, *Women in Shaker Community and Worship: A Feminist Analysis of the Uses of Religious Symbolism*, Studies in Women and Religion, vol. 16 (Lewiston, N.Y.: Edwin Mellen Press, 1985), 150–51.

16. Benjamin S. Youngs, *The Testimony of Christ's Second Appearing Containing a General Statement of All Things Pertaining to the Faith and Practice of the Church of God in this Latter-day* (New Lebanon, Ohio: Press of John M'Clean, 1808), 9–10, 39, 433, 527, 535–37; Calvin Green and Seth Y. Wells, *Summary View of the Millennial Church, or United Society of Believers, (Commonly Called Shakers.) comprising the Rise, Progress and Practical Order of the Society; together with the General Principles of their Faith and Testimony* (Albany, N.Y.: Packard and Van Benthuysen, 1823), 91–92.

17. [Seth Y. Wells], *Millennial Praises, containing a Collection of Gospel Hymns, in four parts; adapted to the Day of Christ's Second Appearing Composed for the Use of His People* (Hancock, Mass.: Josiah Talcott, Jr., 1813), 51, 73.

18. Youngs, 39–40; Procter-Smith, *Women in Shaker Community*, 150–51.

19. George H. Tavard, "Theology and Sexuality," in *Women in the World's Religions, Past and Present*, ed. Ursula King, God, The Contemporary Discussion Series (New York: Paragon House, 1987), 76–79.

20. Green and Wells, 86, 51.

21. See Robley Edward Whitson, *The Shakers: Two Centuries of Spiritual Reflection*, The Classics of Western Spirituality (Ramsey, N.J.: Paulist Press, 1983), 207–13.

22. Procter-Smith, *Women in Shaker Community*, 99–111, 145–56; Marjorie Procter-Smith, " 'Who do you say that I am?': Mother Ann as Christ," in *Locating the Shakers: Cultural Origins and Legacies of an American Religious Movement*, ed. Mick Gidley with Kate Bowles, Exeter Studies in American and Commonwealth Arts, no. 3 (Exeter: Univ. of Exeter Press, 1990), 86–87; Marjorie Procter-Smith, *Shakerism and Feminism: Reflections on Women's Religion and the Early Shakers* (Old Chatham, N.Y.: Center for Research and Education, Shaker Museum and Library, 1991), 8–12; Stephen A. Marini, "A New View of Mother Ann Lee and the Rise of American Shakerism, Part II," *Shaker Quarterly* 18 (Fall 1990): 97–111.

Etta M. Madden argues that when Ann Lee preached, she did so in a way that subverted the " 'masculine' method of sermon development." Whereas male ministers began with a biblical text from which they derived personal and practical applications, according to Madden, Ann Lee "read" the physical bodies of her listeners, drew a lesson from what she saw, and then used Scripture to back up her assertions, (*Bodies of Life: Shaker Literature and Literacies*, Contributions to the Study of Religion, no. 52 [Westport, Conn.: Greenwood Press, 1998], 38).

23. Bishop and Wells, 21.

24. Ibid., 94–95, 140–42.

25. "The Order & Succession of the Ministry," WRHS, III A 7; Octavo vol., Harvard, Mass., Shaker Church Records, 78, courtesy of AAS.

26. Grosvenor, "Incidents #2," 146–48, SL; "Testimonies or the Wise Sayings . . . Written by Eunice Bathrick" 292–97, WRHS, V B 11.

27. "Testimonies or the Wise Sayings . . . Written by Eunice Bathrick," 290–91, 293, WRHS, VI B 11; Copy of a letter to Abigail Beach from unidentified Shirley Shaker, 2 April 1795, WRHS, IV A 58.

28. Joan M. Jensen, *Promise to the Land: Essays on Rural Women* (Albuquerque: Univ. of New Mexico Press, 1991), 100.

29. Whitson, xi.

30. The following section has been modified from Thurman, " 'Dearly Loved Mother Eunice,' " 750–61.

31. See Kann, passim.

32. Testimony of Abijah Worster, 13 July 1826, WRHS, IV A 5; Testimony of Nathan Willard, 19 July 1826, WRHS, IV A 8; Testimony of John Robinson, 19 July 1826, WRHS, IV A 8; Testimony of Elijah Wilds [1826], WRHS, IV A 8.

33. Bathrick, "Biographical Sketch of Eunice Wyeth," WRHS, IV A 5; "Hymns and Songs of Praise, Prayer and Thanksgiving By Eunice Wyeth. Copied by Eunice Bathrick in the Seventy-Second Year of her Age, 1865," WRHS, SM286.

34. Bathrick, "Biographical Sketch of Eunice Wyeth," WRHS, IV A 5; Harvard Ministry to Hancock Ministry, 21 Jan. 1830, WRHS, IV A 23.

35. Harvard Ministry to Hancock Ministry, 21 Jan. 1830, WRHS, IV A 23. For manuscript collections of Wyeth's hymns, see "Hymns and Songs of Praise, Prayer and Thanksgiving," WRHS, SM286; "A Choice Collection of Eunice Wyeth's Hymns," WC.

36. Daniel W. Patterson, *The Shaker Spiritual* (Princeton, N.J.: Princeton Univ. Press, 1979), 150, 198, 201.

37. "Hymns and Songs of Praise, Prayer and Thanksgiving," WRHS, SM286.

38. Letter from Lizzie, Shaker Village, N.H., to Eunice Bathrick, Harvard, Mass., n.d., *Shaker Manifesto* 12 (May 1882): 113; Letter from Eunice Bathrick, Harvard, Mass., to Lizzie, Shaker Village, N.H., April 1882, *Shaker Manifesto* 12 (May 1882): 113–14.

5. Labor and Gender

1. Edward Deming Andrews and Faith Andrews, *Work and Worship: The Economic Order of the Shakers* (Greenwich, Conn.: New York Graphic Society, 1974).

2. On the Shakers' use of gendered labor, see Priscilla Brewer, " 'Tho' of the Weaker Sex': A Reassessment of Gender Equality among the Shakers," in *Women in Spiritual and Communitarian Societies in the United States*, ed. Wendy E. Chmielewski, Louis J. Kern, and Marlyn Klee-Hartzell (Syracuse, N.Y.: Syracuse Univ. Press, 1993), 133–49; D'Ann Campbell, "Women's Life in Utopia: The Shaker Experiment in Sexual Equality Reappraised, 1810–1860," *New England Quarterly* 51 (1978): 24–27; Foster, *Religion and Sexuality*, 231–33; Procter-Smith, *Women in Shaker Community*, 58–63; Kern, 129–30.

3. Karen K. Nickless and Pamela J. Nickless, "Trustees, Deacons, and Deaconesses: The Temporal Role of the Shaker Sisters 1820–1890," *Communal Societies* 7 (1987): 18–20; Karen K. Nickless and Pamela J. Nickless, "Sexual Equality and Economic Authority: The Shaker Experience, 1784–1900," in *Women in Spiritual and Communitarian Societies in the United States*, ed. Wendy E. Chmielewski, Louis J. Kern, and Marlyn Klee-Hartzell (Syracuse, N.Y.: Syracuse Univ. Press, 1993), 119–32.

4. Alice Kessler-Harris, *Out to Work: A History of Wage-Earning Women in the United States* (New York: Oxford Univ. Press, 1982), 4, 8–9; Jeanne Boydston, *Home and Work: Housework, Wages, and the Ideology of Labor in the Early Republic* (New York: Oxford Univ. Press, 1990), 5, 18–20.

5. Boydston, *Home and Work*, 20–21. See also Jeanne Boydston, "The Woman Who Wasn't There: Women's Market Labor and the Transition to Capitalism in the United States," in *Wages of Independence: Capitalism in the Early American Republic*, ed. Paul A. Gilje (Madison, Wis.: Madison House, 1997), 23–47.

6. Welter, 151–74; Boydston, *Home and Work*, 18–20.

7. Alice Kessler-Harris, *A Woman's Wage: Historical Meanings and Social Consequences* (Lexington: Univ. Press of Kentucky, 1990), 8–12; Sean Wilentz, *Chants Democratic: New York City and the Rise of the Working Class, 1788–1850* (New York: Oxford Univ. Press, 1984), 248–53; Leon Fink, *Workingmen's Democracy: The Knights of Labor and American Politics* (Urbana: Univ. of Illinois Press, 1983), 10–12; Christine Stansell, *City of Women: Sex and Class in New York, 1789–1860* (Urbana: Univ. of Illinois Press, 1982), 105–29.

8. Kessler-Harris, *Out to Work*, 53, 90–101; Stansell, xii–xiii, 68–74, 25–29, 207–9.

9. Stansell, 130–41; Teresa L. Amott and Julie A. Matthaei, *Race, Gender, and Work: A Multicultural Economic History of Women in the United States* (Boston: South End Press, 1991), 109–15. For a now-classic formulation of the argument that skilled workers fought to protect their

status, see John R. Commons, "American Shoemakers, 1648–1895, A Sketch of Industrial Evolution," *Quarterly Journal of Economics* 24 (1909): 39–84.

10. Jensen, 11; John Mack Faragher, *Women and Men on the Overland Trail* (New Haven, Conn.: Yale Univ. Press, 1979), 49–50, 64–64, 168; Sally McMurray, *Families and Farmhouses in Nineteenth-Century America: Vernacular Design and Social Change* (New York: Oxford Univ. Press, 1988), 88, 123; Sally McMurray, *Transforming Rural Life: Dairying Families and Agricultural Change, 1820–1885* (Baltimore: Johns Hopkins Univ. Press, 1995), 72–99, 148–71.

11. Hansen, 7, 9, 18–19.

12. "A Journal kept by Augustus H. Grosvenor on the Church farm in Harvard, 1838," HSV 99785.A4; "A Journal of the domestic work performed by the Sisters in the Church at Harvard. Kept by the Deaconess Commencing Dec. 1st 1833. Book No. 4," HSV 9785.333.

13. Helen Deiss Irvin, "The Machine in Utopia: Shaker Women and Technology," *Women's Studies International Quarterly* 4, no. 3 (1981): 313–19; Andrews and Andrews, 154.

14. See Suzanne Thurman, " 'No Idle Hands Are Seen': The Social Construction of Work in Shaker Communities," *Communal Societies* 18 (1998): 37–40.

15. "Receipes," [24–35], FM Reel 1.

16. Ruth Schwartz Cowan, *More Work for Mother: The Ironies of Household Technology from the Open Hearth to the Microwave* (New York: Basic Books, 1983), 45, 63.

17. Faragher, 50–65; Joan M. Jensen and Susan Armitage, "Women in the Hop Harvest from New York to Washington," in *Promise to the Land: Essays on Rural Women*, Joan M. Jensen (Albuquerque: Univ. of New Mexico Press, 1991), 98–102; Jensen, 186–205, 250; McMurray, *Families and Farmhouses*, 91–93.

18. Hansen, 91–93.

19. Journal [1816–1829], 12 July, 8 Dec. 1827, 4 Feb. 1828, WRHS, V B 197; Journal 1826–1835, 12 March 1830, WRHS, V B 199. On female friendships, see Rosemary D. Gooden, " 'In the Bonds of True Love and Friendship': Some Meanings of 'Gospel Affection' and 'Gospel Union' in Shaker Sisters' Letters and Poems," in *Women in Spiritual and Communitarian Societies in the United States*, ed. Wendy E. Chmielewski, Louis J. Kern, and Marlyn Klee-Hartzell (Syracuse, N.Y.: Syracuse Univ. Press, 1993), 104–13.

20. Hansen, 75–78, 110–11. On the Sarah Cornell case, see David Richard Kasserman, *Fall River Outrage: Life, Murder, and Justice in Early Industrial New England* (Philadelphia: Univ. of Pennsylvania Press, 1986).

21. [Harvard Shaker] Account Book (Listing Things Bought and Sold or Expenses and Income, 1825–1836), FM Reel 4; "Book No. 2, Jan. 1845-June 1852," Jan. 1845, FM Reel 1.

22. [Harvard Shaker] Account Book, Jan. 1829, FM Reel 4.

23. Ibid., May, June 1829, July 1830.

24. Journal [1816–1829], 10 July, 7 Aug., 15 Oct. 1828, WRHS, V B 197; "A General Journal of the most interesting & important occurrences as taken from the Daily Journals of different Authors kept by the Sisters in the Church at Harvard. Commencing January 1st 1828," 15 July 1828, FM Reel 4; [Harvard Shaker] Account Book, May 1831, FM Reel 4.

25. Journal [1816–1829], 15 Dec. 1828, WRHS, V B 197; Harvard Ministry's Journal 1834–1836, 9 Nov. 1835, WRHS, V B 214.

26. Thomas Dublin, *Transforming Women's Work: New England Lives in the Industrial Revolution* (Ithaca, N.Y.: Cornell Univ. Press, 1994), 46–75; Andrews and Andrews, 123–26.

27. Hansen, 7–9, 15–19.

28. Journal [1816–1829], 12 Mar., 2 Dec. 1827, WRHS, V B 197; Journal 1826–1835, 27 May 1827, WRHS, V B 199; Joseph Hammond's Day Book, No. 8, 6 April 1826, WRHS, V B 200; Jane Freeman Crosthwaite, "Polly Reed: Shaker Artist and Minister" (Paper delivered at the spring meeting of the American Society of Church History, Williamsburg, Virginia, 2 April 1993).

29. "Visions, Spirit Communications, Religious Experience, Narrative Pieces, Poems, And Sketches from different Authors Gathered and Recorded by Eunice Bathrick. 1850," 127–29, ASC.

30. "The Physician's Journal or an Account of the Sickness in the Society at Harvard, No. 2. Commencing Jan. 1st 1834," WRHS, V B 41; Isaac Newton Youngs, "A Concise View of the Church of God and of Christ on Earth, Having Its Foundation in the Faith of Christ's First and Second Appearing, New Lebanon, 1856. 1860," 273, ASC.

31. Journal [1816–1829], 19 Dec. 1825, 18 March 1827, WRHS, V B 197; Joseph Hammond's Day Book, No. 8, 25 April, 24 Sept. 1826, WRHS, V B 200; Joseph Hammond's Day Book, No. 9, 1 Nov. 1827, WRHS, V B 201; Joseph Hammond's Day Book, No. 10, 22 Oct. 1828, WRHS, V B 202; Joseph Hammond's Day Book, No. 11, 13 Jan., 13 Feb. 1829, 27 May, 31 May 1830, WRHS, V B 203; Joseph Hammond's Day Book, No. 12, 30 Dec. 1830, 19 Feb. 1831, WRHS, V B 204; Joseph Hammond's Day Book, No. 13, 22 Oct. 1831, WRHS, V B 205; Joseph Hammond's Day Book, No. 15, 14 Sept. 1834, WRHS, V B 207.

32. On the rigors and dangers of heroic medicine, see Sarah Stage, *Female Complaints: Lydia Pinkham and the Business of Women's Medicine* (New York: W. W. Norton, 1979), 45–63; William G. Rothstein, *American Physicians in the Nineteenth Century: From Sects to Science* (Baltimore: Johns Hopkins Univ. Press, 1972), 42–55; Martin Kaufman, *Homeopathy in America: The Rise and Fall of a Medical Heresy* (Baltimore: Johns Hopkins Univ. Press, 1971), 1–14.

33. Kaufman, 17–19; Stage, 52–55; Rothstein, 159–60.

34. Stage, 53–54; Kaufman, 21.

35. Journal [1816–1829], 20 Nov., 5 Dec. 1827, WRHS, V B 197; Journal 1826–1835, 4 Dec. 1827, WRHS, V B 199.

36. Journal [1816–1829], 5 Dec. 1827, WRHS, V B 197; Joseph Hammond's Day Book, No. 9, 25 Nov., 28 Nov. 1827, WRHS, V B 201; Joseph Hammond's Day Book, No. 11, 24 Jan., 23 Aug. 1829, WRHS, V B 203; Joseph Hammond's Day Book, No. 13, 3 Dec., 7 Dec., 13 Dec. 1831 through 2 Jan. 1832, 7 Jan., 9 Jan. 1832, WRHS, V B 205.

6. Creating an Identity

1. Grove Blanchard's Journal, 1815–1818, 21 April, 18 Aug. 1816, WRHS, V B 196; "A Short Account," WRHS, VI A 5; Asa Brocklebank's Day Book, No. 5, 18 Aug. 1816, WRHS, V B 183.

2. "Collection of Harvard Shaker Manuscripts," succession of ministry, 221–23, FM Reel 1; Harvard Church Records, typescript, 36, FM Reel 1.

3. "Sayings of Mother Ann and the First Elders, taken from Abijah Worster," 20, 22, 29, 45–46, WRHS, VII B 22; "Sayings of Elder John taken down by Susan Channel and Sally Loomis," 2 April 1825, WRHS, VII B 18.

4. "Circular Epistle Concerning a Revision of the general Covenant, Sept. 1829," LC, cont. 5, reel 5, item 89.

5. Rufus Bishop to Elder Ebenezer, Eldress Ruth, and Sister Asenath, 14 July 1828, WRHS, IV A 22; Rufus Bishop to New Lebanon Ministry, 4 Aug. 1828, WRHS, IV A 22; Harvard Ministry's Journal 1818–1830, 9 July, 17 July, 19 July, 1 Aug., 1 Oct. 1828, WRHS, V B 37.

6. "Circular Epistle," LC, cont. 5, reel 5, item 89.

7. Amy Bess Miller, *Shaker Herbs: A History and a Compendium* (New York: Clarkson N. Potter, 1976), 64–65, 75–76; "Garden seeds raised at Shirley and sold by Oliver Burt," 14 Feb. 1811, WC; [Harvard Shaker] Account Book, FM Reel 4; Nourse, *History of the Town of Harvard*, 455.

8. "Sayings of Elder John taken down by Susan Channel and Sally Loomis," 2 April 1825, WRHS, VII B 18; Joseph Hammond's Day Book, No. 8, 26 Dec. 1826, WRHS, V B 200; Joseph Hammond's Day Book, No. 15, 3 Nov. 1834, WRHS, V B 207; Joseph Hammond's Day Book, No. 17, 22 June, 6 Aug., 21 Aug., 31 Aug. 1835, WRHS, V B 209; Joseph Hammond's Day Book, No. 18, 10 June, 14 June, 15 June, 15 July 1836, WRHS, V B 210. See also Asa Brocklebank's daybooks, WRHS, V B 181–89.

9. Stephen Nissenbaum, *Sex, Diet, and Debility in Jacksonian America*, Contributions in Medical History, no. 4 (Westport, Conn.: Greenwood Press, 1980), 13–14, 30–32, 35, 98–101, 105–21; Richard Harrison Shryock, "Sylvester Graham and the Popular Health Movement, 1830–1870," in *Medicine in America: Historical Essays*, by Richard Harrison Shryock (Baltimore: Johns Hopkins Univ. Press, 1966), 111–25.

10. Harvard Ministry to New Lebanon Ministry, 4 March 1828, WRHS, IV A 58; Joseph Hammond's Day Book, No. 15, 11 Feb., 6 Nov. 1834, WRHS, V B 207; Joseph Hammond's Day book, No. 16, 6 Nov. 1834, WRHS, V B 208; Harvard Ministry's Journal 1834–1836, 20 April, 27 April, 8 June 1835, 20 May 1836, WRHS, V B 214; Journal 1826–1835, 4 May 1835, WRHS, V B 199; Philemon Stewart's Daily Journal, No. 3, 6 Sept. 1835, WRHS, V B 130; "Anonymous Journal, Shirley, 1835–1849," 19 Jan., 20 Jan., 21 Jan. 1839, WRHS, V B 215.

For injunctions against alcohol, see Asa Brocklebank's Day Book, No. 8, 28 Feb., 1 March 1828, WRHS, V B 187; Joseph Hammond's Day Book, No. 9, 30 Oct. 1827, WRHS, V B 201; Journal, 1816–1829, 29 Nov. 1827, 25 Feb. 1828, WRHS, V B 197; Joseph Hammond's Day Book, No. 18, 6 July 1836, WRHS, V B 210; Harvard Ministry's Journal 1834–1836, 4 July, 6 July, 11 Aug. 1836, WRHS, V B 214.

11. "Sayings of Mother Ann and the First Elders, taken from Abijah Worster," 20, 29, 45–46, 62, WRHS, VII B 22.

12. Harvard Ministry to New Lebanon Ministry, 4 Aug. 1825, WRHS, IV A 22; "Account of the Persecution at Harvard in the Year 1825," 9, ASC; Harvard Ministry to New Lebanon Ministry, 30 April 1826, WRHS, IV A 22; Harvard Ministry to New Lebanon Ministry, 13 May 1826, WRHS, IV A 22; "Trial of the Shakers," *Berkshire Star* 37: (1), 18 May 1826, reprinted from the *Worcester Spy*. The Shakers considered this account the most accurate and complete (Harvard Ministry to New Lebanon Ministry, 13 May 1826, WRHS, IV A 22).

Seth Babbitt died at the Square House on November 25, 1826, aged sixty-nine, and was buried in the Harvard Shaker cemetery ("Names of those interred in Harvard burying ground," 56, WRHS, III A 11).

13. Harvard Church Records, typescript, 5, FM Reel 1; "A *Journal Record* of the South and East Family of Young Believers at *Harvard*," note at the front of the journal, WRHS, V B 35; "Account of the Persecution at Harvard in the Year 1825," 1, ASC.

14. "Account of the Persecution at Harvard in the Year 1825," 2–5, ASC; "Trial of the Shakers," *Berkshire Star.*

15. Norman Dain, *Concepts of Insanity in the United States, 1789–1865* (New Brunswick, N.J.: Rutgers Univ. Press, 1964), 12–13, 21–25, 43–45; Gerald Grob, *Mental Illness and American Society, 1875–1940* (Princeton, N.J.: Princeton Univ. Press, 1983), 17, 34–36.

16. Harvard Ministry to New Lebanon Ministry, 30 April 1826, WRHS, IV A 22; Harvard Ministry's Journal 1834–1836, 11 Aug. 1835, WRHS, V B 214; Joseph Hammond's Day Book, No. 12, 14 Dec. 1830, 27 Jan. 1831, WRHS, V B 204; D. Hamilton Hurd, comp., *History of Middlesex County, Massachusetts, with Biographical Sketches of Many of Its Pioneers and Prominent Men*, 3 vols. (Philadelphia: J. W. Lewis and Co., 1890), 1: 549.

17. Harvard Ministry's Journal 1818–1830, 26 June, 28 June, 29 June, 1 July, 10 Aug. 1828, WRHS, V B 37; John Warner to New Lebanon Ministry, 17 Jan. 1829, WRHS, IV A 22; Rufus Bishop to Elder Ebenezer, Eldress Ruth, and Sister Asenath, 14 July 1828, WRHS, IV A 22.

18. Harvard Ministry to New Lebanon Ministry, 25 Oct. 1828, WRHS, IV A 22; Harvard Ministry to South Union Ministry, 25 Oct. 1828, WRHS, IV A 22.

19. Harvard Church Records, typescript, 6, FM Reel 1; "A Collection of Harvard Shaker Manuscripts," succession of ministry, 222–24, FM Reel 1.

20. "A General Journal of the most interesting & important occurrences . . . kept by the Sisters in the Church at Harvard," 14 March 1829, 1 Dec. 1832, 20 Nov. 1833, FM Reel 4.

21. "Sayings of Mother Ann and the First Elders, taken from Abijah Worster," 50, WRHS, VII B 22; Harvard Ministry's Journal 1818–1830, 1 Aug. 1829, WRHS, V B 37. The Harvard Shakers had made a similar visit to the site of the beatings with Shaker visitors from Ohio in 1827. Bethiah Willard went along to tell her story ("Sayings of Elder John taken down by Susan Channel and Sally Loomis," entry under the year 1827, WRHS, VII B 18).

22. Draft of a letter from Harvard Ministry to South Union Ministry, 6 Jan. 1834, WRHS, IV A 23.

23. Draft of a letter from Harvard Ministry to South Union Ministry, 6 Jan. 1834, WRHS, IV A 23; draft of a letter from Harvard Ministry to New Lebanon Ministry, 7 May 1835, WRHS, IV A 23; revised letter from Harvard Ministry to New Lebanon Ministry, 7 May 1835, WRHS, IV A 23; Harvard Ministry to New Lebanon Ministry, 10 March 1836, WRHS, IV A 23.

24. Harvard Ministry to New Lebanon Ministry, 6 April 1826, WRHS, IV A 22; Joseph Hammond's Day Book, No. 8, 12 July, 30 July, 5 Oct. 1826, WRHS, V B 200; Joseph Hammond's Day Book, No. 9, 7 Sept., 19 Sept., 19 Oct. 1827, WRHS, V B 201; Harvard Ministry to New Lebanon Ministry, 8 Feb. 1829, WRHS, IV A 58.

Other missionary activity noted in these journals includes additional trips to Pawtucket,

Middleboro, and Cape Cod. See Joseph Hammond's Day Books, Nos. 8–13, WRHS, V B 200-WRHS, V B 205.

25. Harvard Ministry to New Lebanon Ministry, 1 May 1831, WRHS, IV A 23; Harvard Ministry to New Lebanon Ministry, 18 Dec. 1832, WRHS, IV A 23; Harvard Ministry to New Lebanon Ministry, 17 Jan. 1831, WRHS, IV A 23.

26. Harvard Ministry's Journal 1834–1836, 20 July, 21 July, 22 July, 23 July, 25 July, 26 July, 27 July 1836, WRHS, V B 214.

27. Ibid., 29 July, 30 July, 5 Aug., 6 Oct., 8 Oct., 13 Oct., 14 Oct. 1836.

7. The Era of Manifestations

1. Andrews, *People Called Shakers*, 152–53; Stephen J. Stein, 165–66.

2. Harvard Ministry's Journal 1836–1839, 8 Oct., 31 Dec. 1837, 14 Jan. 1838, WRHS, V B 44; Harvard Ministry to New Lebanon Ministry, 24 Jan. 1838, WRHS, IV A 23.

3. Harvard Ministry's Journal 1836–1839, 12 Feb. 1838, WRHS, V B 44; Harvard Ministry to New Lebanon Ministry, 24 Jan. 1838, WRHS, IV A 23; copies of visions of Anna Mayo and Edwin Myrick, enclosed in a letter from the Harvard Ministry to the Canterbury Ministry, received 1 Feb. 1838, WRHS, IV A 4.

4. Harvard Ministry to New Lebanon Ministry, 23 July 1838, WRHS, IV A 23; draft of a letter from Harvard Ministry to New Lebanon Ministry, 14 Nov. 1838, WRHS, IV A 23; Harvard Ministry's Journal 1836–1839, 9 Oct., 25 Nov., 28 Nov., 29 Nov., 30 Nov., 1 Dec. 1838, other dates in Dec. 1838 and Jan. 1839, WRHS, V B 44.

5. "Protest movement" interpretations are based on the work of anthropologist I. M. Lewis, *Ecstatic Religion: An Anthropological Study of Spirit Possession and Shamanism*, Pelican Anthropology Library (Harmondsworth: Penguin Books, 1971).

6. Procter-Smith, *Women in Shaker Communities*, 206–7; Marsha Mihok, "Women in the Authority Structure of Shakerism: A Study of Social Conflict and Social Change" (Ph.D. diss.: Drew Univ., 1989), 188; Brewer, *Shaker Communities*, 123; Lawrence Foster, "Shaker Spiritualism and Salem Witchcraft: Social Perspectives on Trance and Spirit Possession Phenomena," *Communal Societies* 5 (1985): 190–92. Kern emphasizes the sexual component in his interpretation, arguing that the young sisters used ecstatic behavior as a form of sexual release (105–7).

7. Diane Sasson, "Individual Experience, Community Control, and Gender: The Harvard Community During the Era of Manifestations," *Communal Societies* 13 (1993): 49–53, 64–65.

8. Thurman, " 'Dearly Loved Mother Eunice,' " 755; Thurman, "The Windows of Heaven: A Study of Revival Among the Harvard Shakers," unpub. paper, 25–28.

9. Andrews, *People Called Shakers*, 155; Brewer, *Shaker Communities*, 115; Foster, "Shaker Spiritualism," 179; Sally M. Promey, *Spiritual Spectacles: Vision and Image in Mid-Nineteenth Century Shakerism* (Bloomington: Indiana Univ. Press, 1993), 1–13.

10. Harvard Ministry to New Lebanon Ministry, 27 May 1838, WRHS, IV A 23; Eunice Bathrick, "Miscellany Manuscripts No. III," 32–39, WRHS, VIII B 24; Harvard Ministry to New Lebanon Ministry, 14 Nov. 1838, WRHS, IV A 23.

11. Victor Turner, *The Ritual Process: Structure and Anti-Structure* (Chicago: Aldine Pub. Co., 1969), 94–97, 113.

12. Harvard Ministry's Journal 1838–1839, 5 Feb., 6 Feb., 10 Feb., 11 Feb., 17 Feb. 1839, WRHS, V B 44.

13. For examples of individual records of gifts, see "List of presents from the spiritual world given to Augustus H. Grosvenor," Harvard, 1839–1844, WC; "A Record of Spiritual Presents received from Our Holy Father Jehovah and Holy Holy Mother Wisdom And from The Glorious Inhabitants of the Heavenly World In this Great and Marvelous Manifestation by Daniel Myrick," WRHS, VIII B 54; "Record of Spiritual Presents Received From our Holy Father Jehovah, and Holy Holy Mother Wisdom from our Holy Saviour, and from blessed Mother Ann; from our Heavenly Parents and from many other happified spirits in the Eternal World. By Seth Blanchard," WRHS, VIII B 55.

14. "Record of Spiritual Presents," 11 Feb. 1843, WRHS, VIII B 54.

15. Harvard Ministry's Journal 1840–1845, 11 Jan., 12 Jan., 16 Jan. 1841, WRHS, V B 46; "No. A. Inspired Messages. 2 Copy. From Sept. 20, 1829 to April 13, 1841," 14–18, WRHS, VIII B 28; Harvard Ministry to New Lebanon Ministry, 31 Jan. 1842, WRHS, IV A 58.

16. Harvard Ministry's Journal 1840–1845, 1 June 1841, WRHS, V B 46.

17. Ibid., 25 July, 26 July, 27 July, 30 July, 8 Aug., 9 Aug., 10 Aug., 13 Aug., 14 Aug., 15 Aug., 16 Aug., 18 Aug., 19 Aug. 1841; Harvard Ministry to New Lebanon Ministry, 3 Sept. 1841, WRHS, IV A 24.

18. Harvard Ministry to New Lebanon Ministry, 31 Oct. 1842, WRHS, IV A 24.

19. Ibid.; "A Book of Messages Given to Brother Samuel Myrick, 1841–1842," 1 Jan. 1842, WRHS, VIII B 64; "Communications from our Heavenly Parents and other good Spirits in the course of Holy Mother's Second visitation at Harvard. Begins Tuesd. 28th December, and ends with Holy Mother's visit at the 2nd Family forenoon of Frid.," Dec. 31st, 1841, WRHS, IV A 63.

20. "Br. Seth's remarks on the necessity of correct inspiration," 12 Nov. 1842, WRHS, IV A 38.

21. Stephen J. Stein, 175–76; Harvard Ministry's Journal 1840–1845, 5 June 1842, WRHS, IV B 46; Harvard Ministry to New Lebanon Ministry, 20 May 1839, WRHS, IV A 23; Harvard Ministry's Journal 1839–1840, 9 April, 10 April 1839, WRHS, V B 45; "A Journal or Day Book Containing some of the most important transactions of the Church of Harvard. Kept for the use and accommodation of the Sisters; By order of the Ministry and Elders in union with the Church Beginning Nov. 16th 1840," 24 Jan. 1841, WRHS, V B 50.

22. Harvard Ministry's Journal 1840–1845, 27 Aug., 29 Aug. 1842, WRHS, V B 46; "A Statement Of the First Meeting held On the Holy Hill of Zion By the First Orders of the Church at Harvard. August 29th 1842," 1–3, 18–20, 25, 34, 113, WRHS, VIII B 91.

23. Stephen J. Stein, 176; "Extracts from Shirley Church records," 9 Jan. 1843, ASC; Harvard Ministry's Journal 1840–1845, 19 Jan. 1843, WRHS, V B 46.

24. Harvard Ministry's Journal 1840–1845, 10 Aug., 18 Aug., 20 Aug., 1 Sept., 3 Sept., 8 Sept., 15 Sept., 18 Sept., 20 Sept., 21 Sept. 1844, WRHS, V B 46; Harvard Ministry to New Lebanon Ministry, 30 Sept. 1844, WRHS, IV A 58.

25. Theodore Johnson, "Rules and Orders for the Church of Christ's Second Appearing," *Shaker Quarterly* 11 (Winter 1971): 139–41. For a copy of the 1845 *Millennial Laws*, see Andrews, *People Called Shakers*, 249–89. For a copy of the 1821 *Millennial Laws*, see Theodore Johnson, "The 'Millennial Laws' of 1821," *Shaker Quarterly* 7 (Summer 1967): 43–58.

26. Harvard Ministry to New Lebanon Ministry, 3 Feb. 1845, WRHS, IV A 58; Harvard Ministry's Journal 1840–1845, 17 Nov., 15 Dec. 1844, WRHS, V B 46; "No. 4 Family Journal. Gathering Order, Shirley. Commencing on Tuesd. Dec. 1st 1846. And Ending on January 31, 1849," 25 Oct. 1846, WRHS, V B 193; "A Little Book Containing the Songs given by the Shepherdess in the Church at Shirley. Commencing Nov. 3rd, 1844. Each one numbered as they were given," WC; "Journal of meetings commencing Sept. 17, 1851 and ending May 17, 1852," 7 Nov., 15 Nov., 16 Dec., 28 Dec. 1851, 28 March, 17 April, 1852, WC; "Day Book of Meetings, Sept. 11 1853 to May 15 1854," 18 Sept., 24 Sept., 1 Oct., 20 Oct., 29 Oct., 2 Nov. 1853; 14 Jan., 4 Feb., 5 Feb., 12 March, 22 April, 13 May, 15 May, 21 May 1854, WC; Harvard Ministry to New Lebanon Ministry, 24 March 1851, WRHS, V A 59.

27. Ernest Isaacs, "The Fox Sisters and American Spiritualism," in *The Occult in America: New Historical Perspectives*, ed. Howard Kerr and Charles L. Crow (Urbana: Univ. of Illinois Press, 1983), 79–110. See also Earl Wesley Fornell, *The Unhappy Medium: Spiritualism and the Life of Margaret Fox* (Austin: Univ. of Texas Press, 1964).

28. Harvard Ministry to New Lebanon Ministry, 24 March 1851, WRHS, IV A 59.

29. Caroline Walker Bynum, "Introduction: The Complexity of Symbols," in *Gender and Religion: On the Complexity of Symbols*, ed. Caroline Walker Bynum, Stevan Harrell, and Paula Richman (Boston: Beacon Press, 1986), 2.

30. Deignan, 54–56; Bynum, *Holy Feast and Holy Fast*, 172–80, 270–76, Plates 25–30; Caroline Walker Bynum, " ' . . . And Woman His Humanity': Female Imagery in the Religious Writings of the Later Middle Ages," in *Gender and Religion: On the Complexity of Symbols*, ed. Caroline Walker Bynum, Stevan Harrell, and Paula Richman (Boston: Beacon Press, 1986), 262–68.

31. Jean Soler, "The Semiotics of Food in the Bible," in *Food and Drink in History: Selections form the Annales Economies, Sociétés, Civilisations*, ed. Robert Forster and Orest Ranum, trans. Elborg Forster and Patricia M. Ranum (Baltimore: Johns Hopkins Univ. Press, 1979), 126.

32. "A Book Containing a General Statement of the Gifts and Spiritual Presents With the Bountiful Stores of Love and Blessing Received by Eunice Bathrick In the Late Visitation of God To his Children on Earth; Commencing In the year 1839," 15 June, 23 June, 21 July, 22 July 1841, 7 March, 9 Oct., 22 Oct., 29 Oct. 1842, 14 Jan. 1844, NYSL.

33. Ibid., 19 May 1846; "Diary of spiritual activities, 1842–1844," 24 May 1843, WRHS, V B 216; Shirley Church Journal 1843–1860, 12 Jan., 10 Feb. 1843, FM Reel 6. On the power of food as a method of conversion, see Eliot A. Singer, "Conversion Through Foodways Enculturation: The Meaning of Eating in an American Hindu Sect," in *Ethnic and Regional Foodways in the United States: The Performance of Group Identity*, ed. Linda Keller Brown and Kay Mussell (Knoxville: Univ. of Tennessee Press, 1984), 195–214. On food as a way of establishing intimacy and kinship, see Susan Kal ik, "Ethnic Foodways in America: Symbol and the Performance of Identity," in *Ethnic and Regional Foodways in the United States: The Perfor-*

mance of Group Identity, ed. Linda Keller Brown and Kay Mussell (Knoxville: Univ. of Tennessee Press, 1984), 47–49.

34. Karen Voci Zimmerman, "Symbol, Structure and Reality: Forms of Worship of the New England Shakers" (M.A. thesis: American Univ., 1973), 211–12.

35. "Book Containing a General Statement of Spiritual Gifts and Presents," 29 Aug. 1842, NYSL.

36. Bynum, *Holy Feast and Holy Fast*, 118, 127–29, 230–33.

37. Ibid., 236.

38. Message from the Prophet Iddo, 14 Feb. 1843, WRHS, VIII A 11. Several Iddos appear in the Old Testament who could have caught the imagination of the Shakers. Iddo has been variously identified as the son of the prophet Zechariah (I Chronicles 27: 21), the father of Zechariah (Ezra 5: 1, Ezra 6: 14), and the grandfather of Zechariah (Zechariah 1: 1). In 2 Chronicles 9: 29, 12: 15, and 13: 22, Iddo is described as a prophet, seer, and historian, (*The Anchor Bible Dictionary*, s.v. "Iddo").

39. "Message from Eunice Wyeth to the Ministry," 20 April 1842; "A Short communication from Rebekah Proctor," 4 May 1842; "A Roll from Abigail Cooper, in which she writes for a number of the Ancient Sisters," 6 May 1842; "A Roll from Mary Worster directed to Mother's first born Children at Harvard Chh," 13 May 1842; "A Roll from Solomon Cooper directed to the Elders at Harvard Church," 16 May 1842; "A Roll from Childs Whitney Directed to those of the Brethren & sisters who were his former acquaintance on the shores of time," 23 May 1842; "A Roll from Brother Aaron Jewett Directed to the Ministry, Elders, Brethren & sisters, at Harvard Church," 6 June 1842; "A Roll from Deliverance Whittemore to the beloved Ministry, Elders, Brethren & Sisters in the church at Harvard," 13 June 1842, all messages collected under WRHS, VIII A 10.

40. "Communications from the Spirit Land transcribed by Eunice Bathrick, 1842–1843," 94, WRHS, VIII B 93; "No. 4. Inspired Communications From May 22d to June 3d, 1841," 4–5, WRHS, VIII B 33.

41. "Narrative pieces and Historical Sketches from Spirit Land, Transcribed by Eunice Bathrick, 1842–1845," 84–86, WC; "No. B., No. 2. Inspired Messages From April 17th 1841 to September 26th 1841," 13–15, WRHS, VIII B 29; "A List of the different Tribes of Indians and other Nations, which, (through the instrumentality of George Washington, William Penn and others), were brought to the Zion of God on Earth, to learn of Mother's Children, what they must do in order to be happy," WRHS, VIII A 52.

42. Daniel W. Patterson, " 'Bearing for the Dead': A Shaker Belief and Its Impress on the Shaker Spiritual," *Shaker Quarterly* 8 (Winter 1968): 116–28.

43. *Extract from an Unpublished Manuscript on Shaker History (By an Eye Witness.) Giving an Accurate Description of Their Songs, Dances, Marches, Visions, Visits to the Spirit Land, etc.* (Boston: E. K. Allen, 1850), 11.

44. "Spiritual Messages received by Joseph Parker, Second Family, Harvard, Mass., 1842–1843," WC.

45. "A Communication given at Harvard, third family, in the form of a Roll, by Alfred Loomis to his beloved daughter, Sally," 27 Feb. 1842, WRHS, VIII A 14.

46. Spirit Message sent to Lucy Bodge, Shirley, Mass. 1842–1843, 1–14, 21–32, 35–40, 49–57, 78–81, 103–109, ASC.

47. "Collection of Visions given to Minerva L. Hill in the South Family at Harvard," 17 Feb. 1839, WRHS, VIII B 23.

48. "No. 18. Inspired Communications From November 14th to November 21st 1841," 38–42, WRHS, VIII B, 45.

49. "A Roll from the Martyr Polycarp," 8 June 1843, WRHS, VIII A 11; "Life and Sufferings of the Patriarch Joseph," 1 Dec. 1841, WRHS, VIII B 60; [The Lives and Sufferings of Christ, Mother Ann Lee, Father William, Father James, and John Hocknell,] instrument William Leonard, 1841, WRHS, VIII B 68.

50. Harvard Ministry's Journal 1840–1845, 20 April, 4 Dec. 1842, WRHS, V B 46.

51. "A Vision," Eunice Bathrick, 18 March 1842, WRHS, VIII A 10.

52. On the belated reception of gifts in the Church families, see Harvard Ministry to New Lebanon Ministry, 23 Nov. 1840, WRHS, IV A 58.

53. "No. 1. Visions & Insp'd Communications From Jan. 19th 1840 to March 28th 1841," 3, WRHS, VIII B 30; "No. 4. Inspired Communications From May 22nd to June 3d, 1841," 1–3, WRHS, VIII B 33; "No. 5. Inspired Communications Commencing June 4th 1841 And Ending June 7th 1841 inclusive," 9–11, WRHS, VIII B 34; "No. B., No. 2. Inspired Messages From April 17th 1841 to September 26th 1841," 29–30, 51–52, WRHS, VIII B 29.

54. "No. 12. Inspired Communications Commencing September 12th 1841, And Ending September 26th, 1841," 11, WRHS, VIII B 41; "Words of our blessed Parents to the Ministry," 18 April 1843, WRHS, VIII A 11; "No. 1. Visions & Insp'd Communications From Jan. 19th 1840 to March 28th 1841," 3, WRHS, VIII B 30; Harvard Ministry's Journal 1840–1845, 4 Aug. 1844, WRHS, V B 46.

55. "No. 3. Inspired Communications From the 8th to the 20th of May, 1841. Containing the Communications of our Holy Savior & Blessed Mother Ann In their late visitation to us," 6–9, WRHS, VIII B 32; "No. 6. Inspired Communications Commencing June 8th 1841, And Ending June 19th inclusive," 9–13, 20–23, WRHS, VIII B 35.

8. The Woman Question

1. "A Short Account of some of the Sufferings of Christ and Mother Ann and other messages given between July 5 and August 15, [1841]," 34–35, 41, WRHS, VIII B 57.

2. "Words of Holy Mother by the Prophetess Elizabeth to her Daughters in Lovely Vineyard," 6 May 1843, WRHS, VIII A 11.

3. Ann Braude, *Radical Spirits: Spiritualism and Women's Rights in Nineteenth-Century America* (Boston: Beacon Press, 1989), 80–84.

4. Laurie A. Finke, "Mystical Bodies and the Dialogics of Vision," in *Maps of Flesh and Light: The Religious Experience of Medieval Women Mystics*, ed. Ulrike Wiethaus (Syracuse, N.Y.: Syracuse Univ. Press, 1993), 33.

5. "Divine Instructions from Holy Mother Wisdom. Also, Various Communications From the Holy Angels. Harvard, 1841," 11 Dec. 1841, 228–32, LC, cont. 39, reel 31, item 359.

6. "Words of Holy Mother by the Prophetess Elizabeth," 6 May 1843, WRHS, VIII A 11.

7. Ibid. Words in brackets were crossed out in the edited manuscript.

8. "Words to Eldress Betty from Elizabeth," 1 May 1842, WRHS, VIII A 25; "A Roll given to Eldress Betty by Caroline Dunva," 30 April 1842, WRHS, VIII A 25; "No. 19. Inspired Communications. From Nov. 25th to 28th, 1841," 16–23, WRHS, VIII B 46; "A Short Account of some of the Sufferings of Christ and Mother Ann," 31–33, WRHS, VIII B 57.

9. Shaker women's observations that history written by men subsumed women's history preceded current feminist scholarship by more than one hundred years. One of the goals of today's feminist scholars is the recovery of women's voice in history, requiring "a radical restructuring of thought and analysis which once and for all accepts the fact that . . . the experiences, thoughts, and insights of both sexes must be represented" (Lerner, 220). See Marilyn J. Boxer and Jean H. Quataert, "Introduction: Restoring Women to History," in *Connecting Spheres: Women in the Western World, 1500 to the Present*, ed. Marilyn J. Boxer and Jean H. Quataert (New York: Oxford Univ. Press, 1987), 3–17.

10. Procter-Smith, *Women in Shaker Community*, 196–207; Linda A. Mercadante, *Gender, Doctrine, and God: The Shakers and Contemporary Theology* (Nashville: Abingdon Press, 1990), 99, 105–7, 114, 121, 123, 131–32.

11. "A part of the Record of Holy Mother's visit to Lovely Vinyard [sic] in Aug. 1841," 6, 18, 22, WRHS, VIII B 58; "No. 25. Inspired Communications. From the 12th to the 23rd December 1841," 8–18, 31–35, WRHS, VIII B 50; "The Sacred and Solemn Truths of Jehovah. Given in a Roll on the Holy Hill of Zion," WRHS, VIII A 10; "No. 1 Mary Ann Widdifield's Visions, July 25–31, Aug. 4, 1841," 5–6, 11, WRHS, VIII A 10; "A Message from Holy Mother Wisdom to Her Children in Lovely Vineyard," 3 Aug. 1844, WRHS, VIII A 11; "A Short Account of some of the Sufferings of Christ and Mother Ann and other messages given between July 5 and August 15, [1841]," 45–46, WRHS, VIII B 57; Octavo vol., Harvard Mass., Shaker Church Records, 222, courtesy of AAS.

12. "A Communication from Father William, to the Office Sisters at Harvard Church," 26 July 1842, WRHS, VIII A 10.

13. Johnston, 62–65, 67–79; Degler, 144–77; William Leach, *True Love and Perfect Union: The Feminist Reform of Sex and Society* (New York: Basic Books, 1980), 3–15.

14. Basch, 41.

15. Braude, 56–81; Bret E. Carroll, *Spiritualism in Antebellum America*, Religion in North America Series (Bloomington: Indiana Univ. Press, 1997), 101–7. J. R. Hyland devotes a whole chapter to the Shakers as the "spiritual roots of the women's movement" in *Sexism is a Sin: The Biblical Basis of Female Equality* (Sarasota, Fla.: Viatoris Pub., 1995), 115–23.

16. Mary McDaniels to Grove Blanchard, 3 March 1850, WRHS, IV A 25.

17. Harvard Ministry to New Lebanon Ministry, 16 March 1850, WRHS, IV A 25.

18. Day Book No. 3 [Eliza Babbitt], 1 Sept. 1849, WRHS, V B 217; *Notable American Women, 1607–1950: A Biographical Dictionary*, s.v. "Hunt, Harriot K."; Harriot K. Hunt, *Glances and Glimpses; or Fifty Years Social, Including Twenty Years Professional Life* (Boston: John P. Jewett and Co., 1856).

19. Hunt, 219–20, 228–29, 281; Day Book No. 3 [Eliza Babbitt], 1 Sept., 3 Sept., 5

Sept., 9 Sept., 10 Sept. 1849, 3 June, 4 June, 1 July, 30 Aug., 31 Aug. 1850, 10 April, 11 April, 13 May, 8 Sept., 9 Sept., 10 Sept., 18 Oct., 19 Oct., 20 Oct. 1851, WRHS, V B 217; Ministry Journal, 1851–1854, 19 May, 21 May, 22 May, 25 Sept. 1852, WRHS, V B 218; Journal, 15 Feb., 4 May, 15 May, 26 June, 30 June 1856, 24 June, 25 June 1857, 11 April, 6 Aug. 1858, 1 May 1859, WRHS, V B 54; Harvard Ministry to Alfred Ministry, 30 Sept. 1851, SL.

20. Day Book No. 3 [Eliza Babbitt], 10 Sept. 1851, WRHS, V B 217; Ministry Journal, 1851–1854, 19 May, 21 May 1852, WRHS, V B 218; Journal 1856, 24 June 1857, WRHS, V B 54; *Notable American Women*, s.v. "Davis, Paulina Kellogg Wright"; *American Reformers*, s.v. "Fowler, Lydia Folger," "Fowler, Orson Squire"; *Notable American Women*, s.v. "Wells, Charlotte Fowler"; *Dictionary of American Biography*, s.v. "Flagg, Josiah Foster"; Hunt, 254–55.

21. Hunt, 254–55, 277–80; "Journal of a trip from Enfield, Conn., to Shaker Communities in Maine, New Hampshire, and Massachusetts. Aug. 26 to Oct. 8, [1850]," 30 Aug. 1850, ASC.

22. Hunt, 150–59, 229–30, 232–33.

23. Marianne Finch, *An Englishwoman's Experience in America* (London: R. Bentley, 1853), 119–20, 140, 142, 147, 150–52.

24. Lorenzo Dow Grosvenor, *Circular Letter in Defence of the United Society of Believers, Commonly Called Shakers; With a Reply to Correspondents* (Harvard, Mass.: n.p., 1849), 6, 16–17.

25. [Lorenzo Dow Grosvenor], *Testimony of Jesus Concerning Marriage: Marriage,—Jesus and the Shakers* (n.p.: n.d.).

26. A. B. Davis, *True Love: What it is, and what it is not*, Shaker Tracts for the Times, no. 1 (Shirley, Mass.: pub. for the author, 1869), 17.

27. Ibid., 18.

28. Harvard Ministry to New Lebanon Ministry, 4 Oct. 1848, WRHS, IV A 58; William Leonard to Harvard Ministry, 13 Oct. 1849, WRHS, IV A 24; William Leonard to Harvard Ministry, 15 Jan. 1849, WRHS, IV A 24; Ministry Journal, 1851–1854, 26 Nov. 1851, 29 Aug., 17 Oct. 1852, WRHS, V B 218; Sally [Loomis] and Roxalana [Grosvenor] to Eldress Ruth [Landon] and Sister Asenath [Clark], 27 Nov. 1849, WRHS, IV A 58.

29. Abigail Cook to Joseph Tillinghast, 22 Dec. 1851, WRHS, IV A 59; Dennis Pratt to Joseph Tillinghast, 23 Dec. 1851, WRHS, IV A 59.

30. Ministry Journal, 1851–1854, 11 Aug, 11 Oct. 1852, WRHS, V B 218; "A Journal Kept by the Ministry Commencing Feb. 18th/62. Eliza Babbitt commences writing in this book," 7 Jan. 1864, ASC.

31. Harry B. Weiss and Howard R. Kemble, *The Great American Water-Cure Craze: A History of Hydropathy in the United States* (Trenton, N.J.: Past Times Press, 1967), 41; Jane B. Donegan, *"Hydropathic Highway to Health:" Women and Water-Cure in Antebellum America*, Contributions in Medical Studies, no. 17 (New York: Greenwood Press, 1986), 5–7; Harvard Ministry to New Lebanon Ministry, 3 Feb. 1845, WRHS, IV A 58.

32. Weiss and Kemble, 126–28; "No. 4 Family Journal. Gathering Order, Shirley," 20 July 1847, WRHS, V B 193; "Anonymous Journal, Shirley 1835–1849," 20 July, 24 Sept. 1847, 2 May 1849, WRHS, V B 215; Journal, 16 Nov 1848, 26 May, 28 May 1849, WRHS, V B 53; "No. 5 Family Journal. Gathering Order, Shirley, Commencing on Thursday Febry 1st 1849," 8 July 1851, WRHS, V B 194; Day Book No. 3, [Eliza Babbitt], 4 Sept. 1851,

WRHS, V B 217; Ministry Journal, 1851–1854, 30 Sept., 7 Oct., 15 Dec., 19 Dec. 1851, 13 Jan., 17 Jan., 21 May, 1 June, 1 Nov. 1852, 17 April, 21 April, 10 Sept. 1853, WRHS, V B 218; Susan E. Cayleff, *Wash and Be Healed: The Water-Cure Movement and Women's Health*, Health, Society, and Policy (Philadelphia: Temple Univ. Press, 1987), 84–86.

33. Donegan, passim; Cayleff, passim.

34. Sally Loomis to Eldress Asenath and Sister Samantha, 11 Feb. 1851, WRHS, IV A 25.

35. Ibid.

36. Ministry Journal, 1851–1854, 18 Feb. 1852, WRHS, V B 218; Sally Loomis to Eldress Asenath and Sister Samantha, 11 Feb. 1851, WRHS, IV A 25.

37. Sally Loomis to Samuel H. Myrick, 28 Dec. 1851, WRHS, IV A 25.

38. Seth Wells, "Temperance the best preserver of Health," c. 1846, 3, 6, 9, 12–15, 17–22, 26–27, 50, LC, cont. 27, items 313–15; copy of a letter from Seth Wells to Sally Loomis, 3 Oct. 1846, LC, cont. 27, item 315.

39. Verbrugge, 16–23; Carroll Smith-Rosenberg and Charles Rosenberg, "The Female Animal: Medical and Biological Views of Woman and Her Role in Nineteenth-Century America," *Journal of American History* 60 (Sept. 1973): 332–56; Diane Price Herndl, *Invalid Women: Figuring Feminine Illness in American Fiction* (Chapel Hill: Univ. of North Carolina Press, 1993).

40. Frances B. Cogan, *All-American Girl: The Ideal of Real Womanhood in Mid-Nineteenth-Century America* (Athens: Univ. of Georgia Press, 1989), 3–26.

41. Verbrugge, 1–10.

42. Beverly Gordon, "Dress in American Communal Societies," *Communal Societies* 5 (1985): 123, 132; Youngs, "A Concise View," 303–7, 317, ASC; "Memorandum on Changes of Sisters' Gowns," WRHS, I A 24; Katherine Morris Lester and Rose Netzorg Kerr, *Historic Costume: A Résumé of Style and Fashion from Remote Times to the Nineteen-Sixties*, 6th ed. (Peoria, Ill.: Chas. A. Bennett Co., 1967), 186–91; Valerie Steele, *Fashion and Eroticism: Ideals of Feminine Beauty from the Victorian Era to the Jazz Age* (New York: Oxford Univ. Press, 1985), 51–56, 145–58, 161–91; Donegan, 135–61.

43. Donegan, 137–56, 191.

44. "A Bundle of Letters Reflecting Correspondence Between Sister Eunice and Jeremiah Hacker," extracts of a letter from Eunice Bathrick to Jeremiah Hacker, 1864, 57, FM Reel 5.

45. Central Ministry's Journal, 1850–1859, 15 May 1859, NYPL.

9. Embracing the World

1. I contend that the Shakers' move to embrace the world was a positive result of the revitalization of the Era of Manifestations, and not, as Priscilla Brewer has argued, the result of disillusionment with the revival (*Shaker Communities*, 158).

2. Calvin Green to Elder Lorenzo Grosvenor, 11 April 1852, SL.

3. See Michael Barkun, *Crucible of the Millennium: The Burned-Over District of New York in the 1840s*, A New York State Study (Syracuse, N.Y.: Syracuse Univ. Press, 1986); Lawrence Foster, "Had Prophecy Failed?: Contrasting Perspectives of the Millerites and Shakers," in *The*

Disappointed: Millerism and Millenarianism in the Nineteenth Century, ed. Ronald L. Numbers and Jonathan M. Butler, Religion in North America (Bloomington: Indiana Univ. Press, 1987), 173–88.

4. Journal, July 1845-September 1847, 12 Sept., 13 Sept., 25 Sept., 26 Sept., 27 Sept. 1846, 4 Jan. 1847, FM Reel 2. The ban on public Sabbath meetings instituted by the Central Ministry in 1842 was lifted three years later.

5. Harvard Ministry to New Lebanon Ministry, 5 Jan. 1847, WRHS, IV A 58; Journal, July 1845-September 1847, 13 Feb., 11 March, 19 March, 20 March, 21 March, 17 April, 18 April, 4 June 1847, FM Reel 2; Harvard Ministry to New Lebanon Ministry, 8 Feb. 1847, WRHS, IV A 24; Harvard Ministry to New Lebanon Ministry, 19 May 1847, WRHS, IV A 24; "Anonymous Journal, Shirley 1835 to 1849," 13 Jan., 30 May, 5 June, 6 June, 7 Sept, 26 Sept. 1847, WRHS, V B 215; "No. 4 Family Journal. Gathering Order, Shirley," 12 Sept. 1847, WRHS, V B 193.

6. Daniel Ricketson, *The History of New Bedford, Bristol County, Massachusetts: Including A History of the Old Township of Dartmouth and the Present Townships of Westport, Dartmouth, and Fairhaven, From Their Settlement to the Present Time* (New Bedford, Mass.: pub. by the author, 1858), 37, 41–42; Leonard Bolles Ellis, *History of New Bedford and Its Vicinity, 1602–1892* (Syracuse, N.Y.: D. Mason and Co., 1892), 456, 511, 513, 517, 520, 600–601.

7. William Leonard to Harvard Ministry, 15 Jan. 1849, WRHS, IV A 24; William Leonard to Harvard Ministry, 16 Jan. 1849, WRHS, IV A 24; Harvard Ministry to New Lebanon Ministry, 16 Jan. 1849, WRHS, IV A 24; Joseph Tillinghast to Grove Blanchard, 24 Jan. 1849, WRHS, IV A 24; Joseph Tillinghast to Grove Blanchard, 2 Oct. 1850, WRHS, IV A 25; Joseph Tillinghast to Grove Blanchard, 12 Jan. 1852, WRHS, IV A 25; Joseph Tillinghast to Grove Blanchard, 14 March 1850, WRHS, IV A 25; Joseph Tillinghast to Grove Blanchard, 12 June 1850, WRHS, IV A 25; William Leonard to James McNemar, 21 July 1850, LC, cont. 35, item 351 c2.

8. "No. 4 Family Journal. Gathering Order, Shirley," 5 Jan., 25 Jan., 29 Jan., 30 Jan., 31 Jan. 1849, WRHS, V B 193; "No. 5 Family Journal. Gathering Order, Shirley," 3 Feb., 10 Feb., 6 March, 9 March, 21 March 1849, WRHS, V B 194; Harvard Ministry to New Lebanon Ministry, 16 Jan. 1849, WRHS, IV A 24.

9. Joseph Tillinghast to Grove Blanchard, 14 March 1850, WRHS, IV A 25; Mary Babbitt to Joseph Tillinghast, 1 Aug. 1851, WRHS, IV A 25; Joseph Tillinghast to Grove Blanchard, 3 Jan. 1851, WRHS, IV A 25; Moses Tenney to Joseph Tillinghast, 6 March 1851, WRHS, IV A 25; John [Tillinghast] to Joseph Tillinghast, 11 Sept. 1851, WRHS, IV A 25; Lorenzo Grosvenor to Joseph Tillinghast, 15 Aug. 1853, WRHS, IV A 26; Grove Blanchard to Joseph Tillinghast, 17 March 1854, WRHS, IV A 26; Joseph Tillinghast to Samuel Myrick, 30 June 1851, WRHS, IV A 25.

10. Joseph Tillinghast to Grove Blanchard, 25 March 1850, WRHS, IV A 25; Joseph Tillinghast to Grove Blanchard, 12 April 1851, WRHS, IV A 25; Joseph Tillinghast to Grove Blanchard, 12 May 1851, WRHS, IV A 25; Grove Blanchard to Joseph Tillinghast, 20 Jan. 1852, WRHS, IV A 59; Grove Blanchard to Joseph Tillinghast, 24 Jan. 1857, WRHS, IV A 59; Nancy Orsement to Joseph Tillinghast, 5 Aug. 1851, WRHS, IV A 25; Joseph Tillinghast to Grove Blanchard, 14 Nov. 1842, WRHS, IV A 25.

11. William Wetherbee to Joseph Tillinghast, 2 June 1852, WRHS, IV A 59.

12. Harvard Ministry to Grove Wright, 13 April 1849, ASC; William Leonard to Joseph Tillinghast, 17 Feb. 1858, WRHS, IV A 27; [Joseph Tillinghast], *Brief and Useful Moral Instructions for the Young. By a Friend of Youth and Children* (Worcester, Mass.: Chas. Hamilton, 1858).

13. Joseph Tillinghast to Grove Blanchard, 16 Jan 1853, WRHS, IV A 26.

14. Journal, 21 Aug. 1848, WRHS, V B 53; Jeremiah Hacker to Joseph Tillinghast, 9 Sept. 1848, WRHS, IV A 24; Moses Tenney to Joseph Tillinghast, 6 March 1851, WRHS, IV A 25.

15. Central Ministry's Journal, 1839–1850, 2 July 1847, NYPL; Journal, 21 Aug. 1848, WRHS, V B 53; Jeremiah Hacker to Joseph Tillinghast, 9 Sept. 1848, WRHS, IV A 24; Joseph Hacker to Joseph Tillinghast, 27 Oct. 1857, WRHS, IV A 27; Jeremiah Hacker to Joseph Tillinghast, 2 Nov. 1857, WRHS, IV A 27; Jeremiah Hacker to Joseph Tillinghast, June 1860, WRHS, IV A 87.

16. See, for example, Priscilla Brewer, "Emerson, Lane, and the Shakers: A Case of Converging Ideologies," *New England Quarterly* 55 (1982): 254–75.

17. Charles Lane and Bronson Alcott, letter, *Herald of Freedom*, 8 Sept. 1843, quoted in Clara Endicott Sears, comp., *Bronson Alcott's Fruitlands* (Boston: Houghton Mifflin, 1915), 44–45.

18. Ibid., 45–46.

19. Brewer, "Emerson, Lane, and the Shakers," 256–62; Ralph Waldo Emerson, *Journals of Ralph Waldo Emerson: With Annotations*, ed. Edward Waldo Emerson and Waldo Emerson Forbes, 10 vols. (Boston: Houghton Mifflin, 1911),6: 27 Sept. 1842; R.W.E. to William Emerson, 22 May 1852, *The Letters of Ralph Waldo Emerson*, ed. Ralph L. Husk, 6 vols. (New York: Columbia Univ. Press, 1939), 4: 294.

20. Braude, 82–116; Mary Farrell Bednarowski, "Women in Occult America," in *The Occult in America: New Historical Perspectives*, ed. Howard Kerr and Charles L. Crow (Urbana: Univ. of Illinois Press, 1983),177–95; Howard Kerr, *Mediums, and Spirit-Rappers, and Roaring Radicals: Spiritualism in American Literature, 1850–1900* (Urbana: Univ. of Illinois Press, 1972); Alex Owen, *The Darkened Room: Women, Power and Spiritualism in Late Victorian England* (Philadelphia: Univ. of Pennsylvania Press, 1990), passim.

21. Carroll, 112–13; William Leonard to Isaac Youngs, 16 Nov. 1851, WRHS, IV A 25; "Journal of meetings commencing Sept. 17, 1851 and ending May 17, 1852," 7 Nov. 1851, WC.

22. Ministry Journal, 1851–1854, Sept. and Oct. 1852, 19 Jan. 1854, WRHS, V B 218; Journal 1856, 5 Jan. 1856, 7 Feb., 17 Aug., 15 Sept. 1858, WRHS, V B 54; William Leonard to Joseph Tillinghast, 29 March 1858, WRHS, IV A 27.

23. [Seth Wells] to Br. Rufus [Bishop], 7 Oct. 1843, LC, cont. 1, item 14; "The Word of the Lord to *His* chosen people," 10 Aug. 1844, WRHS, VIII A 11. According to Seth Wells' letter, the doctrine of two orders was revealed over the course of several years in inspired messages but seems to have become widely known only after its appearance in *A Holy, Sacred and Divine Roll and Book*, published in 1843. New Lebanon Shaker Philemon Stewart wrote the text by "divine revelation" the year before, (Stephen J. Stein, 174, 177, 180).

24. Stephen J. Stein, 205–7, 213–14, 331–37.

25. Braude, 32–55; Carroll, 101–7; Frederick Evans, "Pre-Existence of Christ," *The Shaker Manifesto* 10 (Jan. 1880): 3–4.

26. William Leonard to Frederick Evans, 9 Oct. 1853, WRHS, IV A 26.

27. Ibid.

28. David A. Christie-Murray, *A History of Heresy* (1976; reprint; Oxford: Oxford Univ. Press, 1989), 26, 45–55; Robert C. Gregg and Dennis E. Groh, *Early Arianism: A View of Salvation* (Philadelphia: Fortress Press, 1981), 9, 22–24.

29. William Leonard to Frederick Evans, 9 Oct. 1853, WRHS, IV A 26.

30. William Leonard, *A Discourse on the Order and Propriety of Divine Inspiration and Revelation, Showing the Necessity Thereof in All Ages, to Know the Will of God. Also, a Discourse on the Second Appearing of Christ, in and through the Order of the Female. And a Discourse on the Propriety and Necessity of a United Inheritance in All Things, in Order to Support a True Christian Community* (Harvard, Mass.: United Society of Believers, 1853), 1, 42; Diane Sasson, *The Shaker Spiritual Narrative* (Knoxville: Univ. of Tennessee Press, 1983), 129–32.

31. William Leonard to Frederick [Evans], 14 April 1853, WRHS, IV A 26.

32. Elder William Leonard to Elder Frederick Evans, 9 Dec. 1867, SL.

33. William Leonard to Eldress Antoinette [Doolittle], 15 Feb. 1858, WRHS, IV A 27.

34. "A Journal Containing some of the most important events of the day kept for the use and convenience of the Brethren in the Church In union with the Ministry & Elders. Harvard, Nov. 1840," 17 Nov., 21 Dec. 1840, 5 Jan., 3 Feb., 16 March, 3 Sept., 6 Sept., 27 Sept., 5 Oct., 6 Oct., 12 Oct., 1 Nov. 1841, FM Reel 2; Harvard Ministry's Journal, 1839–1840, 29 Oct. 1840, WRHS, V B 45.

35. Journal, July 1845-September 1847, 27 March, 10 June, 23 June, 8 July 1846, 1 May, 3 May, 12 May 1847, FM Reel 2; "Items of a Journey to Harvard," 6 Aug., 10 Aug., 11 Aug. 1846, WRHS, V B 140; "A Journal of an Eastern Tour of Visitors [by members of the Second family at Watervliet. June, 1847]," 13 June 1847, WRHS, V B 332; "Journal of a trip to various Societies, Sept. 1854-Oct. 1854," 12 Sept. 1854, WRHS, V B 250.

36. Harvard Ministry's Journal, 1840–1845, 2 Dec. 1840, WRHS, V B 46; "A Journal Record of the South and East Family of Young Believers at *Harvard*," 19 March, 25 March 1846, 31 Dec. 1853, WRHS, V B 35.

37. Nourse, *History of the Town of Harvard*, 168–69; Harvard Ministry's Journal, 1836–1839, 1 Nov. 1837, 9 April, 28 Oct. 1838, WRHS, V B 44; Harvard Ministry's Journal, 1839–1840, 9 March, 8 April, 29 April, 23 Aug. 1839, WRHS, V B 45; "Journal, Thomas Hammond, Harvard, Mass., Not belonging to the Chh. Records," 17 July 1839, WRHS, V B 40; "No. 2, Family Journal. For the North Family or Gathering Order, at Shirley, Commencing on Friday, Jan. 1st, 1836 and Ending Aug. 31, 1844," 12 April 1844, WRHS, V B 191; Journal, July 1845-September 1847, 11 Nov., 18 Nov. 1845, 10 Feb., 24 Feb., 22 April, 25 April, 28 April, 15 Aug. 1846, FM Reel 2; "Items of a Journey to Harvard," 11 Aug. 1846, WRHS, V B 140; Journal, 1 Jan. 1848, WRHS, V B 53.

38. Nourse, *History of the Town of Harvard*, 167; Harvard Ministry to New Lebanon Ministry, 7 April 1845, WRHS, IV A 58; Harvard Ministry's Journal, 1840–1845, 6 Jan., 13 May, 23 May, 24 May, 27 May, 5 June, 6 June, 10 June, 11 June 1845, WRHS, V B 46.

39. Journal, July 1845-September 1847, 8 Sept. 1845, 28 Feb. 1846, 11 May 1847, FM Reel 2.

40. Journal, July 1845-September 1847, 24 July, 10 Sept., 11 Sept., 27 Oct., 21 Nov., 5 Dec., 31 Dec. 1845, 16 Jan., 6 March, 23 March, 9 April, 4 June 1846, 13 March, 30 April, 13 May, 19 July 1847, FM Reel 2; "Items of a Journey to Harvard," 12 Aug. 1846, WRHS, V B 140; Journal, 6 Nov. 1848, 26 Jan., 13 Feb., 15 Feb., 16 Feb., 20 March, 1850, WRHS, V B 53; "Journal of a trip from Enfield, Conn., to Shaker Communities in Maine, New Hampshire, and Massachusetts. Aug. 26 to Oct. 8, [1850]," 31 Aug. 1850, ASC.

41. Harvard Ministry to Watervliet Ministry, 29 April 1852, WRHS, IV A 25.

42. Margaret Van Alen Frisbee Sommer, *The Shaker Garden Seed Industry* (Old Chatham, N.Y.: Shaker Museum Foundation, 1972), 14.

43. Amy Bess Miller, 65–66, 71; Journal, 1 Jan. 1849, 30 Nov., 31 Dec. 1850, 4 Feb. 1851, WRHS, V B 53; "A Diary Kept for the use & convenience of the Herb Department. By Elisha Myrick. Harvard Mass. Jan. 1st 1853," 31 Dec. 1853, 31 Dec. 1855, ASC. For a complete list of the herbs available from the Harvard Shakers, see Simon Atherton, *Catalogue of Herbs, Roots, Barks, Powdered Articles, Etc. Prepared in the United Society, Harvard, Mass.* (Boston: C.C.P. Moody, 1868).

44. "Account book of the Herb Dept., Harvard, Mass., 1847–1854," ASC.

45. "A Diary Kept for the use & convenience of the Herb Department," 30 Dec. 1854, 31 Dec. 1855, ASC.

10. The Price of Worldliness

1. Hurd, 1: 457, 463–67; Chandler, 50–51; "No. 6 Family Journal—1852&3," 17 May 1852, WRHS, V B 195; Grove Blanchard to Joseph Tillinghast, 24 May 1852, WRHS, IV A 25.

2. [Giles B. Avery], *Circular Concerning the Dress of Believers* (New Lebanon, N.Y.: n.p., 1866), 3–4.

3. Chandler, 50–51; "Money Received of the Phoenix Factory," 1856–1861, comp. by William Leonard, WRHS, II A 11; Central Ministry's Journal, 1850–1859, 25 March, 27 March, 3 May, 6 May, 7 May 1853, NYPL; Grove Blanchard to Joseph Tillinghast, 29 Sept. 1851, WRHS, IV A 59; Samuel Rodman, *The Diary of Samuel Rodman: A New Bedford Chronicle of Thirty-Seven Years, 1821–1859*, ed. Zephaniah Pease (New Bedford, Mass.: Reynolds Printing Co., 1928), 1 March 1853; Grove Blanchard to Joseph Tillinghast, 4 March 1853, WRHS, IV A 59; Grove Blanchard to Joseph Tillinghast, 10 March 1853, WRHS, IV A 26; Joseph Tillinghast to Grove Blanchard, 12 March 1853, WRHS, IV A 26; Harvard Ministry to New Lebanon Ministry, 23 March 1853, WRHS, IV A 26.

4. Harvard Ministry to New Lebanon Ministry, 30 May 1853, WRHS, IV A 26; Rodman, 7–19 July 1856; Chandler, 51–52; *Phoenix Cotton Manufacturing Company* v. *Samuel Hazen and Another*, 118 Mass. 350 (1875); "Money Received of the Phoenix Factory Company," WRHS, II A 11; Central Ministry's Journal, 1850–1859, 15 Jan., 4 Aug. 1857, NYPL; Harvard Ministry to Mount Lebanon Ministry, 10 Feb. 1864, WRHS, IV A 59; Samuel Rodman to Jonas Nutting, 23 Feb. 1857, WRHS, IV A 59.

5. William Leonard to [Mount Lebanon] Ministry, 5 April 1861, WRHS, IV A 28; Central Ministry's Journal, 1859–1874, 8 April 1861, NYPL; "Money Received of the Phoenix Factory Company," WRHS, II A 11; Harvard Ministry to Mount Lebanon Ministry, 10 Feb. 1864, WRHS, IV A 59; Shirley Shaker Journal, 1866–1881, 2 July, 4 Oct. 1866, 7 July 1881, FM Reel 7; Chandler, 51–52; Rodman, 6.

6. Central Ministry's Journal, 1859–1874, 15 Oct. 1863, NYPL.

7. Ibid., 14 Oct 1863; "Circular to Believers Universally. 1864. Mount Lebanon, N.Y," ASC.

8. Harvard Ministry to New Lebanon Ministry, 23 Dec. 1833, WRHS, IV A 23; "Items of a Journey to Harvard," 6 Aug., 12 Aug., 13 Aug., 14 Aug., 16 Aug. 1846, WRHS, V B 140.

9. Brewer, *Shaker Communities*, 215–16; William Sims Bainbridge, "Shaker Demographics 1840–1900: An Example of the Use of U.S. Census Enumeration Schedules," *Journal for the Scientific Study of Religion* 21 (1982): 355.

10. Brewer, *Shaker Communities*, 216; Bainbridge, 355; "Journal of trip to eastern societies by the ministry of Pleasant Hill and South Union," 23 July, 26 July 1869, WRHS, V B 228; Nourse, *History of the Town of Harvard*, 397, 404.

11. "A Journal kept by Alfred Collier," 19 May, 21 May, 27 May, 3 June 1859, January 1860, FM Reel 2.

12. Central Ministry's Journal, 1850–1859, 8 May 1859, NYPL; Central Ministry's Journal, 1859–1870, 9 May 1870, NYPL.

13. Grove Blanchard to Joseph Tillinghast, 25 April 1862, WRHS, IV A 28; "A Journal kept by Alfred Collier, 1859," 21 Dec. 1860, FM Reel 2; Central Ministry's Journal, 1859–1874, 14 Jan. 1862, NYPL.

14. "List of all mail [*sic*] members in the United Society of Shakers in Harvard Mass. liable to do Military duty. 1863," ASC; Jonas Nutting to Benjamin Gates, 11 June 1863, ASC; Jonas Nutting to Benjamin Gates, 26 July 1863, ASC; Elder William Leonard to Sylvester Russell, 21 Oct. 1863, WRHS, IV A 59; H. S. Tabor to Elder John [Whiteley], 28 Sept. 1863, WRHS, IV A 59; H. S. Tabor to Elder John [Whiteley], 29 Sept. 1863, WRHS, IV A 59; copy of a letter from Horace Tabor to Elder William [Wetherbee], 2 Oct. 1863, WRHS, IV A 59; Deposition of Dr. Nathaniel Kingsbury before Isaac Kimball, Justice of the Peace, 2 Oct. 1863, WRHS, IV A 59; Horgan, 111–12.

15. John [Tillinghast] to Joseph Tillinghast, 11 Sept. 1851, WRHS, IV A 25; Ministry Journal, 1851–1854, 2 July 1852, WRHS, V B 218; Lorenzo Grosvenor to Joseph Tillinghast, 15 Jan. 1852. WRHS, IV A 25; Grove Blanchard to Joseph Tillinghast, 4 April 1855, WRHS, IV A 59.

16. "A Journal kept by Alfred Collier, 1859," 21 April, 23 May 1861, FM Reel 2; Journal, 15 April 1861, WRHS, V B 55; Olive Chandler to Joseph Tillinghast, 3 Nov. 1862, WRHS, IV A 28; William Leonard to Joseph Tillinghast, 23 July 1861, WRHS, IV A 28.

17. "Day Book No. 3 [1859–1862] For the United Society at Shirley, Kept by Samuel Augustus Burns, Church," 22 March, 2 April 1862, FM Reel 6; "Day Book No. 7 [1863–1869] For the United Society at Shirley. Kept by Samuel A. Burns, Church," 15 May 1863, FM Reel 6.

18. William Leonard, "Non-Resistance," *The Manifesto* 14 (Nov. 1888): 241–43.

19. Much of this section on the Grosvenor heresy appeared previously in Suzanne Thurman, "Shaker Women and Sexual Power: Heresy and Orthodoxy in the Shaker Village of Harvard, Massachusetts," *Journal of Women's History* 10 (Spring 1998): 70–87.

20. "Account of the Grosvenors [*sic*] Family Coming to Harvard 1819," CAN.

21. John C. Spurlock, *Free Love: Marriage and Middle-Class Radicalism in America, 1825–1860,* The American Social Experience, 13 (New York: New York Univ. Press, 1988), 90–98, 107–38, 143; Braude, 127–41; Owen, 35–38.

22. Spurlock, 4–22.

23. Central Ministry's Journal, 1859–1874, 15 May 1864, NYPL.

24. Youngs, 43–48, 54, 60–71.

25. The Shakers understood the possibility of such an interpretation, but they refused to recognize it as legitimate. At the Free Convention, held in Rutland, Vermont, in 1858, Elder Frederick Evans identified lust as the central, and inherent, problem in the institution of marriage. Therefore, one could not "reform" marriage simply by changing the frequency of or motivation for intercourse. Evans argued that the only solution to the problem of marriage was to "*crucify* the old man, with all his lusts; then you will put the axe to the root of the tree, then you will go down to the bottom of the evil." The only "remedy for all the troubles of the marriage relation" was "a life of virgin purity" (*Proceedings of the Free Convention, Held at Rutland, Vt., July 25th, 26th, and 27th, 1858* [Boston: Yerrinton and Sons, 1858], 62–63).

26. Central Ministry's Journal, 1859–1874, 15 May, 27 Sept. 1864, NYPL.

27. "Deposition and testimonies of Shakers in Grosvenor v. United Society of Believers," testimony of Olive Hatch, CAN.

28. "Deposition and testimonies of Shakers in Grosvenor v. United Society of Believers," deposition of Sylvia Persons, CAN.

29. "Deposition and testimonies of Shakers in Grosvenor v. United Society of Believers," testimony of Maria Foster, testimony of Ellen E. Anthony, CAN; Extract of a letter from the Harvard Ministry to the Mount Lebanon Ministry, 17 July 1864, copied by Giles Avery, (hereafter cited as Grosvenor letter 1864), CAN; Extract of a letter from the Harvard Ministry to the Mount Lebanon Ministry, 27 May 1863, copied by Giles Avery, (hereafter cited as Grosvenor letter 1863), CAN.

30. Grosvenor letter 1863, CAN; "Deposition and testimonies of Shakers," deposition of Sylvia Persons, testimony of Elizabeth E. Grover, testimony of Ann Elizabeth Persons, CAN; Journal, 7 Jan., 7 Feb., 9 Feb., 17 Feb., 12 March, 13 March 1857, WRHS, V B 219.

31. "Deposition and testimonies of Shakers," deposition of Sylvia Persons, CAN; Harvard Ministry's Journal, 1862–1865, 17 Dec., 23 Dec. 1862, 6 Jan., 2 July, 31 July, 14 Oct., 16 Oct., 11 Dec. 1863, 2 Feb., 10 March, 27 April, 29 April, 8 June, 9 June, 26 June, 28 July, 4 Sept., 7 Nov., 29 Dec. 1864, 19 March 1865, ASC; Grosvenor letter 1863, CAN; Grosvenor letter 1864, CAN.

32. After 1861 the New Lebanon, New York, Shaker village officially changed its name to Mount Lebanon.

33. Central Ministry's Journal, 1859–1874, 26 July 1865, NYPL; Harvard Church Register, typescript, 24, FM Reel 1; Roxalana L. Grosvenor, *Shakers' Covenant, (Never before Published,) With a Brief Outline of Shaker History* (Boston: W. C. Allan, 1873).

34. [Francis Wayland-Smith], "Grosvenor Suit," *Oneida Circular* 12 (11 Oct. 1875): 324; subpoena, 1871, CAN; Massachusetts Supreme Judicial Court, *Roxelana* [sic] *L. Grosvenor vs. United Society of Believers.*

35. [James William Towner], "Community Contracts," *Oneida Circular* 11 (21 Dec. 1874): 417–18; Carol Weisbrod, *The Boundaries of Utopia* (New York: Pantheon Books, 1980), xii–xiv; Journal, Harvard 1867–1878, 16 Feb., 7 March 1873, 21 April, 22 April, 23 April, 24 April, 2 May 1874, WRHS, V B 57; "Grosvenor Court Case," *Boston Evening Transcript,* 24 April 1875; *Roxalana L. Grosvenor v. United Society of Believers. Maria F. Grosvenor v. Same,* 118 Mass. 78 (1875); "Defendants' Points in Grosvenor Case," March 1875, CAN. (These last two documents, though dated 1875, refer to the 1874 case.)

36. Journal, Harvard 1867–1878, 24 April, WRHS, V B 57.

37. John [Tillinghast] to Joseph Tillinghast, 11 Sept. 1851, WRHS, IV A 25; William Leonard to Frederick Evans, 24 Oct. 1853, WRHS, IV A 26; copy of a letter from Anna Dodgson to Elder Sister Roxalana Grosvenor, 2 June 1853, FM Reel 3. Four collections by Roxalana Grosvenor may be found at SL, including "Incidents Related by Jemima Blanchard of her experience and Intercourse with Mother Ann and our first Parents," and "A Collection of Particulars respecting the daily walk and conversation of Mother Ann, Father William and Father James as related by those who enjoyed the privilege of being with them, together with some of their own experience, 1850." See also "Incidents Related by some of the Ancient Believers of Their experience & intercourse with Mother & the Elders together with some other Interesting Statements, collected & recorded by Roxalana Grosvenor," WRHS, VI B 9.

38. Roxalana Grosvenor to Joseph Tillinghast, 16 Oct. 1859, WRHS, IV A 59; Roxalana Grosvenor to Joseph Tillinghast, 8 April 1860, WRHS, IV A 59; Roxalana Grosvenor to Joseph Tillinghast, 7 Oct. 1860, WRHS, IV A 59; "A Bundle of Letters," Jeremiah Hacker to Eunice Bathrick, 9 April 1864, 5, FM Reel 5; Hunt, 228; Journal 1856–1859, 15 Feb. 1856, WRHS, V B 54; Finch, 144, 146.

39. Grosvenor letter 1863, CAN.

40. "Deposition and testimonies of Shakers," CAN; Grosvenor letter 1863, CAN.

41. Stephen J. Stein, 205, 236–37.

42. "A Bundle of Letters," Eunice Bathrick to Jeremiah Hacker, 5 June 1864, 40, Eunice Bathrick to Jeremiah Hacker, 14 June 1864, 49, FM Reel 5.

43. "A Bundle of Letters," Eunice Bathrick to Jeremiah Hacker, 5 June 1864, 40, FM Reel 5.

44. Eunice Bathrick to Eldress Betsey Bates, 24 June 1866, WRHS, IV A 28; Stephen J. Stein, 232, 237.

11. The Dissolution of Harvard and Shirley

1. W. D. Howells, "A Shaker Village," *Atlantic Monthly* 37, no. 224 (June 1876): 702, 710.

2. Joel M. Jones, "A Shaker Village Revisited: The Fading of the Familial Ideal in the World of William Dean Howells," *The Old Northwest* 8 (Summer 1982): 86–87, 97–98. See also James W. Mathews, "Howells and the Shakers," *Personalist* 44 (Jan. 1963): 212–19; Alma

J. Payne, "The Family in the Utopia of William Dean Howells," *Georgia Review* 15 (Summer 1961): 217–29; Allen F. Stein, "Marriage in Howells's Novels," *American Literature* 48 (Jan. 1977): 501–24. W. D. Howells's four Shaker novels are: *The Undiscovered Country* (Boston: Houghton Mifflin, 1880); *A Parting and a Meeting* (New York: Harper and Brothers, 1896); *The Day of Their Wedding* (New York: Harper and Brothers, 1896); and *The Vacation of the Kelwyns: An Idyll of the Middle Eighteen-Seventies* (New York: Harper and Brothers, 1920).

3. Journal of Olive Chandler, 1860–1884, 3 Feb., 16 Feb., 27 May, 3 June 1882, 31 May, 1 June, 14 June, 18 June, 23 June 1883, FM. (N.B. Parts of the Fruitlands Collection are not cataloged by reel number).

4. Ibid., 5 Dec. 1882; John Whiteley's Journal 1887, 10 March 1887, FM Reel 11.

5. John Whiteley's Journal 1881, 29 May 1881, FM Reel 10; John Whiteley's Journal 1882, 8 Jan. 1882, FM Reel 10; Shirley Shaker Journal, 1882–1894, 15 Aug. 1886, FM Reel 7.

6. Stephen Paterwic, comp., "An Extract of Names, Ages, and Occupations from the U.S. Census 1850–1900 and from the Massachusetts State Census 1855 and 1865 for Lovely Vineyard, Massachusetts, the Shaker Society at Harvard," HSV; Stephen Paterwic, comp., "Extract of Names, Ages, and Occupations from the US Census 1850–1900 and from the Massachusetts State Census 1855 and 1865 for Pleasant Garden, Massachusetts, the Shaker Society at Shirley," HSV. Compilations are used with Paterwic's permission.

7. Central Ministry's Journal, 1874–1890, 4 April, 12 April 1880, NYPL; Stephen Paterwic, "The Last of the Harvard Shakers," *Shaker Quarterly* 20 (Summer 1992): 69–70, 79 n. 15.

8. John Whiteley to E. P. Bangs, 15 Aug. 1899, John Whiteley's Letterbook, 1898–1901, OC 8833; "A Journal Written by Maria Foster. Commencing, August 1st 1893," 7 May 1898, FM Reel 3.

9. "A Journal Written by Maria Foster," information found on last page of journal, FM Reel 3; John Whiteley's Journal 1883, 5 May, 6 May, 7 May 1883, FM Reel 10; Paterwic, "Last of the Harvard Shakers," 71.

10. Harvard Church Records, typescript, 7, FM Reel 1; "A Journal Written by Maria Foster," 26 Feb. 1900, (after Maria Foster's death in September 1898, Annie Walker continued the journal), FM Reel 3; "Order and Succession of the Ministry and other lists," WRHS, III A 7; John Whiteley to Elder Joseph, 10 Oct. 1900, John Whiteley's Letterbook, 1898–1901, OC 8833; Paterwic, "Last of the Harvard Shakers," 71.

11. "A Journal Written by Maria Foster," 15 Aug. 1904, FM Reel 3; "Order and Succession of the Ministry and other lists," WRHS, III A 7.

12. Andrew [Barrett] to Giles Avery, 29 Sept. 1889, WRHS, IV A 28.

13. Ibid.

14. "A Journal Written by Maria Foster," 20 Jan. 1909, FM Reel 3; Paterwic, "Last of the Harvard Shakers," 71.

15. Charles Edson Robinson, *A Concise History of the United Society of Believers Called Shakers* (East Canterbury, N.H.: United Society of Shakers, 1893), 57; Nourse, *History of Harvard*, 269–70; John Whiteley's Journal 1900, 16 Nov. 1900, SL; Glenn H. Miller, Jr., "The Hawkes Papers: A Case Study of a Kansas Mortgage Brokerage Business, 1871–1888," *Business History Review* 32 (Autumn 1958): 294, 308–9; John Whiteley to Charles M. Hawkins [sic], 9 Dec. 1898, John Whiteley to Hon. George F. Hoar, United States Senate, 24 Feb. 1899, John

Whiteley to Charles M. Hawkes, 9 Dec. 1899, John Whiteley to Charles Hawkes, 5 Dec. 1900, John Whiteley to Charles M. Hawkes, 5 Jan. 1901, John Whiteley's Letterbook, 1898–1901, OC 8833.

16. John Whiteley's Journal 1884, 1 Sept. 1884, FM Reel 10; Shirley Shaker Journal, 1882–1894, 3 April 1882, 3 Dec. 1883, 1 Sept., 11 Nov. 1884, FM Reel 7; John Whiteley's Journal 1881, 18 Feb., 9 March 1881, FM Reel 10.

17. Account Book of Employees of Harvard Shakers, 1876–1908, 26, NYSL; Shirley Shaker Journal, 1866–1881, 21 April 1875, FM Reel 7; John Whiteley's Journal 1895, 8 March 1895, FM Reel 11; "A Journal Written by Maria Foster," 2 April 1907, FM Reel 3.

18. John Whiteley's Journal 1885, 3 Feb., 17 Feb., 18 Feb. 1885, FM Reel 10; John Whiteley's Journal 1883, 30 Nov. 1883, FM Reel 10; John Whiteley's Journal 1895, 4 June, 3 Sept. 1895, FM Reel 11; Shirley Shaker Journal, 1882–1894, 1 Dec. 1883, 7 Jan. 1884, FM Reel 7.

19. Account Book of Employees of Harvard Shakers, 1876–1908, NYSL; "B. J. Goss in account with Harvard Shakers, Jan. 1, 1897," NYSL; "A Journal Written by Maria Foster," 23 Oct. 1893, 2 April, 18 May 1894, 2 May, 25 Dec. 1896, 17 Sept. 1904, FM Reel 3.

20. "Order and Succession of the Ministry and other lists," WRHS, III A 7; John Whiteley's Journal 1881, 19 Jan. 1881, FM Reel 10; John Whiteley's Journal 1882, 18 Jan. 1882, FM Reel 10.

21. Central Ministry's Journal, 1874–1890, 2 May, 3 May 1883, 25 Jan., 26 Jan. 1884, NYPL; John Whiteley's Journal 1884, 22 Jan., 27 Jan. 1884, FM Reel 10.

22. John Whiteley to Mount Lebanon Ministry, 10 Jan. 1886, OC 9741.

23. "A Journal Written by Maria Foster," last page, FM Reel 3; "Order and Succession of the Ministry and other lists," WRHS, III A 7. On the shift to female trustees among the Shakers, see Nickless and Nickless, "Trustees, Deacons, and Deaconesses."

24. Shirley Shaker Journal, 1882–1894, 23 Jan., 15 May 1883, FM Reel 7; Elder John Whiteley's Journal 1883, 25 Nov. 1883, FM Reel 10; Elder John Whiteley's Journal 1884, 27 Jan. 1884, FM Reel 10; Elder John Whiteley's Journal 1885, 6 Nov. 1885, FM Reel 10.

25. John Whiteley's Journal 1882, 9 Jan., 10 Jan. 1882, FM Reel 10; Shirley Shaker Journal, 1882–1894, 9 Jan., 10 Jan., 11 Jan. 1882, FM Reel 7.

26. Elizabeth D. Grover to Friends Gertrude and Henry, 5 Oct. 1908, FM IV A, Harvard 1901–1910; Norbert Wiener, *Ex-Prodigy: My Childhood and Youth* (New York: Simon & Schuster, 1953), 86–87, 90. See also Beverly Gordon, "Shaker Fancy Goods: Women's Work and Presentation of Self in the Community Context in the Victorian Era," in *Women in Spiritual and Communitarian Societies in the United States*, ed. Wendy E. Chmielewski, Louis J. Kern, and Marlyn Klee-Hartzell (Syracuse, N.Y.: Syracuse Univ. Press, 1993), 89–103.

27. "Sisters' Account Book, 1875–1905," OC 8839. The sisters were not always systematic in their record keeping, and for some years, particularly the later ones, it is difficult, if not impossible, to figure statistics for the sale of their work.

28. John Whiteley's Journal 1881, 18 April 1881, FM Reel 10; John Whiteley's Journal 1882, 8 Sept., 3 Nov. 1882, FM Reel 10; John Whiteley's Journal 1883, 16 June 1883, FM Reel 10; "Sisters' Account Book," 1881, OC 8839.

29. John Whiteley's Journal 1882, 16 April 1882, FM Reel 10.

30. Journal of Olive Chandler, 22 July, 28 Aug. 1883, FM; John Whiteley's Journal 1881, 23 Jan., 10 April 1881, FM Reel 10.

31. "Deposition and testimonies of Shakers," testimony of Ann Elizabeth Persons, CAN.

32. John Whiteley's Journal 1877, 17 Aug., 19 Aug. 1877, OC 8826; Journal of Olive Chandler, 25 Sept., 26 Sept. 1882, FM. For a discussion of the Rural Home, see Horgan, 126, and Larry Anderson, "The Rural Home: It Broke Augustus Grosvenor's Heart," *The Harvard Post*, 21 May 1976.

33. John Whiteley's Journal 1888, 7 Nov. 1888, FM Reel 11; "A Journal Written by Maria Foster," 13 Oct., 17 Oct. 1893, 9 Jan. 1895, FM Reel 3; obituary for Roxalana Grosvenor, Boston *Evening Transcript*, 8 Jan. 1895; funeral notice for Roxalana Grosvenor, Boston *Evening Transcript*, 10 Jan. 1895.

34. John Whiteley's Journal 1899, 24 Nov. 1899, FM Reel 11; John Whiteley's Journal 1900, 8 March, 1 Nov. 1900, SL.

35. Horgan, 141–42; Copy of a deed for the sale of Shirley to the state of Massachusetts, 18 Sept. 1908, OC; "Records Book No. 2," 1825–1929, Oct. 1908, NYPL; "A Book of Records of the Church of the United Society In Harvard Massachusetts. Commencing January 1791," 6 Jan. 1909, OC 10340; "A Journal Written by Maria Foster," 6 Jan. 1909, FM Reel 3.

36. "A Journal Written by Maria Foster," 16 Oct., 29 Dec. 1908, 10 March 1909, FM Reel 3.

37. Ibid., 20 Sept. 1894, 28 Oct., 31 Oct., 6 Nov. 1895, 12 April, 8 May 1896, FM Reel 3. The trial of H. H. Holmes, a mass murderer convicted of torturing and killing more than forty women, was highly publicized. He was executed on 7 May 1896 (Carl Sifakis, *The Encyclopedia of American Crime* [New York: Smithmark, 1992], 343).

38. Real estate sale notice, Ayer, Mass., *Turner's Public Spirit*, 19 April 1890; Deed from Joseph Holden, Annie Walker, and Josephine Jilson to Harvard Medical Co., 16 March 1912, OC; "A Book of Records of the Church of the United Society In Harvard Massachusetts. Commencing January 1791," Jan. 1913, OC 10340.

39. Paterwic, "Last of the Harvard Shakers," 74–76; Horgan, 151, 154–55; "Records Book No. 2," 1825–1929, 29 July 1918, NYPL; Copy of a deed for the sale of Harvard to Fiske Warren, 22 April 1918, OC.

40. "Records Book, No. 2," 1825–1929, 29 July 1918, NYPL; "Release of Hattie M. Whitney," 3 Aug. 1918, OC; "Things taken from the Society of Shakers of Harvard, Mass. June 1918 by Hattie M. Whitney," OC; "Releasement of Mary Jane Maxwell," 15 June 1918, OC; "Releasement of Almira E. McLean," 8 June 1918, OC; "Inventory of things taken from the Shaker Society of Harvard Mass. by Myra McLain—May 1918," OC; "Release of All Demands," Bessie Bailey, 4 June 1918, OC; "Inventory of things taken from the Society of Shakers, Harvard, by Bessie Baily [*sic*]. June 1918," OC.

41. "Records Book No. 2," 1825–1929, 29 July 1918, NYPL; M. Catherine Allen to Clara Endicott Sears, 18 Aug. 1918, FM IV A, Mount Lebanon 1918.

42. Josephine Jilson to Clara E. Sears, 6 April 1919, FM IV A, Mount Lebanon 1919; M. Catherine Allen to Clara E. Sears, 28 Dec. 1919, FM IV A, Mount Lebanon 1919; M.

Catherine Allen to Clara E. Sears, 18 Nov. 1918, FM IV A, Mount Lebanon 1918; Paterwic, "Last of the Harvard Shakers," 77; Horgan, 152.

43. M. Catherine Allen to Clara E. Sears, 28 Dec. 1919, FM IV A, Mount Lebanon 1919; obituary for Lottie Tremper Gillette, Ayer, Mass., *Turner's Public Spirit*, no. 16, 7 Dec. 1929.

44. Lottie Tremper Gillette to Gertrude Sanderson, 7 Jan. 1920, FM IV A, Mount Lebanon 1920; obituary for Lottie Tremper Gillette; Horgan, 157–58.

45. Josephine Jilson to Clara E. Sears, 27 July 1922, FM IV A, Mount Lebanon 1922; Paterwic, "Last of the Harvard Shakers," 77–78; Horgan, 159, 167.

Conclusion

1. Beth Wade, "MCI at Shirley: Today and Tomorrow," Ayer, Mass. *The Public Spirit*, 18 Aug. 1983; *Guide to the Shirley Shaker Village* (Shirley, Mass.: Shirley Historical Society, [1995]).

2. Larry Anderson, 21 May 1976; Elijah Myrick, *Shaker Medicinal Spring Water* (Boston: n.p., 1880); Robert C. Anderson, *Directions of a Town: A History of Harvard, Massachusetts* (Harvard, Mass.: Harvard Common Press, 1976), 160–61.

3. Robert C. Anderson, 169–70; Communal Studies Association, *Newsletter* 20 (Summer 1995), 5; Maggie Stier and Ralph N. Fuller, *Shaker Sites in Harvard: A Guide for the Harvard Shaker Bicentennial, 1791–1991* (Harvard, Mass.: Shaker 200 Committee, [1991]); "Shaker Eldresses Visit Harvard for Holy Hill Dedication," *The Harvard Post*, 28 May 1976.

4. Daniel Fraser and John Whiteley, *The Divine Afflatus: A Force in History* (Boston: Rand, Avery and Co., 1875), 14–15; Elijah Myrick, *The Celibate Shaker Life* (Mt. Lebanon, N.Y.: n.p., 1889).

Appendix A

1. The following sources were used to compile the membership rosters.

Published: Bishop and Wells; Caleb Butler, *The History of the Town of Groton, Including Pepperell and Shirley, From the First Grant of Groton Plantation in 1655* (Boston: T. R. Marvin, 1848); Chandler; Rev. Edwin R. Hodgman, *History of the Town of Westford, In the County of Middlesex, Massachusetts, 1659–1883* (Lowell, Mass.: Westford Town History Assoc., 1883); Hudson; Kidder; William Little, *The History of Weare, New Hampshire, 1735–1888* (Lowell, Mass.: S. W. Huse and Co., 1888); Marvin; Nourse, *The Birth, Marriage and Death Register . . . of Lancaster*; Nourse, *History of the Town of Harvard*; Paige; Paterwic, "Necrology"; *Vital Records of Cambridge, Massachusetts, To the Year 1850*, 2 vols., comp. Thomas W. Baldwin (Boston: Wright and Potter Printing Co., 1914); *Vital Records of Chelmsford, Massachusetts, To the End of the Year 1849* (Salem, Mass.: Essex Institute, 1914); *Vital Records of Harvard, Massachusetts, To the Year 1850*, comp. Thomas W. Baldwin (Boston: Wright and Potter Printing Co., 1917); *Vital Records of Petersham, Massachusetts, To the End of the Year 1849* (Worcester, Mass.: Franklin P. Rice, 1904); *Vital Records of Sutton, Massachusetts, To the End of the Year 1849* (Worcester, Mass.: Franklin P. Rice, 1907); *Vital Records of Upton, Massachusetts, To the End of the Year 1849* (Worcester, Mass.: Franklin P. Rice, 1904); Waters.

Unpublished: "A Book, Containing the Records of the Church, In the United Society; Shirley, Mass. Transcribed in the Month of February 1844," OC; "A Book of Records of the Church of the United Society In Harvard Massachusetts. Commencing January 1791," OC; "Church Records, 1791–1835," typescript, FM Reel 1; "Circumstances respecting the Square House—related by Abel Jewett, Jonathan Clark, Jr. & others," WRHS, VII A 2; "A Collection of Harvard Shaker Manuscripts," FM Reel 8; "A Collection of Particulars respecting the daily walk and conversation of Mother Ann, Father William and Father James," SL; "Family history of Hannah Lion, written by her," WRHS, III A 11; Grosvenor, "Incidents #1," SL; Hammond, "Sketches of Ireland," WRHS, VII B 27; Harvard land deeds, 26 June 1752; 24 Jan. 1755, WRHS, I A 7; "Incidents Related by some of the Ancient Believers . . . collected by Roxalana Grosvenor," WRHS, VI B 9; Indenture of Artemus Coolidge, 29 Nov. 1813, WRHS, I A 14; "Index Nominum," SL; List of births and deaths, Shirley, Mass., WRHS, III A 11; "Manifest Journal," FM Reel 1; Miscellaneous documents, WRHS, II A 11; "Names and places of Interment Of Those who Deceased in the United Society At Harvard. Commencing in the year 1784," WRHS, III B 8; "Names of those gathered into the Church and Societies of Harvard and Shirley; from the gathering of the people into order in the year 1791, to the present date. Harvard December 2, 1860 Together with their births, place of nativity, admittance, Death & removals etc," ASC; "Record of deaths in the Church since the first gathering. New Lebanon," WRHS, III A 8; "Record of the Church . . . in Shirley," WRHS, I B 62; "Sayings of Elder John taken down by Susan Channel and Sally Loomis," WRHS, VII B 18; "Sayings of Mother Ann and the First Elders, taken from Abijah Worster," WRHS, VII B 22; Shirley Church Register, CAN; Shirley discharges, 11 Jan. 1811, 13 April 1815, WRHS, I A 14; Shirley land deeds, 8 Dec. 1772, 30 May 1785, 28 Jan. 1794, WRHS, I A 14; "Testimonies And Wise Sayings . . . transcribed by Eunice," WRHS, VI B 10; "Testimonies concerning the character and ministry of Mother Ann Lee and the first witnesses of the gospel of Christ's second appearing; given by some of the aged Brethren & Sisters of the United Society, including a few sketches of their own religious experience; approved by the Church, comp. Seth Y. Wells, New Lebanon, May 1, 1827," WRHS, VI B 52; Testimonies of Patience Crouch, John Robinson, Elizabeth Woodward, Oliver Burt, Sarah Burt, Nathan Willard, VI A 8; "Testimonies or the Wise Sayings . . . Written by Eunice Bathrick,", VI B 11; Testimony of Abijah Worster, VI A 5; Thomas Hammond's receipt of inheritance, 1 April 1793, OC.

Bibliography

Shaker Manuscript Collections

American Antiquarian Society. Worcester, Mass.
Andrews Shaker Collection. Henry Francis du Pont Winterthur Museum. Winterthur, Del.
Canterbury Shaker Village. Canterbury, N.H.
Emma B. King Library. Shaker Museum. Old Chatham, N.Y.
Fruitlands Museums. Harvard, Mass.
Hancock Shaker Village, Inc. Hancock, Mass.
Library of Congress. Washington, D.C.
Manuscripts and Special Collections. New York State Library. Albany, N.Y.
Shaker Collection. Williams College Archives and Special Collections. Williams College
    Library. Williams College. Williamstown, Mass.
Shaker Library. United Society of Shakers. Sabbathday Lake, Maine.
Shaker Manuscript Collection. Manuscript and Archives Division, New York Public Library.
    Astor, Lenox, and Tilden Foundations.
Western Reserve Historical Society. Cleveland, Ohio.

Published Sources

American Reformers. Edited by Alden Whitman. New York: H.W. Wilson Co., 1985.
Amott, Teresa L., and Julie A. Matthaei. *Race, Gender, and Work: A Multicultural Economic History
    of Women in the United States.* Boston: South End Press, 1991.
The Anchor Bible Dictionary. Edited by David Noel Freedman et al. 6 vols. New York: Double-
    day, 1992.
Anderson, Robert C. *Directions of a Town: A History of Harvard, Massachusetts.* Harvard, Mass.:
    Harvard Common Press, 1976.
Andrews, Edward Deming. *The Gift to Be Simple: Songs, Dances and Rituals of the American Shakers.*
    1940. Reprint. New York: Dover, 1962.
————. *The People Called Shakers: A Search for the Perfect Society.* Enl.ed. New York: Dover, 1963.

Andrews, Edward Deming, and Faith Andrews. *Work and Worship: The Economic Order of the Shakers.* Greenwich, Conn.: New York Graphic Society, 1974.

Armstrong, Karen. *The Gospel According to Woman: Christianity's Creation of the Sex War in the West.* 1986. Reprint. New York: Doubleday, 1987.

Atherton, Simon. *Catalogue of Herbs, Roots, Barks, Powdered Articles, Etc. Prepared in the United Society,* Harvard, Mass. Boston: C. C. P. Moody, 1868.

[Avery, Giles B.] *Circular Concerning the Dress of Believers.* New Lebanon, N.Y.: n.p., 1866.

Backus, Isaac. *A History of New-England, with Particular Reference to the Denomination of Christians called Baptists. Containing The first principles and settlement of the Country; the rise and increase of the Baptist Churches therein; The intrusion of Arbitrary Power under the cloak of Religion; The Christian Testimonies of the Baptists and others against the same, with their Sufferings under it, from the Begining [sic] to the present Time. Collected from most authentic Records and Writings, both Ancient and Modern.* 3 vols. Boston: Edward Draper, 1777; Providence, R.I.: John Carter, 1784; Boston: Manning and Loring, 1796.

Bainbridge, William Sims. "Shaker Demographics 1840–1900: An Example of the Use of U.S. Census Enumeration Schedules." *Journal for the Scientific Study of Religion* 21 (1982): 352–65.

Barkun, Michael. *Crucible of the Millennium: The Burned-Over District of New York in the 1840s. A New York State Study.* Syracuse, N.Y.: Syracuse Univ. Press, 1986.

Basch, Norma. *In the Eyes of the Law: Women, Marriage, and Property in Nineteenth-Century New York.* Ithaca, N.Y.: Cornell Univ. Press, 1982.

Bednarowski, Mary Farrell. "Women in Occult America." In *The Occult in America: New Historical Perspectives,* edited by Howard Kerr and Charles L. Crow, 177–95. Urbana: Univ. of Illinois Press, 1983.

Bem, Sandra. "The Measurement of Psychological Androgyny." *Journal of Consulting and Clinical Psychology* 42 (April 1974): 155–62.

Bentley, William. *The Diary of William Bentley, D. D.* 4 vols. Salem, Mass.: Essex Institute, 1905–1914.

Binford, Henry C. *The First Suburbs: Residential Communities on the Boston Periphery, 1815–1860.* Chicago: Univ. of Chicago Press, 1985.

Bishop, Rufus, and Seth Y. Wells, eds. *Testimonies of the Life, Character, Revelations and Doctrines of Our Blessed Mother Ann Lee, and the Elders with Her; Through Whom the Word of Eternal Life was Opened in this Day of Christ's Second Appearing: Collected from Living Witnesses, By Order of the Ministry in Union with the Church.* Hancock, Mass.: Tallcott and Deming, 1816.

Bolton, Ethel Stanwood. *Shirley Uplands and Intervales: Annals of a Border Town of Old Middlesex County, with Some Genealogical Sketches.* Boston: George Emery Littlefield, 1914.

Boxer, Marilyn J., and Jean H. Quataert. "Introduction: Restoring Women to History." In *Connecting Spheres: Women in the Western World, 1500 to the Present,* edited by Marilyn J. Boxer and Jean H. Quataert, 3–17. New York: Oxford Univ. Press, 1987.

Boydston, Jeanne. *Home and Work: Housework, Wages, and the Ideology of Labor in the Early Republic.* New York: Oxford Univ. Press, 1990.

———. "The Woman Who Wasn't There: Women's Market Labor and the Transition to Capitalism in the United States." In *Wages of Independence: Capitalism in the Early American Republic,* edited by Paul A. Gilje, 23–47. Madison, Wis.: Madison House, 1997.

Brady, Marilyn Dell. "The New Model Middle-Class Family (1815–1930)." In *American Families: A Research Guide and Historical Handbook*, edited by Joseph M. Hawes and Elizabeth I. Nybakken, 83–123. Westport, Conn.: Greenwood Press, 1991.

Braude, Ann. *Radical Spirits: Spiritualism and Women's Rights in Nineteenth-Century America*. Boston: Beacon Press, 1989.

Brewer, Priscilla. "Emerson, Lane, and the Shakers: A Case of Converging Ideologies." *New England Quarterly* 55 (1982): 254–75.

———. *Shaker Communities, Shaker Lives*. Hanover, N.H.: Univ. Press of New England, 1986.

———. "'Tho of the Weaker Sex': A Reassessment of Gender Equality among the Shakers." In *Woman in Spiritual and Communitarian Societies in the United States*, edited by Wendy E. Chmielewski, Louis J. Kern, and Maryln Klee-Hartzell, 133–49.

Brown, Thomas. *An Account of the People Called Shakers: Their Faith, Doctrines, and Practice, Exemplified in the Life, Conversations, and Experience of the Author during the Time He Belonged to the Society. To Which is Affixed a History of their Rise and Progress to the Present Day*. 1812. Reprint. New York: AMS Press, 1972.

Broyles, Michael. *"Music of the Highest Class": Elitism and Populism in Antebellum Boston*. New Haven, Conn.: Yale Univ. Press, 1992.

Burns, Deborah E. *Shaker Cities of Peace, Love, and Union: A History of the Hancock Bishopric*. Hanover, N.H.: Univ. Press of New England, 1993.

Butler, Caleb. *The History of the Town of Groton, Including Pepperell and Shirley, From the First Grant of Groton Plantation in 1655*. Boston: T.R. Marvin, 1848.

Bynum, Caroline Walker. "'. . . And Woman His Humanity': Female Imagery in the Religious Writings of the Later Middle Ages." In *Gender and Religion: On the Complexity of Symbols*, edited by Caroline Walker Bynum, Stevan Harrell, and Paula Richman, 257–88.

———. *Holy Feast and Holy Fast: The Religious Significance of Food to Medieval Women*. The New Historicism: Studies in Cultural Poetics, 1. Berkeley and Los Angeles: Univ. of California Press, 1987.

———. "Introduction: The Complexity of Symbols." In *Gender and Religion: On the Complexity of Symbols*, edited by Caroline Walker Bynum, Stevan Harrell, and Paula Richman, 1–20. Boston, Beacon Press, 1986.

———. *Jesus as Mother: Studies in the Spirituality of the High Middle Ages*. Berkeley and Los Angeles: Univ. of California Press, 1984.

Campbell, D'Ann. "Women's Life in Utopia: The Shaker Experiment in Sexual Equality Reappraised, 1810–1860." *New England Quarterly* 51 (1978): 23–38.

Carroll, Bret E. *Spiritualism in Antebellum America*. Religion in North America Series. Bloomington: Indiana Univ. Press, 1997.

Cayleff, Susan E. *Wash and Be Healed: The Water-Cure Movement and Women's Health*. Health, Society, and Policy. Philadelphia: Temple Univ. Press, 1987.

Chandler, Seth. *History of the Town of Shirley, Massachusetts, From Its Early Settlement to A.D. 1882*. Shirley, Mass.: pub. by the author, 1883.

Christie-Murray, David. *A History of Heresy*. 1976. Reprint. Oxford: Oxford Univ. Press, 1989.

Clark, Christopher. *The Roots of Rural Capitalism: Western Massachusetts, 1780–1860*. Ithaca, N.Y.: Cornell Univ. Press, 1990.

Clark, George Faber. *A History of the Town of Norton, Bristol County, Massachusetts, From 1669 to 1859.* Boston: Crosby, Nichols, and Co., 1859.

Cogan, Frances B. *All-American Girl: The Ideal of Real Womanhood in Mid-Nineteenth-Century America.* Athens: Univ. of Georgia Press, 1989.

Commons, John R. "American Shoemakers, 1648–1895, A Sketch of Industrial Evolution." *Quarterly Journal of Economics* 24 (1909): 39–84.

Communal Studies Association. *Newsletter* 20 (Summer 1995).

Cook, Ellen Piel. *Psychological Androgyny.* Pergamon General Psychology Series, 133. New York: Pergamon, 1985.

Coontz, Stephanie. *The Social Origins of Private Life: A History of American Families, 1600–1900.* Haymarket Series. London: Verso, 1988.

Cott, Nancy F. *The Bonds of Womanhood: "Woman's Sphere" in New England, 1778–1835.* New Haven, Conn.: Yale Univ. Press, 1977.

———. *The Grounding of Modern Feminism.* New Haven, Conn.: Yale Univ. Press, 1987.

Cowan, Ruth Schwartz. *More Work for Mother: The Ironies of Household Technology from the Open Hearth to the Microwave.* New York: Basic Books, 1983.

Crawford, Patricia. "Divine Androgyny and Female Activism: Gender and Religion in Early Modern History." *Gender and History* 10 (Aug. 1998): 303–6.

Crosthwaite, Jane Freeman. "Polly Reed: Shaker Artist and Minister." Paper delivered at the spring meeting of the American Society of Church History, Williamsburg, Virginia, 2 April 1993.

Dain, Norman. *Concepts of Insanity in the United States, 1789–1865.* New Brunswick, N.J.: Rutgers Univ. Press, 1964.

Daly, Mary. *Gyn/Ecology: The Metaethics of Radical Feminism.* Boston: Beacon Press, 1978.

Davis, A. B. *True Love: What it is, and what it is not.* Shaker Tracts for the Times, no. 1. Shirley, Mass.: pub. for the author, 1869.

Degler, Carl N. *At Odds: Women and the Family in America from the Revolution to the Present.* New York: Oxford Univ. Press, 1980.

Deignan, Kathleen. *Christ Spirit: The Eschatology of Shaker Christianity.* ATLA Monograph Series, no. 29. Methuen, N.J.: Scarecrow Press, 1992.

Desroche, Henri. *The American Shakers: From Neo-Christianity to Presocialism.* Translated and edited by John K. Savacool. Amherst: Univ. of Massachusetts Press, 1971.

Dictionary of American Biography. Edited by Dumas Malone. 10 vols. New York: Charles Scribner's Sons, 1936.

Donegan, Jane B. *"Hydropathic Highway to Health": Women and Water-Cure in Antebellum America.* Contributions in Medical Studies, no. 17. New York: Greenwood Press, 1986.

Douglas, Ann. *The Feminization of American Culture.* New York: Alfred A. Knopf, 1977.

Dublin, Thomas. *Transforming Women's Work: New England Lives in the Industrial Revolution.* Ithaca, N.Y.: Cornell Univ. Press, 1994.

Ellis, Leonard Bolles. *History of New Bedford and Its Vicinity, 1602–1892.* Syracuse, N.Y.: D. Mason and Co., 1892.

Emerson, Ralph Waldo. *Journals of Ralph Waldo Emerson: With Annotations.* Edited by Edward Waldo Emerson and Waldo Emerson Forbes. 10 vols. Boston: Houghton Mifflin, 1911.

———. *The Letters of Ralph Waldo Emerson.* Edited by Ralph L. Husk. 6 vols. New York: Columbia Univ. Press, 1939.

Evans, Frederick. "Pre-Existence of Christ." *The Shaker Manifesto* 10 (Jan. 1880): 3–4.

Extract from an Unpublished Manuscript on Shaker History (by an Eye Witness.) Giving an Accurate Description of Their Songs, Dances, Marches, Visions, Visits to the Spirit Land, etc. Boston: E. K. Allen, 1850.

Faragher, John Mack. *Women and Men on the Overland Trail.* New Haven, Conn.: Yale Univ. Press, 1979.

Farrell, Betty G. *Elite Families: Class and Power in Nineteenth-Century Boston.* SUNY Series in the Sociology of Work. Albany: State Univ. Press of New York, 1993.

Finch, Marianne. *An Englishwoman's Experience in America.* London: R. Bentley, 1853.

Fink, Leon. *Workingmen's Democracy: The Knights of Labor and American Politics.* Urbana: Univ. of Illinois Press, 1983.

Finke, Laurie A. "Mystical Bodies and the Dialogics of Vision." In *Maps of Flesh and Light: The Religious Experience of Medieval Women Mystics,* edited by Ulrike Wiethaus, 28–44. Syracuse, N.Y.: Syracuse Univ. Press, 1993.

Fischer, David Hackett. *Albion's Seed: Four British Folkways in America.* New York: Oxford Univ. Press, 1989.

Fornell, Earl Wesley. *The Unhappy Medium: Spiritualism and the Life of Margaret Fox.* Austin: Univ. of Texas Press, 1964.

Foster, Lawrence. "Had Prophecy Failed?: Contrasting Perspectives of the Millerites and Shakers." In *The Disappointed: Millerism and Millenarianism in the Nineteenth Century,* edited by Ronald L. Numbers and Jonathan M. Butler, 92–117. Religion in North America. Bloomington: Indiana Univ. Press, 1987.

———. *Religion and Sexuality: Three American Communal Experiments of the Nineteenth Century.* New York: Oxford Univ. Press, 1981.

———. "Shaker Spiritualism and Salem Witchcraft: Social Perspectives on Trance and Possession Phenomena." *Communal Societies* 5 (Fall 1985): 176–93.

Fraser, Daniel, and John Whiteley. *The Divine Afflatus: A Force in History.* Boston: Rand, Avery and Co., 1875.

Garrett, Clarke. *Spirit Possession and Popular Religion: From the Camisards to the Shakers.* Baltimore: Johns Hopkins Univ. Press, 1987.

Gelpi, Barbara Charlesworth. "The Politics of Androgyny." *Women's Studies* 2 (1974): 151–60.

Gibbons, B. J. *Gender in Mystical and Occult Thought: Behmenism and its Development in England.* Cambridge: Cambridge Univ. Press, 1996.

Ginzberg, Louis. *The Legends of the Jews.* 7 vols. Philadelphia: Jewish Publication Society of America, 1925.

Godbeer, Richard. "'Love Raptures': Marital, Romantic, and Erotic Images of Jesus Christ in Puritan New England, 1670–1730." In *A Shared Experience: Men, Women, and the History of Gender,* edited by Laura McCall and Donald Yacovone, 51–77. New York: New York Univ. Press, 1998.

Goen, C. C. *Revivalism and Separatism in New England, 1740–1800: Strict Congregationalists and Separate Baptists in the Great Awakening.* New Haven, Conn.: Yale Univ. Press, 1962.

Gooden, Rosemary D. "'In the Bonds of True Love and Friendship': Some Meanings of 'Gospel Affection' and 'Gospel Union' in Shaker Sisters' Letters and Poems." In *Women in Spiritual and Communitarian Societies in the United States,* edited by Wendy E. Chmielewski, Louis J. Kern, and Marlyn Klee-Hartzell, 104–13. Syracuse, N.Y.: Syracuse Univ. Press, 1993.

Gordon, Beverly. "Dress in American Communal Societies." *Communal Societies* 5 (1985): 122–36.

———. "Shaker Fancy Goods: Women's Work and Presentation of Self in the Community Context in the Victorian Era." In *Women in Spiritual and Communitarian Societies in the United States,* edited by Wendy E. Chmielewski, Louis J. Kern, and Marlyn Klee-Hartzell, 89–103. Syracuse, N.Y.: Syracuse Univ. Press, 1993.

Green, Calvin, and Seth Y. Wells. *Summary View of the Millennial Church, or United Society of Believers, (Commonly Called Shakers.) comprising the Rise, Progress and Practical Order of the Society, together with the General Principles of their Faith and Testimony.* Albany, N.Y.: Packard and Van Benthuysen, 1823.

Gregg, Robert C., and Dennis E. Groh. *Early Arianism: A View of Salvation.* Philadelphia: Fortress Press, 1981.

Grob, Gerald. *Mental Illness and American Society, 1875–1940.* Princeton, N.J.: Princeton Univ. Press, 1983.

Gross, Robert A. "Culture and Cultivation: Agriculture and Society in Thoreau's Concord." *Journal of American History* 69 (June 1982): 42–61.

———. *The Minutemen and Their World.* New York: Hill and Wang, 1976.

Grossberg, Michael. *Governing the Hearth: Law and the Family in Nineteenth-Century America.* Studies in Legal History. Chapel Hill: Univ. of North Carolina Press, 1985.

Grosvenor, Lorenzo Dow. *Circular Letter in Defence of the United Society of Believers, Commonly Called Shakers; With a Reply to Correspondents.* Harvard, Mass.: n.p., 1849.

[———]. *Testimony of Jesus Concerning Marriage: Marriage,—Jesus and the Shakers.* N.p.: n.d.

Grosvenor, Roxalana L. *The Shakers' Covenant, (Never before Published,) With a Brief Outline of Shaker History.* Boston: W. C. Allan, 1873.

Guide to the Shirley Shaker Village. Shirley, Mass.: Shirley Historical Society [1995].

Hammond, Joseph. "Account of the Shakers." In *A Gazetteer of Massachusetts Containing a General View of the State, With an Historical Sketch of the Principal Events from Its Settlement to the Present Time, and Notices of the Several Towns Alphabetically Arranged,* compiled by Jeremiah Spofford, 211–12. Newburyport, Mass.: Charles Whipple, 1828.

Hansen, Karen V. *A Very Social Time: Crafting Community in Antebellum New England.* Berkeley and Los Angeles: Univ. of California Press, 1994.

Harris, Daniel A. "Androgyny: The Sexist Myth in Disguise." *Women's Studies* 2 (1974): 171–84.

Heilbrun, Carolyn. *Toward a Recognition of Androgyny.* New York: Alfred A. Knopf, 1973.

Herndl, Diane Price. *Invalid Women: Figuring Feminine Illness in American Fiction.* Chapel Hill: Univ. of North Carolina Press, 1993.

Hessinger, Rodney. "Problems and Promises: Colonial American Child Rearing and Modernization Theory." *Journal of Family History* 21 (April 1996): 125–43.

Hoch-Smith, Judith, and Anita Spring. "Introduction." In *Women in Ritual and Symbolic Roles*, edited by Judith Hoch-Smith and Anita Spring, 1–23. New York: Plenum Press, 1978.

Hodgman, Rev. Edwin R. *History of the Town of Westford, in the County of Middlesex, Massachusetts, 1659–1883.* Lowell, Mass.: Westford Town History Assoc., 1883.

Horgan, Edward R. *The Shaker Holy Land: A Community Portrait.* Harvard, Mass.: Harvard Common Press, 1982.

Howells, W. D. *The Day of Their Wedding.* New York: Harper and Brothers, 1896.

———. *A Parting and a Meeting.* New York: Harper and Brothers, 1896.

———. "A Shaker Village." *Atlantic Monthly* 37, no. 224 (June 1876): 699–710.

———. *The Undiscovered Country.* Boston: Houghton Mifflin, 1880.

———. *The Vacation of the Kelwyns: An Idyll of the Middle Eighteen-Seventies.* New York: Harper and Brothers, 1920.

Hudson, Charles. *History of the Town of Lexington, Middlesex County, Massachusetts, From Its First Settlement to 1868.* 2 vols. Rev. and cont. to 1912 by the Lexington Historical Society. Boston: Houghton, Mifflin Co., 1913.

Humez, Jean M. " 'Weary of Petticoat Government': The Specter of Female Rule in Early Nineteenth-Century Shaker Politics." *Communal Societies* 11 (1991): 1–17.

———. " 'A Woman Mighty to Pull You Down': Married Women's Rights and Female Anger in the Anti-Shaker Narratives of Eunice Chapman and Mary Marshall Dyer." *Journal of Women's History* 6 (Summer 1994): 90–110.

Hunt, Harriot K. *Glances and Glimpses; or Fifty Years Social, Including Twenty Years Professional Life.* Boston: John P. Jewett, 1856.

Hurd, D. Hamilton, comp. *History of Middlesex County, Massachusetts, with Biographical Sketches of Many of Its Pioneers and Prominent Men.* 3 vols. Philadelphia: J. W. Lewis, 1890.

Hyland, J. R. *Sexism is a Sin: The Biblical Basis of Female Equality.* Sarasota, Fla.: Viatoris Pub., 1995.

"Introduction." In *A Shared Experience: Men, Women, and the History of Gender,* edited by Laura McCall and Donald Yacovone, 1–15. New York: New York Univ. Press, 1998.

Irvin, Helen Deiss. "The Machine in Utopia: Shaker Women and Technology." *Women's Studies International Quarterly* 4, no. 3 (1981): 313–19.

Isaac, Rhys. *The Transformation of Virginia, 1740–1790.* Chapel Hill: Univ. of North Carolina Press for the Institute of Early American History and Culture, Williamsburg, Virginia, 1982.

Isaacs, Ernest. "The Fox Sisters and American Spiritualism." In *The Occult in America: New Historical Perspectives,* edited by Howard Kerr and Charles L. Crow, 79–110. Urbana: Univ. of Illinois Press, 1983.

Jensen, Joan M. *Promise to the Land: Essays on Rural Women.* Albuquerque: Univ. of New Mexico Press, 1991.

Jensen, Joan M., with Susan Armitage. "Women in the Hop Harvest from New York to Washington." In *Promise to the Land: Essays on Rural Women,* by Joan M. Jensen, 97–109. Albuquerque: Univ. of New Mexico Press, 1991.

Johnson, Theodore. "The 'Millennial Laws' of 1821." *Shaker Quarterly* 7 (Summer 1967): 35–58.

————. "Rules and Orders for the Church of Christ's Second Appearing." *Shaker Quarterly* 11 (Winter 1971): 139–65.

Johnston, Carolyn. *Sexual Power: Feminism and the Family in America.* Tuscaloosa: Univ. of Alabama Press, 1992.

Jones, Joel M. "A Shaker Village Revisited: The Fading of the Familial Ideal in the World of William Dean Howells." *The Old Northwest* 8 (Summer 1982): 85–100.

Kaltik, Susan. "Ethnic Foodways in America: Symbol and the Performance of Identity." In *Ethnic and Regional Foodways in the United States: The Performance of Group Identity,* edited by Linda Keller Brown and Kay Mussell, 37–65. Knoxville: Univ. of Tennessee Press, 1984.

Kann, Mark E. *A Republic of Men: The American Founders, Gendered Language, and Patriarchal Politics.* New York: New York Univ. Press, 1998.

Kanter, Rosabeth Moss. *Commitment and Community: Communes and Utopias in Sociological Perspective.* Cambridge, Mass.: Harvard Univ. Press, 1972.

Kasserman, David Richard. *Fall River Outrage: Life, Murder, and Justice in Early Industrial New England.* Philadelphia: Univ. of Pennsylvania Press, 1986.

Kaufman, Martin. *Homeopathy in America: The Rise and Fall of a Medical Heresy.* Baltimore: Johns Hopkins Univ. Press, 1971.

Kerber, Linda K. *Women of the Republic: Intellect and Ideology in Revolutionary America.* Chapel Hill: Univ. of North Carolina Press for the Institute of Early American History and Culture, Williamsburg, Virginia, 1980.

Kern, Louis. *An Ordered Love: Sex Roles and Sexuality in Victorian Utopias—The Shakers, the Mormons, and the Oneida Community.* Chapel Hill: Univ. of North Carolina Press, 1981.

Kerr, Howard. *Mediums, and Spirit-Rappers, and Roaring Radicals: Spiritualism in American Literature, 1850–1900.* Urbana: Univ. of Illinois Press, 1972.

Kessler-Harris, Alice. *Out to Work: A History of Wage-Earning Women in the United States.* New York: Oxford Univ. Press, 1982.

————. *A Woman's Wage: Historical Meanings and Social Consequences.* Lexington: Univ. Press of Kentucky, 1990.

Kidder, Frederic. *The History of New Ipswich, from Its First Grant in MDCCXXXVI, to the Present Time: With Genealogical Notes of the Principal Families, and Also the Proceedings of the Centennial Celebration, September 11, 1850.* Boston: Gould and Lincoln, 1852.

Kitch, Sally L. " 'As a Sign That All May Understand': Shaker Gift Drawings and Female Spiritual Power." *Winterthur Portfolio* 24 (Spring 1989): 1–28.

————. *Chaste Liberation: Celibacy and Female Cultural Status.* Urbana: Univ. of Illinois Press, 1989.

Lane, Charles, and Bronson Alcott. Letter. *Herald of Freedom* 8 Sept. 1843. Quoted in Clara Endicott Sears, comp., *Bronson Alcott's Fruitlands,* 44–45. Boston: Houghton Mifflin, 1915.

Leach, William. *True Love and Perfect Union: The Feminist Reform of Sex and Society.* New York: Basic Books, 1980.

Leonard, William. *A Discourse on the Order and Propriety of Divine Inspiration and Revelation, Showing the Necessity Thereof in All Ages, to Know the Will of God. Also, a Discourse on the Second Appearing of Christ, in and through the Order of the Female. And a Discourse on the Propriety and Necessity of a United Inheritance in All Things, in Order to Support a True Christian Community.* Harvard, Mass.: United Society of Believers, 1853.

————. "Non-Resistance." *The Manifesto* 14 (Nov. 1884): 241–43.

Lerner, Gerda. *The Creation of Patriarchy. Women in History*, vol. 1. New York: Oxford Univ. Press, 1986.

Lester, Katherine Morris, and Rose Netzorg Kerr. *Historic Costume: A Resumé of Style and Fashion from Remote Times to the Nineteen-Sixties*. 6th ed. Peoria, Ill.: Chas. A. Bennett Co., 1967.

Levy, Barry. *Quakers and the American Family: British Settlement in the Delaware Valley*. New York: Oxford Univ. Press, 1988.

Lewis, I. M. *Ecstatic Religion: An Anthropological Study of Spirit Possession and Shamanism*. Pelican Anthropology Library. Harmondsworth: Penguin, 1971.

Little, William. *The History of Weare, New Hampshire, 1735–1888*. Lowell, Mass.: S. W. Huse and Co., 1888.

Lockridge, Kenneth A. "Land, Population, and the Evolution of New England Society 1630–1800." *Past and Present* 39 (1968): 62–80.

Lovejoy, Richard. "Shun Thy Father and All That: The Enthusiasts' Threat to the Family." *New England Quarterly* (March 1987): 71–85.

Madden, Etta M. *Bodies of Life: Shaker Literacies and Literature*. Contributions to the Study of Religion, no. 52. Westport, Conn.: Greenwood Press, 1998.

Main, Jackson Turner. *The Social Structure of Revolutionary America*. Princeton, N.J.: Princeton Univ. Press, 1965.

Marini, Stephen A. "A New View of Mother Ann Lee and the Rise of American Shakerism, Part II." *Shaker Quarterly* 18 (Fall 1990): 95–114.

————. *Radical Sects of Revolutionary New England*. Cambridge, Mass.: Harvard Univ. Press, 1982.

Marvin, Abijah P. *History of the Town of Lancaster, Massachusetts: From the First Settlement to the Present Time, 1643–1879*. Lancaster, Mass.: pub. by the town, 1879.

Massachusetts Supreme Judicial Court, Suffolk SS. *Roxelana [sic] L. Grosvenor vs. United Society of Believers, Mary F. Grosvenor vs. Same. Plaintiff's Brief*. Boston: n.p., 1871.

Mathews, James W. "Howells and the Shakers." *Personalist* 44 (Jan. 1963): 212–19.

McLoughlin, William G. *New England Dissent, 1630–1833: The Baptists and the Separation of Church and State*. 2 vols. Cambridge, Mass.: Harvard Univ. Press, 1971.

McMahon, Sarah F. "A Comfortable Subsistence: The Changing Composition of Diet in Rural New England, 1620–1840." 3d ser. *William and Mary Quarterly* 42 (January 1985): 26–65.

McMurry, Sally. *Families and Farmhouses in Nineteenth-Century America: Vernacular Design and Social Change*. New York: Oxford Univ. Press, 1988.

————. *Transforming Rural Life: Dairying Families and Agricultural Change, 1820–1885*. Baltimore: Johns Hopkins Univ. Press, 1995.

[Meacham, Joseph.] *A Concise Statement of the Principles of the Only True Church, according to the Gospel, of the Present Appearance of Christ. As Held to and Practiced upon by the True Followers of the Living Saviour, at New-Lebanon, &c. Together with a Letter from James Whittaker, Minister of the Gospel in this Day of Christ's Second Appearance, to his Natural Relations in England*. Bennington, Vt.: Haswell and Russell, 1790.

Mercadante, Linda A. *Gender, Doctrine, and God: The Shakers and Contemporary Theology*. Nashville: Abingdon Press, 1990.

Mihok, Marsha. "Women in the Authority Structure of Shakerism: A Study of Social Conflict and Social Change." Ph.D. diss., Drew Univ., 1989.

Miller, Amy Bess. *Shaker Herbs: A History and a Compendium*. New York: Clarkson N. Potter, 1976.

Miller, Jr., Glenn H. "The Hawkes Papers: A Case Study of a Kansas Mortgage Brokerage Business, 1871–1888." *Business History Review* 32 (Autumn 1958): 293–310.

Mintz, Steven, and Susan Kellogg. *Domestic Revolutions: A Social History of American Family Life.* New York: Free Press, 1988.

Mitterauer, Michael, and Reinhard Sieder. *The European Family: Patriarchy to Partnership from the Middle Ages to the Present.* Translated by Karla Oosterveen and Manfred Hörzinger. Chicago: Univ. of Chicago Press, 1982.

Moore, R. Laurence. *Religious Outsiders and the Making of Americans*. New York: Oxford Univ. Press, 1986.

Myrick, Elijah. *The Celibate Shaker Life*. Mt. Lebanon, N.Y.: n.p., 1889(?).

———. *Shaker Medicinal Spring Water*. Boston: n.p., 1880.

Nazzari, Muriel. "The 'Woman Question' in Cuba: An Analysis of Material Constraints on Its Solution." *Signs* 9, no. 2 (1983): 246–63.

Neal, Julia. *By Their Fruits: The Story of Shakerism in South Union, Kentucky*. Chapel Hill: Univ. of North Carolina Press, 1947.

———. "Trustees, Deacons, and Deaconesses: The Temporal Role of the Shaker Sisters 1820–1890." *Communal Societies* 7 (1987): 16–24.

Nissenbaum, Stephen. *Sex, Diet, and Debility in Jacksonian America*. Contributions in Medical History, no. 4. Westport, Conn.: Greenwood Press, 1980.

Nordhoff, Charles. *The Communistic Societies of the United States: From Personal Visit and Observation.* 1875. Reprint. New York: Dover, 1966.

Norton, Mary Beth. *Liberty's Daughters: The Revolutionary Experience of American Women, 1750–1800*. 1980. Reprint. Ithaca, N.Y.: Cornell Univ. Press, 1996.

Notable American Women, 1607–1950: A Biographical Dictionary. Edited by Edward T. James, Janet Wilson James, and Paul S. Boyer. 3 vols. Cambridge, Mass.: Belknap Press, 1971.

Nourse, Henry S., ed. *The Birth, Marriage and Death Register, Church Records and Epitaphs of Lancaster, Massachusetts. 1643–1850*. Lancaster, Mass.: n.p., 1890.

———. *History of the Town of Harvard, Massachusetts, 1732–1893*. Harvard, Mass.: Warren Hapgood, 1894.

Oberholzer, Emil, Jr. *Delinquent Saints: Disciplinary Action in the Early Congregational Churches of Massachusetts*. Columbia Studies in the Social Sciences, no. 590. New York: Columbia Univ. Press, 1956.

O'Flaherty, Wendy Doniger. *Women, Androgynes, and Other Mythical Beasts*. Chicago: Univ. of Chicago Press, 1980.

Owen, Alex. *The Darkened Room: Women, Power and Spiritualism in Late Victorian England*. The New Cultural Studies Series. Philadelphia: Univ. of Pennsylvania Press, 1990.

Paige, Lucius R. *History of Cambridge, Massachusetts, 1630–1877. With a Genealogical Register.* Boston: Houghton and Co., 1877.

Paterwic, Stephen. "The Last of the Harvard Shakers." *Shaker Quarterly* 20 (Summer 1992): 67–79.

———. "Necrology for the Shaker Society at Shirley, Massachusetts." *Shaker Quarterly* 20 (Fall 1992): 94–108.

Patterson, Daniel W. " 'Bearing for the Dead': A Shaker Belief and Its Impress on the Shaker Spiritual." *Shaker Quarterly* 8 (Winter 1968): 116–28.

———. *The Shaker Spiritual*. Princeton, N.J.: Princeton Univ. Press, 1979.

Payne, Alma J. "The Family in the Utopia of William Dean Howells." *Georgia Review* 15 (Summer 1961): 217–29.

Pease, William H., and Jane H. Pease. *The Web of Progress: Private Values and Public Styles in Boston and Charleston, 1828–1843*. New York: Oxford Univ. Press, 1985.

Phoenix Cotton Manufacturing Company v. Samuel Hazen and Another. 118 Mass. 350 (1875).

Plumer, William. "The Original Shaker Communities in New England." Edited by F. B. Sanborn. *The New England Magazine*, n.s., 22 (May 1900): 303–9.

Porterfield, Amanda. *Mary Lyon and the Mount Holyoke Missionaries*. New York: Oxford Univ. Press, 1997.

Proceedings of the Free Convention, Held at Rutland, Vt., July 25th, 26th, and 27th, 1858. Boston: Yerrinton and Sons, 1858.

Procter-Smith, Marjorie. *Shakerism and Feminism: Reflections on Women's Religion and the Early Shakers*. Old Chatham, N.Y.: Center for Research and Education, Shaker Museum and Library, 1991.

———. " 'Who do you say that I am?': Mother Ann as Christ." In *Locating the Shakers: Cultural Origins and Legacies of an American Religious Movement*, edited by Mick Gidley with Kate Bowles, 83–95. Exeter Studies in American and Commonwealth Arts, no. 3. Exeter: Univ. of Exeter Press, 1990.

———. *Women in Shaker Community and Worship: A Feminist Analysis of the Uses of Religious Symbolism*. Studies in Women and Religion, vol. 16. Lewiston, N.Y.: Edwin Mellen Press, 1985.

Promey, Sally M. *Spiritual Spectacles: Vision and Image in Mid-Nineteenth Century Shakerism*. Bloomington: Indiana Univ. Press, 1993.

Pruitt, Bettye Hobbs. "Self-Sufficiency and the Agricultural Economy of Eighteenth-Century Massachusetts." 3d ser. *William and Mary Quarterly* 41 (July 1984): 333–64.

Raymond, Janice G. *The Transsexual Empire: The Making of the She-Male*. Boston: Beacon Press, 1979.

Reuther, Rosemary Radford. *Sexism and God-Talk: Toward a Feminist Theology*. Boston: Beacon Press, 1983.

Ricketson, Daniel. *The History of New Bedford, Bristol County, Massachusetts: Including A History of the Old Township of Dartmouth and the Present Townships of Westport, Dartmouth, and Fair-haven, From Their Settlement to the Present Time*. New Bedford, Mass.: pub. by the author, 1858.

Robinson, Charles Edson. *A Concise History of the United Society of Believers Called Shakers*. East Canterbury, N.H.: United Society of Shakers, 1893.

Rodman, Samuel. *The Diary of Samuel Rodman: A New Bedford Chronicle of Thirty-Seven Years, 1821–1859*. Edited by Zephaniah W. Pease. New Bedford, Mass.: Reynolds Printing Co., 1927.

Rothenberg, Winifred B. "The Market and Massachusetts Farmers, 1750–1855." *Journal of Economic History* 41 (June 1981): 283–314.

Rothstein, William G. *American Physicians in the Nineteenth Century: From Sects to Science.* Baltimore: Johns Hopkins Univ. Press, 1972.

Roxalana L. Grosvenor v. United Society of Believers. Maria F. Grosvenor v. Same. 188 Mass. 78 (1875).

Sasson, Diane. "Individual Experience, Community Control, and Gender: The Harvard Community During the Era of Manifestations." *Communal Societies* 13 (1993):45–70.

———. *The Shaker Spiritual Narrative.* Knoxville: Univ. of Tennessee Press, 1983.

Sears, Clara Endicott. "The Shakers of Harvard, Massachusetts." Paper read at the Bay State Historical League, Harvard, Mass., 22 July 1939.

Shaw, Teresa M. *The Burden of the Flesh: Fasting and Sexuality in Early Christianity.* Minneapolis: Fortress Press, 1998.

Shryock, Richard Harrison. "Sylvester Graham and the Popular Health Movement, 1830–1870." In *Medicine in America: Historical Essays,* by Richard Harrison Shryock, 111–25. Baltimore: Johns Hopkins Univ. Press, 1966.

Sifakis, Carl. *The Encyclopedia of American Crime.* New York: Smithmark, 1992.

Singer, Eliot A. "Conversion Through Foodways Enculturation: The Meaning of Eating in an American Hindu Sect." In *Ethnic and Regional Foodways in the United States: The Performance of Group Identity,* edited by Linda Keller Brown and Kay Mussell, 195–214. Knoxville: Univ. of Tennessee Press, 1984.

Smith, William L. *Families and Communes: An Examination of Nontraditional Lifestyles.* Thousand Oaks, Calif.: Sage Pub., 1999.

Smith-Rosenberg, Carroll, and Charles Rosenberg. "The Female Animal: Medical and Biological Views of Woman and Her Role in Nineteenth-Century America." *Journal of American History* 60 (Sept. 1973): 332–56.

Soler, Jean. "The Semiotics of Food in the Bible." In *Food and Drink in History: Selections from the Annales Economies, Sociétés, Civilisations,* edited by Robert Forster and Orest Ranum, and translated by Elborg Forster and Patricia M. Ranum, 126–38. Baltimore: Johns Hopkins Univ. Press, 1979.

Sommer, Margaret Van Alen Frisbee. *The Shaker Garden Seed Industry.* Old Chatham, N.Y.: Shaker Museum Foundation, 1972.

Spurlock, John C. *Free Love: Marriage and Middle-Class Radicalism in America, 1825–1860.* The American Social Experience, 13. New York: New York Univ. Press, 1988.

Stage, Sarah. *Female Complaints: Lydia Pinkham and the Business of Women's Medicine.* New York: W. W. Norton, 1979.

Stansell, Christine. *City of Women: Sex and Class in New York, 1789–1860.* Urbana: Univ. of Illinois Press, 1982.

Steele, Valerie. *Fashion and Eroticism: Ideals of Feminine Beauty from the Victorian Era to the Jazz Age.* New York: Oxford Univ. Press, 1985.

Stein, Allen F. "Marriage in Howells's Novels." *American Literature* 48 (Jan. 1977): 501–24.

Stein, Stephen J. *The Shaker Experience in America: A History of the United Society of Believers.* New Haven, Conn.: Yale University Press, 1992.

Stier, Maggie, and Ralph N. Fuller. *Shaker Sites in Harvard: A Guide for the Harvard Shaker Bicentennial, 1791–1991*. Harvard, Mass.: Shaker 200 Committee [1991].

Stone, Lawrence. "The Rise of the Nuclear Family in Early Modern England: The Patriarchal Stage." In *The Family in History*, edited by Charles E. Rosenberg, 13–57. Philadelphia: Univ. of Pennsylvania Press, 1975.

Tavard, George H. "Theology and Sexuality." In *Women in the World's Religions, Past and Present*, edited by Ursula King, 68–80. God, the Contemporary Discussion Series. New York: Paragon House, 1987.

Taylor, Amos. *A Narrative of the Strange Principles, Conduct and Character of the People known by the Name of Shakers*. Worcester, Mass.: Printed for the author, 1792.

Thurman, Suzanne. " 'Dearly Loved Mother Eunice': Gender, Motherhood, and Shaker Spirituality." *Church History* 66 (Dec. 1997): 750–61.

———. " 'No Idle Hands are Seen': The Social Construction of Work in Shaker Communities." *Communal Societies* 18 (1998): 36–52.

———. "Shaker Women and Sexual Power: Heresy and Orthodoxy in the Shaker Village of Harvard, Massachusetts." *Journal of Women's History* 10 (Spring 1998): 70–87.

———. "The Windows of Heaven: A Study of Revival Among the Harvard Shakers, 1837–1845." Unpublished paper, 1989.

[Tillinghast, Joseph.] *Brief and Useful Moral Instruction for the Young. By a Friend of Youth and Children*. Worcester, Mass.: Chas. Hamilton, 1858.

Tower, Henry M. *Historical Sketches Relating to Spencer, Mass.* 4 vols. Spencer, Mass.: W.J. Heffernan-Spencer Leader Print, 1902.

[Towner, James William.] "Community Contracts." *Oneida Circular* 11 (21 Dec. 1874): 417–18.

Turner, Victor. *The Ritual Process: Structure and Anti-Structure*. Chicago: Aldine Pub. Co., 1969.

Tuveson, Ernest Lee. *Redeemer Nation: The Idea of America's Millennial Role*. Chicago: Univ. of Chicago Press, 1968.

Tyler, Alice Felt. *Freedom's Ferment: Phases of American Social History to 1860*. Minneapolis: Univ. of Minnesota Press, 1944.

U.S. Bureau of the Census. *Heads of Families at the First Census of the United States Taken in the Year 1790, Massachusetts*. Washington, D.C.: U.S. Government Printing Office, 1908.

Verbrugge, Martha H. *Able-Bodied Womanhood: Personal Health and Social Change in Nineteenth-Century Boston*. New York: Oxford Univ. Press, 1988.

Vital Records of Cambridge, Massachusetts, To the Year 1850. 2 vols. Compiled by Thomas W. Baldwin. Boston: Wright and Potter Printing Co., 1914.

Vital Records of Chelmsford, Massachusetts, To the End of the Year 1849. Salem, Mass.: Essex Institute, 1914.

Vital Records of Harvard, Massachusetts, To the Year 1850. Compiled by Thomas W. Baldwin. Boston: Wright and Potter Printing Co., 1917.

Vital Records of Petersham, Massachusetts, To the End of the Year 1849. Worcester, Mass.: Franklin P. Rice, 1904.

Vital Records of Sutton, Massachusetts, To the End of the Year 1849. Worcester, Mass.: Franklin P. Rice, 1907.

Vital Records of Upton, Massachusetts, To the End of the Year 1849. Worcester, Mass.: Franklin P. Rice, 1904.

Warren, Mary Anne. "Is Androgyny the Answer to Sexual Stereotyping?" In *"Femininity," "Masculinity," and "Androgyny": A Modern Philosophical Discussion,* edited by Mary Vetterling-Braggin, 170–86. Totowa, N.J.: Littlefield, Adams and Co., 1982.

Waters, Wilson. *History of Chelmsford, Massachusetts.* Lowell, Mass.: Courier-Citizen, 1917.

[Wayland-Smith, Francis.] "Grosvenor Suit." *Oneida Circular* 12 (11 Oct. 1875): 324.

Weis, Virginia. "Women in Shaker Life." Paper delivered at the Bicentennial Conference, Sabbathday Lake, Maine, 1974. Quoted in Flo Morse, *The Shakers and the World's People,* 101. 1980. Reprint. Hanover, N.H.: Univ. Press of New England, 1987.

Weisbrod, Carol. *The Boundaries of Utopia.* New York: Pantheon Books, 1980.

Weiss, Harry B., and Howard R. Kemble. *The Great American Water-Cure Craze: A History of Hydropathy in the United States.* Trenton, N.J.: Past Times Press, 1967.

[Wells, Seth Y.] *Millennial Praises, containing a Collection of Gospel Hymns, in four parts, adapted to the Day of Christ's Second Appearing Composed for the Use of His People.* Hancock, Mass.: Josiah Talcott, Jr., 1813.

Welter, Barbara. "The Cult of True Womanhood, 1820–1860." *American Quarterly* 18 (1966): 151–74.

Whitson, Robley Edward, ed. *The Shakers: Two Centuries of Spiritual Reflection.* The Classics of Western Spirituality. Ramsey, N.J.: Paulist Press, 1983.

Wiener, Norbert. *Ex-Prodigy: My Childhood and Youth.* New York: Simon & Schuster, 1953.

Wilentz, Sean. *Chants Democratic: New York City and the Rise of the Working Class, 1788–1850.* New York: Oxford Univ. Press, 1984.

Wolford, John Brenton. "The South Union, Kentucky, Shakers and Tradition: A Study of Business, Work, and Commerce." Ph.D. diss., Indiana Univ., 1992.

Wood, Gordon S. *The Creation of the American Republic, 1776–1787.* 1969. Reprint. New York: W. W. Norton, 1972.

Yacovone, Donald. "'Surpassing the Love of Women': Victorian Manhood and the Language of Fraternal Love." In *A Shared Experience: Men, Women, and the History of Gender,* edited by Laura McCall and Donald Yacovone, 195–221. New York: New York Univ. Press, 1998.

Youngerman, Suzanne. "'Shaking is No Foolish Play': An Anthropological Perspective on the American Shakers—Person, Time, Space, and Dance–Ritual." Ph.D. diss.: Columbia Univ., 1983.

Youngs, Benjamin S. *The Testimony of Christ's Second Appearing Containing a General Statement of All Things Pertaining to the Faith and Practice of the Church of God in this Latter-day.* Lebanon, Ohio: Press of John M'Clean, 1808.

Zimmerman, Karen Voci. "Symbol, Structure and Reality: Forms of Worship of the New England Shakers." M.A. thesis, American University, 1973.

Index

Women and Gender in North American Religions
Amanda Porterfield *and* Mary Farrell Bednarowski, *Series Editors*

Building Sisterhood: A Feminist History of the Sisters, Servants of the Immaculate Heart of Mary
Sisters, Servants of the Immaculate Heart of Mary, Monroe, Michigan

Emma Newman: A Frontier Woman Minister
Randi Jones Walker

Moon Sisters, Krishna Mothers, Rajneesh Lovers: Women's Roles in New Religions
Susan J. Palmer

Moravian Women's Memoirs: Spiritual Narratives, 1750–1820
Katherine M. Faull, trans. & ed.

Rational Mothers and Infidel Gentlemen: Gender and American Atheism, 1865–1915
Evelyn Kirkley

The Religious World of Antislavery Women: Spirituality in the Lives of Five Abolitionist Lecturers
Anna M. Speicher

A Still Small Voice: Women, Ordination, and the Church
Frederick W. Schmidt

Windows of Faith: Muslim Women Scholar-Activists of North America
Gisela Webb, ed.